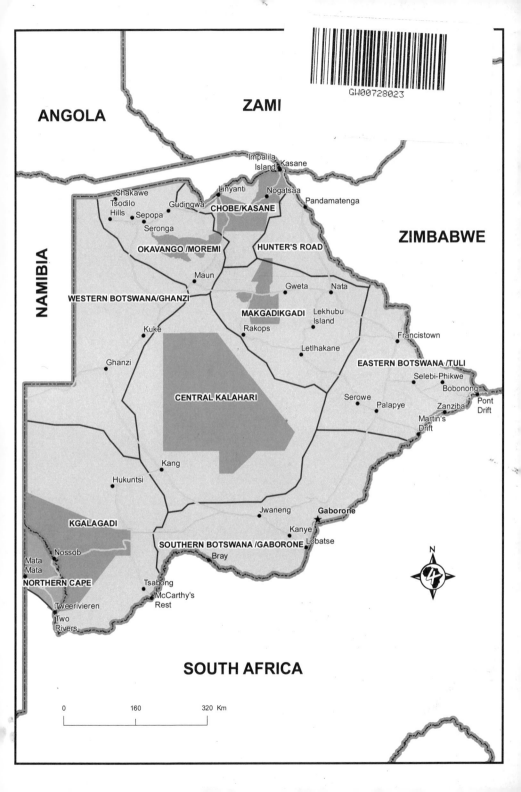

BOTSWANA

SELF-DRIVE

TRAVEL GUIDE

Travel Africa Informed

Foreword

We at Tracks4Africa are a community of people who are passionate about travelling Africa. The essence of any community is to share in the true Ubuntu spirit, which is inherent to Africa. That is indeed what we have aimed for with this guide book.

This book is not about the personal experience of one person, but about the culminated experiences of a whole community of travellers. We believe that the only way to preserve the beauty and splendour of Africa for the next generation is to inform the people who want to explore it. They need to travel informed so that they will not exploit it.

We asked ourselves what kind of information a self-drive traveller needs, and we aimed to combine that in an easy-to-use guide which is enjoyable to browse through. This guide book is the result.

This, our first guide book, was in a sense a journey like any other journey in Africa. We had to plan our route thoroughly but not too rigidly. We had to manoeuvre many potholes along the road as well as a few unexpected delays, and sometimes we had to find new routes.

But, like any journey into Africa, this was an exciting and gratifying one. I feel privileged to have been part of it and I want to thank my fellow travellers on this journey. On the acknowledgements page we mention all the people who contributed towards this guide, but I need to make special mention of Peter Levey who undertook a dedicated research trip for us.

I hope that you enjoy this guide book and your travels to Botswana just as much as we enjoyed compiling it for you, our fellow traveller.

The face of Africa changes continuously – embrace that as part of the beauty of Africa! Sometimes you just have to go with the flow when you are in Africa. The Tracks4Africa community travels far and wide to give you the most up-to-date maps and information possible, but still, Africa keeps changing her face. Occasionally you will find that our data is not one hundred percent up to date. Please let us know at newdata@tracks4africa.co.za if you find any discrepancies in this guide or on any of our maps.

Enjoy our beloved continent, Africa!

Karin Theron
EDITOR

Go to the book website to stay up to date with new information and accommodation updates since the book was published:
http://botswana-self-drive-guide.tracks4africa.co.za/

Acknowledgements

You are holding this guide book, **Tracks4Arica's** first of hopefully many fully fledged guide books, in your hands because of the vision of Johann Groenewald and Wouter Brand. Without their dream of publishing the ultimate guide book for self-drive tourists, this book would never have come into fruition.

We believe that this guide book is different from others because it was written by a whole community of travellers. We bring you the collective experience of many hard-core travellers, not just the perception of an individual traveller.

Like all other **Tracks4Africa** products, this one would not have existed if it wasn't for the Tracks4Africa community. This is a community of travellers who love sharing their travel experiences with other people.

Although the whole **Tracks4Africa** community contributed in some way to this guide book, special mention needs to be made of the following members who made specific contributions:

Aubrey Moore, Alan Rielander, Abrie Stoltz, Bessie Brand, Chris Smit, David Smith, Deon Kotze, Darryl Lampert, dr. Dirk von Delft, Dries Boshoff, Eddie von Bargen, Emmanuel Berger, Eric Sommer, Francois Visagie, Glen Roberts, dr. Grahame Stewart, Hannes Thirion, Hugo Potgieter, Ivan Marais, Jakes Louw, dr. James Berkley, Johan Cloete, Johan Snyman, Lizette Swart, Marc Hall, Michael Knott, Mike Nieuwoudt, Mike Lauterbach, Peter Levey, dr. Riaan van der Colf, Robert Shadford, Tony Robertson and Willie Solomon.

Apart from the **Tracks4Africa** Community Forum (www.tracks4africa.co.za) we also relied on the travel experience of the SA 4x4 Community Forum (www.4x4community.co.za).

Behind the scenes the **Tracks4Africa** team did a lot of research themselves, specifically on the towns and accommodation listings.

Janine Reyneke and her data research team consisting of Anet Bosman, Liezel Kriel, Hester Gikas and Faith Mandere spent endless hours of phoning and searching for the right information. Erick Ndava created the exquisite maps for this book. This book was indeed one huge team effort!

First published 2013
ISBN: 978-0-9921829-5-3

Published by
Tracks4Africa (Pty) Ltd
Unit 8, Innovation Center 1, Meson Street
Technopark, Stellenbosch, 7599
SOUTH AFRICA
www.tracks4africa.co.za

Design by Different Designers, Elsa Cade

Reproduction by Hirt & Carter (Pty) Ltd, Cape Town

Print production: SA Media Services, Les Martens
Printed by: WKT Company Limited, China

Let us know what you think
Tracks4Africa is essentially a community driven project and we collect, collate and process the travel experience of a wide variety of travellers into various products. Your input to the data on any of our platforms, be it this book, our website or our maps, are highly valued.

Should you come across any errors in this book or find new and interesting places to stay, please contact us. You can e-mail us at newdata@tracks4africa.co.za, or visit our website to post your photographs, comments or corrections on existing listings.

If you are interested in making contributions to our maps, go to Submit Data on our website.
www.tracks4africa.co.za

How to use this guide

TOWNS OR DESTINATIONS

Facilities available in towns or at destinations

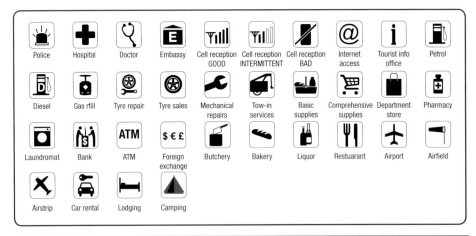

Please note that these facilities are not necessarily indicated on the town maps as they might not have been marked on our T4A GPS maps. If some facilities are listed but not indicated on the town map, just ask around town to find it.

Accommodation Listings

Lodging

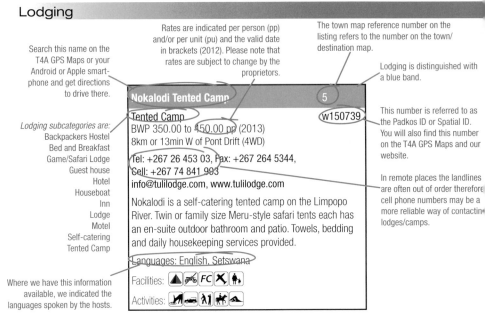

Search this name on the T4A GPS Maps or your Android or Apple smartphone and get directions to drive there.

Rates are indicated per person (pp) and/or per unit (pu) and the valid date in brackets (2012). Please note that rates are subject to change by the proprietors.

The town map reference number on the listing refers to the number on the town/destination map.

Lodging is distinguished with a blue band.

Lodging subcategories are:
Backpackers Hostel
Bed and Breakfast
Game/Safari Lodge
Guest house
Hotel
Houseboat
Inn
Lodge
Motel
Self-catering
Tented Camp

This number is referred to as the Padkos ID or Spatial ID. You will also find this number on the T4A GPS Maps and our website.

In remote places the landlines are often out of order therefore cell phone numbers may be a more reliable way of contacting lodges/camps.

Where we have this information available, we indicated the languages spoken by the hosts.

Nokalodi Tented Camp — 5

Tented Camp — w150739
BWP 350.00 to 450.00 pp (2013)
8km or 13min W of Pont Drift (4WD)

Tel: +267 26 453 03, Fax: +267 264 5344,
Cell: +267 74 841 993
info@tulilodge.com, www.tulilodge.com

Nokalodi is a self-catering tented camp on the Limpopo River. Twin or family size Meru-style safari tents each has an en-suite outdoor bathroom and patio. Towels, bedding and daily housekeeping services provided.

Languages: English, Setswana

Facilities:

Activities:

Lodging facilities

Where the following icons are shown, it indicates that the facilities are offered on the premises of the listing, with the exception of landing strips which can be close by.

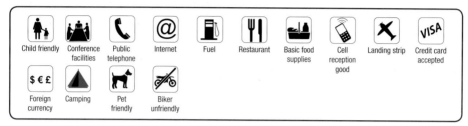

Child friendly	Conference facilities	Public telephone	Internet	Fuel	Restaurant	Basic food supplies	Cell reception good	Landing strip	Credit card accepted

Foreign currency	Camping	Pet friendly	Biker unfriendly

Accommodation Listings
Camping

If accommodation is situated in a town or city, we provide the street address. For accommodation in the countryside, we provide the nearest town and the distance, time and spatial position from it. The distance and time is calculated using T4A GPS Maps and is a fair indication of how long it will take you to drive from the nearest town.

Where you see 4WD in the address line, it means that the lodge/camp is only reachable by 4x4. Where 4WD is not indicated, a sedan vehicle may in some cases be sufficient to gain access, but in some cases you may need a 4x2 to reach the lodge/camp.

No self-drive access means that guests are not allowed to or are unable to drive to the lodge.

Camping listings are distinguished with a green band.

Camping subcategories are:
Camping (ordinary camp)
4WD Trail Camp
Caravan Park
Community Camp
Farm Camp
Hiking Trail Camp
Holiday Resort
Lodge Camp
Park Camp
Tour Operator Camp
Transit Camp
Wilderness Camp

Khama Rhino Sanctuary EEC Camp   3

Park Camp   w189286
BWP 50.00 to 67.00 pp (2012)
31km or 28min NNE of Serowe

Tel: +267 463 0713, Fax: +267 463 5808,
Cell: +267 73 965 655, krst@khamarhinosanctuary.org.bw
www.khamarhinosanctuary.org.bw

The camp at the Environmental Education Centre (EEC) of Khama Rhino Sanctuary has clean ablution blocks. Campers can use the facilities at the entrance gate to the sanctuary. Support this community based wildlife project.

Facilities:

Activities:

The yellow paw indicates that this listing is a community camp or wildlife foundation. Tracks4Africa supports community efforts and conservation therefore we would in this way like to give extra free exposure to them.

How to use this guide

Camping facilities

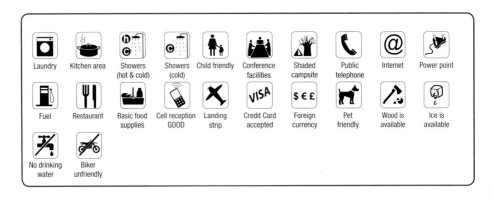

Please note that the descriptions are highly summarised. For more information you can go to our other information platforms like the T4A Travel Guide on your GPS (it comes with your T4A maps), our website or our Nokia, Android and Apple applications

Lodging and camping activities

Please note that the activities indicated may not necessarily be offered by the lodge/camp itself, but may be offered in the nearby vicinity, eg. balloon trips.

All the information about towns and listings in this guide book is listed on www.tracks4africa.co.za. Please post any corrections, comments or photos on this website. We have done thorough research on all towns and listings, but as you know change is inevitable.

 Wherever you see this icon in the book, we have given you a noteworthy tip.

THE USE OF THE INFORMATION CONTAINED HERIN IS SOLELY AT YOUR OWN RISK.

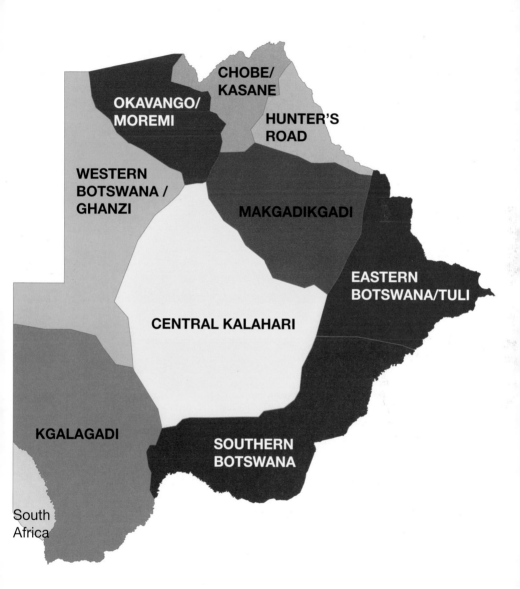

CHOBE/
KASANE

OKAVANGO/
MOREMI

HUNTER'S
ROAD

WESTERN
BOTSWANA /
GHANZI

MAKGADIKGADI

EASTERN
BOTSWANA/TULI

CENTRAL KALAHARI

KGALAGADI

SOUTHERN
BOTSWANA

South
Africa

All regions are colour coded for quick reference. Colour strips make it easy to find a specific region when you page through the book.

contents

Preparing for your Trip

contents

Preparing for your Trip

contents
Regions

GENERAL INFORMATION

GLOSSARY

We have used certain words in this guide that are lingua franca in Africa but might be unfamiliar to Europeans:

Boma: an outdoor, enclosed entertainment area.

Lapa: an enclosure where people get together and normally eat together. It is usually thatched with open sides.

Braai: barbeque (frying meat on an open fire).

Long drop: a pit toilet.

Mokoro: a type of canoe made by digging out a tree trunk.

Meru-style tents: large tents with covered verandas.

Giraffe in the Kgalagadi Transfrontier Park. (Karin Theron)

Botswana

Botswana is a largely wild and untouched country, dominated by the Kalahari Desert and home to the Okavango Delta, a magnificent wetland fed by water from the Angolan highlands.

The Okavango is the largest inland delta in the world and is a maze of lagoons, secret waterways and palm-dotted islands abound with hippos, crocodiles, antelopes and, of course, a huge variety of birds and smaller animals.

It is a unique oasis of life right in the centre of the Kalahari Desert which covers 84% of the country. The word desert is a misnomer, as the Kalahari is indeed covered by vegetation including stunted thorn and scrub bush, trees and grassland. The Kalahari is more arid savannah than desert. The largely unchanging flat terrain is occasionally interrupted by gentle descending valleys, sand dunes, large numbers of pans and isolated hills.

About 17% of Botswana is national reserves, and wildlife has never been imported or controlled in any way. The protected areas are unfenced; therefore Botswana offers you a true wilderness experience. Much of Botswana is remote and remains accessible to only a small number of visitors.

Botswana is not a cheap country, as the government has taken a high-cost, low-volume approach to tourism to protect the country's natural assets. However, there are quite a number of campsites available that offer good value for money and makes Botswana affordable for over-landers.

Botswana lies to the north of South Africa and is bordered on the west by Namibia and on the east by Zimbabwe. It connects with Zambia at one point of Namibia's Caprivi Strip that stretches out like an arm over the northern part of Botswana. Thanks to its diamonds, Botswana is one of the richest countries in Africa.

Botswana has a small population and although Gaborone is the capital, Maun and Kasane are the main tourist hubs.

CLIMATE

Botswana is hot and dry as it is classified as a semi-arid country. Rain falls mainly in summer, between October and March. During the peak rain months, December to February, the humidity can get as high as 80%. Downpours are usually short but heavy. During summer, daytime temperatures are around 37°C and in winter it is on average 10° lower. During nighttime, temperatures below freezing and ground frosts are common. In the central Kalahari it can even drop to -12°C.

In summer you should wear lightweight, light-coloured clothing, good sunglasses, a hat and suntan lotion with a high UV protection factor. People with fair and sensitive skins should even take these precautions in winter. Avoid synthetic materials and black clothing, as they increase perspiration and discomfort.

Garments of neutral colours that blend with the bush and forest are advisable for safaris and game viewing. Warm jerseys and jackets are vital for morning and evening game drives, especially in winter. Closed, comfortable walking shoes are a must in all seasons.

BEST TIME TO VISIT

Because of the heat in summer, most people find April to October a more comfortable time to visit Botswana. You also need to bear in mind that roads can become very treacherous during the rainy season, therefore you should be extremely cautious if you want to travel Botswana between December and March.

April and May are lovely months with only the odd afternoon showers. June and July are the coldest months. From August to September temperatures gradually rise and the humidity stays below 40%. During October and November temperatures rise even more, humidity builds up and rain showers often occur in the late afternoon. Because of the clouds and rain, some days are cooler than others. During December, afternoon showers are a regular occurrence, the humidity is around 60% and temperatures can rise to 40°C.

It can be very difficult to get bookings in the national parks; therefore you should plan your itinerary at least a year in advance.

MONEY

The Botswana currency is the pula. One pula is divided into 100 thebe. In few places US dollar and South African rand are accepted, but it is always best to have enough pula in cash on hand, especially in the rural areas.

Credit cards are accepted and work in the cities and bigger towns. Just remember to let your bank know that you are travelling, and to increase your credit limit for the duration of the trip if needed. Visa debit/credit cards are more widely accepted than MasterCard, and you will be able to withdraw money from ATMs with a Visa card only.

It is advisable to have more than one credit card between your travel party in case it gets lost or stolen, and, if possible, both Visa and MasterCard. It is a good idea to split your money between your group members so that you don't carry all your cash with you. Never ever carry all your money on you in one place, especially not in your wallet.

Fuel stations do not accept petrol/garage cards, but credit cards are accepted in the bigger towns. In smaller towns they only accept cash.

Even places that normally do accept

A shop in Gweta selling local arts and crafts. (Hannes Thirion)

credit cards may have connectivity problems from time to time, so it is best to always have enough cash with you. You do not need to carry cash for the whole trip, as most big towns do have ATMs. This guide will indicate to you which towns have ATMs so that you can plan ahead.

Travellers' cheques and foreign currency may be changed at banks, bureaux de change, and authorised hotels. The US dollar, euro, British pound and the South African rand are the most easily convertible currencies.

Banking hours are:
Monday to Friday 8:30 - 15:30 and Saturday 8:30 - 10:45.

Value Added Tax (VAT) in Botswana is 12% on goods and services and is included in the price of goods. Foreign tourists who have spent more than P5 000 may reclaim VAT at all major border posts and airports. You need a tax invoice stating VAT paid, your passport number and your bank account details. It is always advisable to keep a copy of the VAT form as a record for any follow-up on the transaction.

LANGUAGE

Setswana, the national language, is spoken by about 79% of the population. However, English is the official language in Botswana.

PEOPLE

The population of just over two million is divided into the main ethnic groups of Tswana people (79%), Kalanga people (11%), and San (or Bushmen) (3%). The remaining 7% consist of other peoples, including some speaking the Kgalagadi language, and 1% of non-African people.

The San were the first people in Botswana. Their rock paintings and engravings can still be seen at Tsodilo Hills. The San, who were hunter-gatherers, were later joined by the Khoi who were herders that kept domesticated animals.

People from central Africa only arrived via the Chobe River in the first or second centuries AD and spread down the eastern side of the country. They were stock and grain farmers. Herero and Himba people arrived from the west via Angola and Namibia, and the Bayei river people from the Congo and Zambia in mokoros.

By around 1300 AD the Tswana people had become the dominant people of the eastern Kalahari. Today the ethnic Tswana is split up among eight tribes: Bamangwato, Bakwena, Bangwaketsi, Bakgatla, Barolong, Bamalete and Batlokwa.

During the early 1800's Europeans came to hunt and trade ivory, leather and ostrich feathers. Later white Voortrekkers who fled from British rule in the Cape Colony, arrived from South Africa, followed by missionaries like Robert Moffat and David Livingstone. In 1885 Botswana (then Bechuanaland) was proclaimed a British protectorate after the leader of the Batswana people appealed to Britain for assistance against the Boers from the neighbouring Transvaal.

In 1966 the independent Republic of Botswana was established after the first democratic elections with Sir Seretse Khama as the first president. Botswana has a stable and democratic political system.

CONSERVATION

With 38% of its total land area devoted to national parks, reserves and wildlife management areas, Botswana offers some of the best wildlife areas on the African continent. These areas are mostly unfenced, allowing animals to roam wild and free.

The Okavango is the world's largest intact inland Delta and the Central Kalahari Game Reserve is the world's second largest game reserve. The Makgadikgadi have uninhabited pans the size of Portugal and the Chobe National Park boasts prolific wildlife.

Botswana is the last stronghold for a number of endangered bird and mammal species, including Wild Dog, Cheetah, Brown Hyena, Cape Vulture, Wattled Crane, Kori Bustard and Pel's Fishing Owl.

In Botswana you will experience vast expanses of uninhabited wilderness stretching from horizon to horizon, the sensation of limitless space, astoundingly rich wildlife and bird viewing, night skies littered with stars and heavenly bodies of an unimaginable brilliance, and stunning sunsets of indescribable beauty.

Local communities get involved in and also want to benefit from tourism. If you visit these villages, you can experience their rich cultural heritage firsthand. If you only pass through these villages you do not need to pay, but if you stop to take

Yellowbilled Storks in Moremi Game Reserve. (Lindy Lourens)

pictures or camp somewhere around there, you will be expected to pay a fee to the chief of the village. Always ask before you just setup camp.

USEFUL CONTACT NUMBERS

Botswana uses the following toll-free numbers for the emergency services and visitors are encouraged to use these numbers.
Ambulance 997
Fire brigade 998
Police 999
Medical rescue 911
Medical Air Rescue +267 390 1601
Okavango Air Rescue 995

FOOD AND DRINK

Tap water throughout the country is safe to drink. However, if you doubt the source of the water, treat the water by adding chemicals or boil-

ing it, or drink bottled water. Bottled mineral water is readily available in most shops and supermarkets, and at camps and lodges.

Using water purification tablets is a cheap and simple way to kill bugs in drinking water; just ensure that you wait 20 to 30 minutes for the tablets to work before you drink the water. A better tasting alternative is using one of the many water filtration devices available.

Tourists travelling by road are advised to carry sufficient water at all times as daytime in Botswana can be exceedingly hot in summer and hot in winter.

Every small village in Botswana has a shop where basic food can be purchased. If you require anything more

Deep sand track in the Kgalagadi Transfrontier Park. (Karin Theron)

exotic than the basics, you should stock up at supermarkets in bigger towns.

ROAD CONDITIONS

Botswana's highways are all paved (also referred to as surfaced or tarred roads) and form a basic network of major access routes around the country. As soon as you leave the main highways, you are faced with sandy tracks that require an off-road vehicle with good ground clearance and 4WD. In some places these sandy tracks can turn into deep sand tracks.

The main attractions of Botswana are within its majestic game parks and these are reached by sandy to deep sand tracks for which a proper off-road vehicle is required. Therefore, unless you are just passing through, you really do need a 4x4 for travelling Botswana.

If you don't have a 4x4, you can visit one of the few wildlife places with easy access, like Khama Rhino Sanctuary, or do a safari with a local operator from Maun or Kasane.

During the rainy season places like Moremi and Makgadikgadi will flood and many of the smaller tracks will become muddy, water logged or even impossible to drive. If you plan on travelling during the rainy season, you need to inquire about road conditions from lodge/camp owners or fellow travellers. If you are unsure, rather do not attempt to cross muddy tracks as you can get hopelessly stuck.

When you go on game drives, let the lodge/camp owners know that you are going for a drive, which route you plan on taking and what time you expect to be back.

Botswana's roads are not fenced and domestic animals such as cattle, donkeys, goats and dogs are free to roam the roads. Cattle has right of way.

📍 *When travelling from Kasane to Nata, the grass next to the road is very high and you will be unable to see any animals wandering next to the road. It is recommended that you travel at 80 km/h most of the way.*

The rules

- You must at all times carry a valid driver's license (issued in English) with you. If your licence is not in English, you will have to get an international driver's licence.
- According to the Automobile Association of South Africa (AA) it is compulsory for any vehicle, caravan or trailer registered in South Africa to have a ZA sign displayed when it crosses any border. The ZA sign must be placed in a visible position on the rear of each vehicle, caravan and trailer, and may not be within 150 mm of the rear number plate.
- Drive on the left side of the road.
- The general speed limit is 60 km/h in towns and villages, 80 km/h when passing intersections or villages on the main roads and 120 km/h outside urban areas.

They are very strict on enforcing speed limits and visitors are advised to always adhere to the speed limits which are always very clearly marked.

- All passengers must wear safety belts.
- The use of cell phones when driving is illegal.

Advice

- Always be on the lookout for stray animals.
- Never drive at night because of the danger of stray animals crossing the road.
- Before you leave on your trip for the day, ensure that your vehicle's tyre pressures are correct for the kind of roads you plan on travelling, as well as the amount of luggage and passengers that you will be carrying.
- If at all possible, carry two spare tyres.
- A tyre repair kit can help you out of a lot of trouble.
- Keep your lights on at all times, so you can be seen in dusty or low visibility conditions.
- If you don't have any 4WD experience, you should seriously consider doing a course before you venture into remote areas.
- You should always drive with a tyre compressor and pressure gauge with you so you can adjust tyre pressure as needed.

Driving on gravel roads

If you deflate your tyres to about 1,8 bar, it will soften the ride and ensure better grip on gravel roads. Although the speed limit is 100 km/h on gravel roads, it is advisable to drive at 80 km/h as they can be unpredictable and it is easy to lose control.

People with little gravel driving experience should never drive faster than 80 km/h on gravel roads, because they can be very slippery. If you overtake someone on a gravel road, drive to the far right and stay there until you are well clear. Do not overtake through dust as your visibility will be impaired.

When you encounter badly corrugated roads, do not skirt around on the sides of the road, making it wider and wider and causing what they call vehicle track pollution. Be careful of the road edges; sometimes there is a very abrupt camber that can pull you straight off the road.

Driving in thick sand

Driving on soft sand requires lowering tyre pressure to 1,2 bar, or maybe even as low as 0,8 bar. Do not reduce radial tyres less than 0,8 bar and cross-ply tyres less than 1,2 bar. Note that the pressure depends on the load of your vehicle.

You need a 4WD to drive in thick sand. Select first gear, low range. Thick sand requires momentum, you should therefore always keep moving. If you need to stop in sand, don't use the brakes but rather roll to a halt. Applying brakes will cause a wall of sand to be built up in front of the wheels, which will make pulling away very difficult.

If possible, drive thick sand as early in the day as possible. As the day gets hotter, the sand gets softer and your speed is slower and your fuel consumption higher.

Driving over rough terrain

There is no clear-cut recommended tyre pressure for driving over terrain with sharp rocks and stones. Reducing tyre pressure can improve traction, but will expose the tyres to possible damage. On the other hand, increasing tyre pressure will protect the tyre but will compromise on traction. Therefore it is best to keep the tyre pressure as recommended by the manufacturer.

You need a 4WD to drive rough terrain. Select first gear, low range. It is always best to drive very slowly directly over sharp rocks instead of trying to avoid them, because damage happens when the sidewalls of your tyre, which is only a few millimetres thick, ride up against a knife-edged rock. The tread of a tyre is much thicker and is built to deal with these rocks.

Driving in mud

Mud usually has a firm base underneath and the trick is to let the tyres cut through the mud to get traction on the firm base underneath. Narrower tyres and high tyre pressure will normally be better than wide tyres that are aired down.

Encountering mud in the Makgadikgadi Pans. (Willie Solomon)

You need a 4WD to drive in mud. Select second gear, low range. In most cases driving through mud requires momentum and speed that is high enough to get you through the obstacle but not too high to be unsafe.

Do not hold the steering wheel too tightly; feel the feedback from the tyres to the steering wheel and move with it rather than to fight it.

(Sources: Enduro Namibia, Association of All Wheel Drive Clubs of Southern Africa, 4x4 Community Forum)

FUEL

Fuel is available in most towns and generally speaking reliable and of good quality. A very good rule is to fill up at each and every fuel station that you pass, regardless of how full your tank is. The distances between towns can be great and sometimes towns run out of fuel or pumps might be out of order.

This is especially true when the demand for fuel is highest, like during the holiday season when small places need more fuel than normal to be able to supply in tourist demand. Therefore it is best to always carry at least 40 ℓ of extra fuel.

Keep in mind that low sulphur diesel (50 ppm) is not available everywhere. You will only find it in the main centres. You should in any case only buy 50 ppm diesel from fuel stations with reputable names as some travellers have found, at great cost, that not all diesel sold to them was pure.

The fuel price is regulated in Botswana. However, there might be marginal price differences from town to town. On date of going to press the fuel prices in Gaborone were: Lead Replacement 93 = 960 thebe, Unleaded 95 = 970 thebe and diesel = 976 thebe. Please note that, where fuel is sold in containers, prices will be a bit higher.

CAMPING ETIQUETTE

Botswana is the ideal destination for people who love to camp. Botswana offers a wide variety of camping options, which are all listed in this guide book. There are well equipped campsites in and around most of the bigger towns of Botswana, which allows you to camp in relative luxury such as good ablutions with hot showers and electricity. These are great if you need to clean up and sort your equipment before you go on the next leg of your trip.

The real gems for camping are the bush camps situated in many of the nature reserves and/or conservancy areas. These may be very rustic with some having absolutely no facilities apart from a designated long drop. However, these camps offer you the solitude that so many people come to seek in Botswana, and they are well worth exploring.

Botswana also has quite a few community camps. These are initiatives by the tourism industry of Botswana to assist local communities to run campsites in their areas. Some are

brilliant and others not. Please support these community camps by staying there. You should offer constructive criticism which would enable these entrepreneurs to improve their offering.

For most campsites with a reception, it is pretty obvious what the rules for the camp are. Be a good neighbour and remember that people go camping because they want to relax and enjoy nature. They are not interested in listening to your music or generator (ever!).

For bush camping and some of the remote community camps, we would like to suggest a few guidelines as these are not always managed properly. If we as campers do not take control of keeping these scenic places in a serene condition, they will deteriorate.

Camp in designated areas

When you camp you interfere with nature, so try to disturb the environment as little as possible by camping in the designated area only. Never camp near a waterhole. Animals go there to drink and your presence will deter them. The next waterhole may be very far for them. Also be on the lookout for animal trails to the waterholes and do not camp on or near their paths.

Honour bookings

Some camps may be very remote and un-manned, but still require bookings. There is nothing as bad as arriving at your booked campsite to find a squatter occupying it.

Fires

Most of these campsites will have a designated fire pit or place where previous campers made fire. Try to stick to one place otherwise the camp will be littered with leftover coals. Bring your own firewood or preferably charcoal. Never collect wood around the camp; it is simply not sustainable and in most of the national parks it is not allowed. Before you go to bed, make sure your fire is put out completely. A wind during the night could cause the fire to spread.

Waste management

These camps are in the wilderness and may be visited by officials only once a month. Under no circumstances should you leave your garbage even if bins are provided. Take along strong plastic bags or containers in order to carry your garbage out with you. Leave absolutely nothing behind; do NOT bury your garbage! Also, do not throw the leftover food or bones into the veld, thinking that you are doing the local animal population a favour. They become dependent on these rations and will over time become a nuisance to campers. Rather burn leftovers in your campfire.

The toilet

These bush camps will most probably have a designated long drop and although these are not always the nicest of places to visit, it is in everyone's interest that you do so. The breakdown of organic matter in these toilets is a natural process which should not be interfered with by adding chemicals like antiseptics, disinfectants, or anything else, to reduce bad odours.

Designated campsites probably experience quite a bit of traffic; hence if no toilet facility is provided, go into the bush and bury your business. Paper should ideally be burned instead of buried, but be careful not to start a veld fire. It is quite difficult to burn wet toilet paper, therefore it is best to put it in a bag that you can either burn in your campfire or store with the rest of your garbage.

If you are a big party, consider managing your bush etiquette as follows:

1. Dig a small ditch approximately 150 mm wide (small spade width), 200 mm deep and 5 to 20 m long (depending on the number of people and duration of stay) at an appropriate place.
2. Agree with all campers that this is the ONLY place that will be used to relief yourselves.
3. Start to use it from one side. After using it each member closes the part he/she has used. A toilet chair (toilet seat with legs) can also be used.

Cover the whole ditch with sand before your party leaves and within a short time even the toilet paper will have decomposed.

GENERAL SAFETY AND PRECAUTION

An unfortunate incident can really spoil your long-awaited holiday; therefore you need to consider a few general points on safety and precaution.

RULE NUMBER ONE

Rule number one for travelling anywhere in Africa is to be as well informed as possible. Before your trip, read up as much as possible about the areas which you will be visiting. There are various overland forums on the internet where you can ask experienced travellers just about anything you need to know.

You would also be wise to make sure that you have a good basic understanding of your vehicle and the equipment which you will be using on your trip. If you're planning a trip into remote areas, it's a good idea to do a bush mechanic course, or at least watch some video clips on the internet on how to fix some basic mechanical problems.

Make sure that your travel partner can also drive your vehicle, in case something happens to you. Familiarise him/her with the basics of the vehicle, like where to open the bonnet, how to change a tyre, etc.

Once again, if something happens to you, does your travel partner know where you keep your important information like emergency contact numbers?

Photo: Lindy Lourens

BEWARE OF GROUP TRAVEL

Some people prefer to travel on their own and some prefer to travel in a group. Whichever way you prefer, always remember rule number one and stay cautious.

Very often people are recommended not to travel alone to remote places. Group travel is, however, no guarantee for safety! If you prefer to travel in a group because you like the company or find it more convenient or economical, then do so. But never become complacent because you travel in a group. You are still responsible for every aspect of your own safety.

Sometimes group travel can be just as dangerous as travelling alone because people tend to do things that they would never have dreamt of doing when alone. They seem to be over confident because they feel safer travelling in a group. Also, most damage to vehicles occurs because people want to prove their own driving skills or the capability of their vehicles to the group.

Whether you travel alone or in a group, avoid having to admit to yourself afterwards that a disaster happened because of your own stupidity.

If you do travel in a group, give the spare keys for your vehicle to another driver in your group, just in case you lose yours. Don't forget to take it back before you split up at the end of your journey.

CARRY WITH YOU

Carry your passport with you at all times, as well as copies of all your documents. Don't leave it in your tent or wherever you stay.

TRAVELLING REMOTE AREAS

When you travel remote areas a satellite phone is a must. See our special section on Communication on page 64.

Apart from extra fuel, it is vital that you take enough extra water and dry food rations, and a few packets of rehydrate solution so that you will be able to survive five extra days in emergency situations. If you really need to, you can ration yourself to 2 ℓ of water per person per day, but remember to take that on top of your normal daily water ration. Under normal circumstances you could work on 6 ℓ of water per person per day for drinking, cooking and dishes. Ideally you should always travel with at least 40 ℓ of water with you.

In case of an emergency, stay at your car as a search party will find it easier than they will find you wandering around, especially if the search is conducted by air.

PERSONAL SAFETY

You should use good common sense when you travel Botswana, like you would when you travel anywhere else in the world. Basically the same can be said for this country as for any other country in the world: A lot of people = a lot of crime. Therefore you should be more cautious when you are in cities.

Crime is mostly confined to thefts like pickpocketing, luggage theft and burglaries. You are a welcome target if you leave your handbag or camera equipment lying openly in your car, especially if you leave your vehicle unattended.

Avoid displaying flashy jewellery and carrying your camera around your neck. Rather carry it in a camera bag over your shoulder.

When you camp, you should rather take your personal belongings with you into the tent at night, especially if the campsite is in or close to a village or town. In case you have a breakdown or accident and you cannot reach your planned destination, it is better not to pitch your tent right next to the road where everybody can see you.

It is always best to pack your loose camping equipment away at night as you never know if a wind will come up during the night.

INSURANCE

Make sure you have appropriate medical and vehicle insurance before you leave, and that your vehicle insurance includes vehicle recovery. You will find the numbers of tow in services in this guide under the towns closest to where you are.

Keep the contact numbers for your insurance with you. Remember that you cannot phone other countries' toll free numbers from Botswana, so ensure that you have direct numbers.

It is advisable to contact your medical aid/insurance prior to your trip to obtain a document which states what you are covered for and what the claim procedure is if you are in a foreign country.

DRIVING THROUGH LONG, DRY GRASS

When driving through long, dry grass, like you often find in the Kgalagadi Transfrontier Park, be very aware of the danger of vehicle burn out. ALWAYS have a fire extinguisher in the vehicle and be on the lookout for Grass Burn Out Risk warnings on your Tracks4Africa GPS map.

Grass collects underneath the vehicle around the exhaust pipe. In a short time it can catch fire and your vehicle can burn out. This risk is higher for petrol than for diesel vehicles because exhaust temperatures are much higher, although turbo diesel engines also generate a lot of heat.

In places where the grass is long, stop every 20 km or so to check for grass collecting near or on the exhaust. The exhaust will be extremely hot, so always have a thick glove, similar to the ones used by welders, in the car. Also, when you stop, don't stop over grass.

♀ *Never install any additional electrical equipment to your vehicle without a proper fuse; not only is it better for the protection of the apparatus, but it also ensures the safety of your car. Always verify the safety of any aftermarket work yourself by checking for any loose electric wiring underneath your vehicle. Sparks combined with a hot exhaust pipe and dry grass are like putting a match to a pile of dry wood.*

WILD ANIMALS

The parks in Botswana are unfenced so the wildlife can wander through. Always keep your eyes open for wild animals, especially at night. Remember that wild animals are wild and that you are entering their territory. It is never safe to leave your vehicle in wildlife areas, even if it is allowed.

It is not a good idea to swim or cool down in any of the rivers in the north of Botswana or in the Okavango Delta as there are many hungry crocodiles.

One should treat any abnormally tame actions by wild animals with suspicion because they might have rabies. Children can easily fall prey when they see these nice little 'doggies' approaching and they want to play with them. Reports were made of jackal, meerkat and even Kudu approaching vehicles and people.

Do not leave bones or other food out to attract animals to take photos. You will cause them to become tame and be shot as they pose a threat to humans. Also, don't leave any refuse bags around your camp as the animals will tear them open.

Pack away all food as wild animals, small or big, will help themselves to your food when you go to bed. Hyenas are known for carrying off or chewing on anything lying around that is foreign to them. In areas where you might encounter them, rather pack away everything at night and when leaving your camp.

A wild elephant wandering through Magotho Camp. (Hannelie Bester)

In areas where there are elephants, you shouldn't have fruit (especially citrus) with you as the elephants will do anything to get to it. Be vigilant of baboons and monkeys around your camp, for they will steal your food. Always ask the local camp warden if they have any problems with monkeys or baboons.

Never ever sleep with your tent open where wild animals roam free – no matter how hot it is – as predators will drag you out of your tent and make a meal of you. As long as your tent is zipped up, you are safe.

In Moremi or near rivers where you can encounter hippos, be aware that they come out to graze at night. Never get between a hippo and the water and do not pitch your tent in their path.

TAKING PHOTOGRAPHS

Remember common decency. You should respect people's privacy; therefore it is always best to first ask before taking photographs of them. Specific groups are especially sensitive to tourists taking photographs of them. It is not uncommon to be expected to pay a fee for each photo you take of someone or his possessions.

In Africa you should rather not take photographs of official buildings like airports or official residences. Road blocks, guard posts and people in uniform are a definite no. You do not want to clash with anybody who is in a position of power.

You should always respect people's privacy. With a digital camera you can show them the photograph that you have taken of them. (Frank Höppener)

TRIP PLANNING

(By Francois Visagie)

People travel for different reasons. Whatever your reason, it is important to put some thought into an upcoming trip before the time. Remember, success loves preparation.

DECIDE WHAT YOU WANT

How flexible is your itinerary?

Some people enjoy planning and travelling to a well-defined itinerary. They might not feel equipped to deal with unforeseen circumstances, or they might not have enough time available to accommodate delays. Others might find a fixed itinerary suffocating. Decide before the time how structured or how flexible you want your itinerary to be.

Do you want to travel in a group or on your own?

If you have never ventured into Africa, it would be wise to join a group of friends who are experienced overlanders, or even a guided tour for your first trip. If thereafter you feel comfortable enough to try it on your own, start with 'easy' routes and places. Travelling in a group can be very enjoyable and helpful, but it can at the same time really spoil your trip if you do not know the people.

What are your personal capabilities?

Be realistic about things like whether you are comfortable with camping, pitching a tent, cooking in the veld and off-road driving.

What type of accommodation do you want?

You might be a rough-and-tough bush camper or prefer camping with amenities. If you are not a camper, you can overnight in self-catering chalets or choose to splash out on luxury accommodation.

Photo: Johann Groenewald

Some people prefer a mix of accommodation options. If you camp, just remember that you need to take along the same equipment, whether you camp for one night or for two weeks.

Your type of overnight accommodation will have a direct influence on deciding where you'll need to aim for each night; it will also determine how much time you will need to settle in after arriving at your destination and how long it will take you to get going again.

How safe are your destinations?

Whether you will be venturing into unfamiliar or familiar territory, it may still pose risks that your party members might not be accustomed to; also check if your vehicle is suited to the kind of terrain. In your planning you must pay attention to the safety of your party and their vehicles. Consider that you may have to recover or repair vehicles.

Cultures differ and it will be worth your while to find out more about the people living in the areas that you want to visit. Find out about things like how to approach someone politely for advice and how to obtain permission to camp on communal land.

What problems can you expect?

If there will be any police or veterinary check points on the way or you will be crossing international borders, you should know what paperwork you need and what items you are allowed to take through and what not. Allow extra time in your itinerary for border crossings and check points.

Do you have time for all this?

Be realistic about the time you have available for your trip. You might not be able to see and do everything you want because of a time limit.

Can you pay for all of this?

Assuming you would consume the equivalent amount of food and refreshments as at home, you will need extra money for fuel, levies, accommodation, park fees, shopping, activities etc. Draw up at least a rough budget for the trip to make sure you can afford it.

PLANNING

1. Make a rough list of attractions you want to visit and activities you want to do. This will form the basis of your trip plan.

2. Read up on your destinations. Many excellent reference sources are available; most countries have official tourism websites and various internet user forums are also dedicated to overland travel. These websites and forums are usually easy to find via search engines like Google, but you can also enquire on the Tracks4Africa forum on http://www.tracks4africa.co.za.

3. Update your destinations. Remove the ones you think might be unsuitable and add any new or interesting ones you came across.

4. Now that you have an idea of where you'll be going, decide how many days of your holiday you are prepared to travel. You may also want to consider building in a day or two for contingencies.

5. Determine how many hours you'll be able to travel per day, taking into account children, people with special needs, lunch stops and the fact that it will take longer to drive scenic routes. If you camp, plan your day to be at your campsite well before nightfall. It is not pleasant to set up camp in the dark. Limit yourself to five hour's driving time per day.

6. Mark your destinations on a map. You can use a paper map for this, or create waypoints in a mapping program like Garmin MapSource. This could be useful later – see the section on Navigation. Viewing your route on Google Earth gives you a good indication of the terrain and population density of the area you will be driving through.

7. Connect your destinations on the map to form the route you'll follow. Try to follow a logical sequence to prevent double-backs that might add unnecessary travelling time. Again, you could use a paper map or something like Garmin MapSource. The T4A paper maps indicate travel time between distances and MapSource also calculates travel time.

8. When you start your detail planning, you will address issues like the following:

- Accommodation and the best time of the year to go.
- Make sure you have identified where you will replenish fuel, water and food, and if your goods will last until you reach these stops.
- Health and safety aspects. See our comprehensive section on health on page 81.
- Plan how much and where you will exchange Pula.
- Current regulations on moving fresh produce.
- Apply for guest licences for your communications equipment like two-way radios.

TRIP PLANNING CHECKLIST

Money matters

- Make sure you have a Visa Card in your travel company.
- Notify your bank that you will be using your cards in Botswana during a certain period.
- Draw up a budget.
- Arrange for adequate amounts of currency from your bank.

Ensure you take the following contact numbers with you

- To report lost or stolen bank cards.
- Medical aid. Remember to take direct dial and not toll free numbers.

- Vehicle insurance in case of an accident.
- Vehicle mechanic or service centre closest to where you will stay.
- A friend who can assist with any emergency arrangements back home.

Paperwork

- Make sure your passport is valid for six months after you are due to leave Botswana.
- Make sure you have a visa, if you need one.
- Make sure you have the correct documents for getting through the border (see page 67 for more information about border post red tape).
- Make sure that you have sufficient medical and vehicle insurance cover and you know the claims procedure.
- Make sure you have all accommodation booking confirmations with you.
- Make copies of your passport and all other documents and keep them separate from the originals.
- Load digital copies of all important documents on a secure online server in order to be able to access them from an internet café.

Medical

- Get the required inoculations and prophylactics for malaria if you're going to the north of Botswana.
- Make sure your first aid kit is well-stocked and that medicines are not past their expiry dates.

Technical stuff

- Load your route onto your GPS and make sure you have the right maps on your GPS.
- If you are taking a two-way radio, make sure it is licensed to be used where you go.
- If you are going into remote areas, rent a satellite phone if you don't have one.

Vehicle

- Make sure your vehicle's services are up to date.
- If you are taking a trailer, have that serviced as well.
- If your overland vehicle is in storage, make sure it was used from time to time.
- Make sure your tyres (for both the vehicle and trailer) are in good condition and less than five years old.
- Check mechanicals like suspension and transmission components and steering linkages, or have them checked by a mechanic.
- Check tyre pressure, oil and coolant levels shortly before you leave.
- Make sure all fuel and water tanks and containers are filled before you leave.
- You need two emergency triangles and a ZA sticker if your vehicle is registered in South Africa.

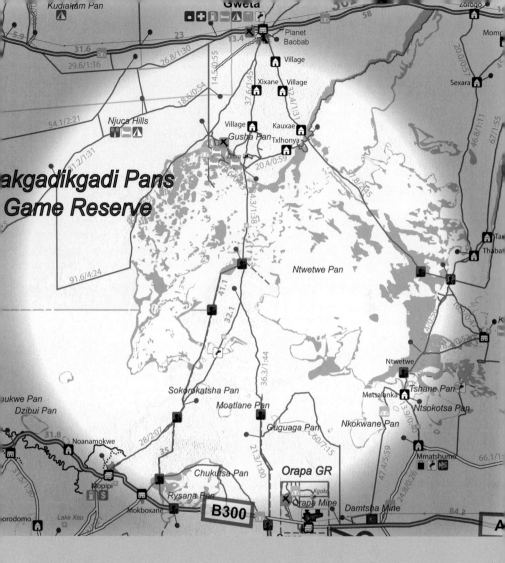

NAVIGATION

(By Francois Visagie, Wouter Brand and Johann Groenewald)

Unlike so many animal species, few of the human species possess a natural ability to navigate. For us, to know where we are and to navigate from point A to point B, usually requires some or other form of intellectual effort to construct or maintain a mental map of where we are in relation with our surroundings.

The human mental map at best is only a relative map. It exists relative to known landmarks. Absolute directions (North, South, East and West) play little or no part in the human mental map. Often people will know in which direction some landmark is, without knowing where an absolute direction like North is.

A good mental map must include absolute orientation. It must know (more or less) where North is. This is essential when travelling to new and unfamiliar places.

The ability to maintain and adjust a mental map to some degree can be called 'navigational skills'. To navigate, one needs to first of all know where you are and then know where you want to go. Fortunately humans, nowadays, have the aid of maps, both on paper and GPS, to help them navigate.

Some people prefer paper maps and others GPS maps; in fact there is a place for both when you are travelling Africa. A paper map allows you to orientate yourself better as to where you are in relation to the bigger picture of the country that you are travelling, while the GPS map can zoom in and navigate you within meters of a point. Where a paper map can give you accurate information within 50 m a GPS can do it within 5 m.

Even if you do not like to rely on a GPS, it may be a good idea to have one as a backup in case you need to

find your location on the map or simply want to retrace your tracks.

Whether you use a paper map or a GPS map or both, invest in the best possible maps that you can get. Before departing, make sure your map has accurate and up-to-date information on the areas you want to travel. This is especially vital if you are travelling remote areas.

Even if you have the best GPS with the most accurate GPS maps, the responsible traveller will still use auxiliary navigational aids such as paper maps and a compass. These are to be consulted from time to time to ensure that the mental map stays intact even after the GPS's batteries have run flat.

Whether you use a GPS or paper map for navigation, pay attention to the surroundings that you travel through. Make a mental note when you take a turn, or maybe even mark it on your map. If you find yourself in a maze of tracks, also consider noting the odometer reading at each turn.

If you're using a GPS, set it to voice-guided navigation - not for letting your mind drift off into day-dreams, but so you can pay better attention to the road and your surroundings. When you pay attention to your changing surroundings, you will have all the information needed to face any decision. If you need to turn back, you will know which way to back-track. If you need to take a detour, you'll know exactly where you are and how best to plan the detour to your destination on the map.

If you do get lost, don't panic. Although you might have missed an important turn-off, you're still a lot better off than someone who got dropped there blind-folded. You will remember quite a bit about the terrain you travelled through, for how long, and so on. Use this information to locate yourself.

You can load Tracks4Africa maps onto your Garmin GPS (Hannes Thirion)

NAVIGATION USING A GPS

Which GPS?

Before you can answer this question you have to consider what you will be using the GPS for. A very different set of requirements are to be considered if you want to use your GPS for a self-drive trip into remote areas than for other activities such as hiking, mountain biking or just normal city navigation.

If you want to travel remote areas, a GPS that can merely get you from point A to B is not good enough. If you are going to use Tracks4Africa GPS maps and want to get the full potential from your navigation system, then you need a GPS that will be compatible with Tracks4Africa maps and display the map in a particular way. If not, you must know and accept that you will not have this information at your disposal when you travel.

In the Garmin range you get the Nuvi models which are mainly intended for city navigation. They will do a perfect job to get you from point A to B, but they do not display road labels or points of interest (POI) on the map screen. The information is embedded in the map, but not displayed.

On the Tracks4Africa maps, road labels will carry information such as "off-road" or "deep sand" which is critical for your decision making. The map also carries POIs which provide additional information, for example seasonal flood warnings or dangerous sections on a trail. You would want to see this type of information on the map as you drive or when you plan a route.

If you intend to record your route with your GPS, then you need a GPS that can record and manage the tracks for the length of your trip. GPS tracks can be used for your trip report afterwards and are also very welcome at Tracks4Africa in order to update or improve our maps.

If you plan to venture into areas which are not covered in detail by the maps you have installed, then you might want to import tracks and waypoints to your GPS which can be used as a guide. This feature is normally only associated with outdoor type GPS units.

You will be using your GPS inside your vehicle and a high sensitivity GPS receiver is required to ensure that your GPS receives signals from the satellites in order to calculate its position. If your GPS does not pick up a signal in your vehicle, consider fitting an external antenna.

On a motorbike you also need to consider that your GPS is water resistant and dust proof and that you will be able to read the maps in direct sunlight.

There is one Garmin model which will tick all of the above boxes. At the time of going to press the Garmin Montana seemed to be a very good choice. It is rugged, has a big enough screen and is a true outdoor GPS which displays all map features and allows superior track management. It is, however, an expensive device and if you are merely looking for routing instructions from A to B on known roads and tracks, then any of the entry level Garmin Nuvi devices will do at a fraction of the price.

Before you go

Never leave the preparation of your GPS and associated maps to the last

minute. If you did proper trip planning, you should already have selected which maps to take on your trip and you would also have studied these maps to make sure that the places you intend to visit are indeed indicated on these maps.

If you intend using a GPS for navigation on your trip, then here are a few things to consider when preparing:

1. Get to know your GPS and all its peripherals before you go into unfamiliar territory. Test the features and maps and consider a basic training course in the use of your GPS.
2. Make sure your GPS is running on the latest firmware from the manufacturer.
3. Get the latest maps installed on your GPS and computer.
4. Make sure the route calculation method of your GPS is set to the desired setting. This would normally be fastest time with no avoidances selected.
5. If you are going to record tracks and your GPS has limited track capacity, you will not be able to record your entire trip. You can download tracks to your computer if you take one with you, otherwise set the recording method to 'wrap' when full. This way the latest recording will remain intact in case you need to track back on your steps.
6. Transfer all waypoints and tracks you would like to use for navigation from your trip planning to the

GPS and make sure you can find them under 'favourites' before you set off.

7. Get a secure mounting bracket for your GPS and find a suitable position in your vehicle. You should be able to glance at the screen without having to look away from the road ahead for too long. It should also be out of the way of other controls of your vehicle. Some units are prone to overheating if left in direct sunlight.

8. The GPS will most probably have to be powered from your vehicle's battery and the most common power supply is via the cigarette lighter plug. For a GPS with an internal battery this will be sufficient. However, an outdoor GPS without a rechargeable battery will be problematic on corrugated roads as the power supply from this connection is intermittent. Therefore it is better to have a permanently wired connection for your GPS. If you are going to use the cigarette lighter plug, take an extra fuse for it.

It is all good and well that you know how to operate the GPS. Now get one of your fellow travellers trained as well, just in case something happens to you or if you want someone to help navigate when you are driving.

On the road

By now your trip planning should have been done and your GPS equipment should be checked and installed properly. You should also have familiarised yourself with the operation of your GPS and associated maps.

Your GPS can serve as more than just a navigation device on the road. Loaded with the correct maps and travel guides, it is a great source of travel information. If, for instance, you are using the Tracks4Africa SD card, you will also have access to the T4A Africa Travel Guide. This is a rich source of information specially designed with the self-drive traveller in mind.

When you search for a place, go to 'Extras' and there you will find the guide. POIs in this guide are categorised and the points nearest to your current location will be listed according to category, like for instance picnic spots, accommodation, etc. You can scroll down and explore the places near you.

If you set your destination, your GPS will also display useful information like 'time to destination' and 'distance to destination' provided you have set up your map screen accordingly. These are very handy when the kids start asking the inevitable question. It is also useful for planning lunch stops.

Operating a GPS while driving is very dangerous. It can be seen in the same category as texting while driving. Rather pull over when you are looking up information on the GPS or let one of your passengers operate the GPS.

To navigate to a desired destination, follow these steps:
1. Make sure the correct map, and only that map, is selected. Your GPS will not configure correctly if you have more than one map selected at a time.
2. Know which route calculation method is selected and that you specifically want this method to be used. The default should be 'Fastest time'. De-select 'All-avoidances'.
3. Find the desired destination. This is based on your trip planning. You will either look up intermediate destinations or waypoints from your 'Favourites'. Then select 'Go' to start navigation on your Garmin device.
4. Review the calculated route to make sure that it takes you on a suitable route. Pay attention to the time to destination. If this is very long in relation to the distance, then you are probably going to do some 4x4 driving. Use your common sense and do not be led astray by technology.
5. Now you can follow the route instructions, but pay careful attention to major turnoffs and always correlate information from the road with what your GPS is suggesting. For instance, does the road sign indicate the same distance as your GPS?

If you do not already have accommodation booked, you would want to start looking for a place to sleep in the afternoon. You can find accommodation around you by simply browsing the contents of this book or you could scroll down to the accommodation category on your GPS to find the accommodation nearest to you. Keep the direction of these places in mind as some may be behind you. Note that the distance indicated is a straight line distance and you first have to set your GPS to navigate to a particular place before it will calculate the proper distance and, more importantly, drive time. In this book we have given distance as well as time on the road.

Also note that when you are stationary, your GPS will not show you which way you should be driving. It is only when you start moving that the GPS will pick up in which direction you are going and can orientate the map accordingly.

There are two ways to set up the map screen of your GPS when it comes to direction. You have north-up where the screen will always position the map with north aligned with the top of the screen, similar to a paper map view. Then there is track-up where the map will be rotated to always have the track you are supposed to be following pointing to the top of the screen. Whichever way you decide to use, is personal preference.

When you are on holiday, you and your family do not necessarily want to hear the GPS guidance voice. You can still use the routing function, but with the voice guidance switched off. You now need to pay attention to the screen to get routing instructions.

NAVIGATION USING A PAPER MAP

Many people consider navigating with a paper map much more exciting than merely following a GPS. This is true, because with a paper map you do not have a GPS signal indicating your position on the map like you have on the digital map of your GPS.

If you use a paper map, you need to be able to correctly orientate yourself on the map. If you are driving major routes, it is easy as they all have signs. However, when you are travelling in remote areas where the landscape is unfamiliar and there are no road signs, it becomes much more difficult to plot your exact position on the map.

If you are going to rely only on a paper map for navigation, you must study the map well before you set off for the day. Look for prominent features that can help you to orientate yourself along the way. These could be things like river crossings, major intersections, villages or mountain passes.

As you drive, plot your progress and mark the last position that you are absolutely sure of on the map. Also keep an eye on the distance you have travelled and jot down odometer readings if necessary.

Pay careful attention to where north is and determine if you are driving in the correct direction.

If you are using a Tracks4Africa paper map, you will find travel time in addition to travel distance indicated on the map. These are handy when planning your trip ahead.

If you get lost, stop and try your best to orientate yourself. You should be able to follow your tracks back by remembering prominent features you have just passed or by even following your own vehicle tracks. We trust that you have stayed on a designated track!

Get yourself to the last known position on the map and then start your route planning all over again.

BE AN ECO-TRAVELLER

Tracks left by vehicles can cause irreparable damage to the environment. It can take hundreds of years for nature to repair the scars of vehicle track pollution. These tracks can be seen clearly from an aeroplane and even on satellite photos.

Responsible travellers not only stick to existing tracks, but to the right tracks. Do not cause track pollution and unnecessary damage to fauna and flora.

There are numerous dead-end tracks leading into unspoilt areas. This is the result of indiscriminate leisure driving and people getting lost over many years. The problem is then made worse where time and time again travellers follow previous erroneous tracks.

Navigating by means of a route or using a routable GPS map is a far safer and environmentally friendly option. This is the only way to ensure that you are indeed taking the right track and therefore limiting track pollution.

Eco-travellers share information so that they can learn from each other's travel experiences. This is the only way in which we can protect and preserve the environment for future generations. If you love travelling Africa, share your tracks and experiences with fellow travellers on one of the many forums designed specifically for that purpose.

Track pollution in Mabuasehube.
(Johann Groenewald)

44

PREPARING YOUR VEHICLE FOR OVERLAND TRAVEL

(By Francois Visagie, Johann Groenewald and Bessie Brand)

When you embark on an overland trip, it is important to realise that you are actually undertaking a vehicle dependent trip. This means that the selection and preparation of your vehicle is critical.

For overland travel you need to make sure that your vehicle is safe and capable of traversing the kind of terrain you plan to cover. It also needs to be equipped for camping (if you plan on camping) and carrying all the supplies you need to take along.

CHOOSING YOUR VEHICLE

You won't be able to access the national parks of Botswana in a normal sedan, as you will encounter a lot of thick sand and water crossings. But that is only one aspect of touring Botswana. There are plenty of destinations in Botswana that are accessible to people touring in a normal sedan or 4x2 vehicle. Places like Maun offer plane trips into and over the delta as well as mokoro trips that can easily be organised from the town.

Photo: Hannelie Bester

Kasane offers fantastic daily boat cruises for game and bird viewing in the national park. There are numerous lodges and hotels that offer decent accommodation as well as transfer services.

Keen bikers believe an off-road bike is the best way to travel. A motorbike is economical and flexible because it gives you access to more roads than a four wheeled vehicle does. You can even take your bike over a river on two mokoros tied together if a ferry has broken down! Also, you don't need to plan for weeks and make lists of all the things that you need to take with, because you simply don't have space. However, you need to be an experienced biker before you venture into Africa on your iron horse.

Remember that motorbikes are not allowed in the national parks of Botswana. In spite of this Botswana is an exciting motorbike destination and offers many other nice places where motorbikes are welcome and the public roads offer enjoyable driving.

PREPARING YOUR MOTORBIKE

If you travel by bike, all you really need is money and your documents. The rest are luxuries. The less weight you carry, the better your motorcycle will handle and the less chance you have of falling and damaging yourself and your bike.

To prepare for a biking expedition, you would prepare more or less like you would for a multi-day hiking trip. Go and look what hikers use for camping, cooking and clothing when not on the bike. You need to drastically cut down on the weight of your equipment.

Extra fittings to your bike

Fuel tank

You should seriously consider fitting a long range fuel tank. If you have a range of 400 km, you will be able to cover most distances between fuel stops. If you need to carry extra fuel, a bladder system is better than extra fuel containers, because it can be easily stored when not in use.

Safety features

Fit hand guards and a bash plate to protect the sump.

Electronics

Fit a dual battery system with two external power outlets for your GPS and other electronic equipment. Most modern bikes have electronic starters; therefore it is best to protect the main battery from possible drainage.

Luggage carrier

The carriage system that you choose should be dust and water proof, and packed as low as possible. Using dry-bags is a better option than rigid boxes. If you fall, a rigid box can get damaged so badly that you cannot use it for the rest of your trip.

The best option is to strap waterproof dry-bags onto the carrier. It is crucial that once your luggage is strapped on and secure, there should be no

Your motorbike will need some extra fittings like a long range fuel tank. (Wouter Brand)

loose straps hanging off that can be caught in the chain or wheels.

Tyres

You will inevitably ride a lot of sandy tracks in Botswana, therefore you should rather fit off-road tyres. If your itinerary consists of mostly tar and good gravel roads, a dual purpose tyre will be adequate. Get specialist advice on tubeless tyres.

Tools and spares

The basic equipment for every bike includes a toolset with the right sizes specific to your bike. A tyre repair kit includes spare tubes, tyre levers, tube patches, valve spanner and, of course, an air pump.

Spares include an assortment of nuts and bolts, a sparkplug, spare clutch and brake cables, epoxy glue and a chain breaker.

Camping equipment

For camping you will need to take a good lightweight and waterproof tent, small but warm sleeping bag, thin inflatable mattress and a groundsheet that can double as an emergency blanket. For cooking, you need a basic pot and pan set, a small gas stove and basic cutlery.

Personal items

You only have space for the bare minimum when it comes to toiletries. You should invest in good protective riding and rain gear. Take one set of riding gear and one set of clothes to wear in the evening.

Water and hydration backpack

You must always carry at least three litres of water and a hydration pack in your backpack. The best way to carry water, is in a plastic bladder in your backpack.

PREPARING YOUR SEDAN OR SUV

If you are going to travel in a sedan car, SUV or a 4x2 pick-up you are most likely not going to venture into rough or remote terrain but will stick to the main roads. This may lead you to think that you do not need to prepare for every eventuality. This may be true, but we urge you to at least consider the following aspects.

Make sure you have a proper spare tyre, not one of the narrow types many vehicles are kitted out with nowadays. Make sure all your tyres

are in good condition. Remember that the mileage on your tyres is not necessarily a prediction of their fitness to travel gravel roads. Bear in mind that tyres have a limited shelf life of about five to six years, irrespective of their mileage.

Ensure that your vehicle's service schedule is up to date before you leave. If you tow a trailer, make sure that its tyres are also in good condition, that you have a spare wheel and that the trailer has been serviced as well.

Always have a container of at least 20 ℓ of drinking water and some dry food rations with you, in case of emergency.

PREPARING YOUR VEHICLE FOR TRAVEL INTO REMOTE AREAS

If you plan on venturing into remote areas, preparing your vehicle is of the utmost importance. You have to make sure that you and your fellow travellers travel safely and that you will be able to survive the ordeal if you do get into trouble.

Basics

You will have to be a self-sufficient and preferably experienced camper. If you have never done an overland trip before, we recommend that you consider renting camping equipment and try it out closer to home first. That is the best way to figure out if you and your travel companions really like camping and what you need and what you don't need. Camping equipment is expensive, and one can easily be lured into buying a lot of unnecessary paraphernalia that will cost you dearly, not only money wise, but also in terms of space and weight.

Make sure you can use all your equipment. Don't take off with stuff you've never used. When the day of reckoning arrives, you don't want to find out it doesn't work for you, or is defective or missing some essential part.

When preparing your vehicle for a trip, the first and utmost important point is to make sure that the manufacturer's services are up to date. If your overland vehicle is kept in storage, you will have to make sure that it is used and serviced regularly.

Ensure that the tyres are of good quality, in good condition and preferably not older than six years, even if they still have enough tread. Take at least one, but preferably two, good spare tyres and a puncture repair kit. Invest in a good quality kit (not the plastic ones) and make sure you know how to use it. Take your tyre compressor and pressure gauge along so that you can adjust tyre pressure as needed.

Thoroughly check your vehicle's mechanicals just before the trip. This is especially important if you haven't used your vehicle much since the previous service. This is a good time for the proverbial "bumper-to-bump-

er" check of suspension and transmission components, steering linkages, healthy engine operation, etc. If you don't have the time, ask your favourite mechanic to do it.

If you have any aftermarket products or equipment fitted to your vehicle, make sure it is in line with your vehicle's specifications. Pay particular attention to electrical equipment that could interfere with the vehicle's safety systems. Also test drive your vehicle to see if you're happy with any non-electrical and non-mechanical equipment fitted to your vehicle, like roof racks. Make sure everything is fitted securely.

Always take cable ties to refasten things that rattled loose. Take duct tape and a basic tool kit as well as a few basic spares like a fan belt and filters. Also take spares for parts that are possibly prone to failure on your vehicle model. Take at least one spare of all the fuses on your vehicle, even for the cigarette lighter plug that

A seed screen will protect your radiator from being blocked. (Peter Levey)

you use for your GPS, mobile phone, etc. Always have a fire extinguisher in your vehicle and make sure that it is full and in working condition.

Prepare your vehicle for specific conditions that you know you will be facing. If you intend driving through long grass, take along a seed screen to protect your radiator from being blocked. Try to use a net that is long enough to cover the radiator at the bottom as well, as most of the seeds are sucked up from below. Don't leave it on your vehicle all the time as it could increase your vehicle's fuel consumption by almost 10%, especially for turbo-diesels that rely on cool intake air.

If you expect having to ford deep water, take along a plastic or tarpaulin radiator cover and consider fitting a snorkel. A snorkel also helps to reduce the amount of dust being sucked into your air filter.

Knowledgeable advice can help ensure you're on the right path without wasting your money.

More than the basics

If you plan on travelling seriously remote areas, you should prepare yourself adequately to be able to repair your vehicle yourself.

If the belts and hoses on your vehicle are more than a few years old, seriously consider taking along replacement belts and hoses. They do

Take at least one, but preferably two, spare tyres on your trip. (Billy Boshoff)

not take up a lot of space and can be packed into a sealed plastic bag; with a bit of silicon spray in the bag it will last for many years. It is, however, good practice to replace rubber components after a few years as they do become brittle.

Take along the following:
- Extra tyre valves, both the inner and the entire unit. When running in thick mud, it is not uncommon for the valves to get damaged, and all the tyre repair kits in the world won't fix that.
- Spare light bulbs for every light on the vehicle: headlights, running lights, indicators, brake lights.
- Fuel filter and oil filter. Air filters are easy to clean, so you can reuse your air filter. However, if you plan on crossing rivers, take a spare one in case yours gets damp. It is better to replace it with a dry one, even if only temporarily.
- Spare oil for the engine, and a couple of litres of gearbox and differential oil.
- If you have a long range fuel pump, get a small spare pump with a hose that you can put into the long range tank and pump over to the main tank should the pump, electrics or switches fail.
- Take spare wire, connectors, fuses and electrical tape, and tools to apply them.
- Tow strap. If you're planning on driving muddy areas, you need a strap longer than 15 meters. Make sure your tow points are sufficiently strong to be towed out of thick

A puncture repair kit, tyre compressor and pressure gauge are essential tools on your trip. (Karin Theron)

sand or mud. The standard ones are inadequate.
- Bow shackles. Make sure they are double the minimum specification required for your vehicle.
- Bottle jacks for changing tyres.
- A hi-lift jack. Make sure you know how to use it as this is a dangerous piece of equipment.
- Plates to prevent the jack from sinking into sand/mud. You have to improvise!
- Jumper cables to charge a run-down battery.
- Make and take a small wire tool with a 'rake' on the end (about 1 m long) for cleaning out the grass from areas around the radiator and under the vehicle.

- If travelling in cold weather, make sure you take along sufficient emergency type gear to keep people warm, dry and visible.

Buying additional equipment

If you decide on fitting any accessories to your vehicle, remember to check your vehicle's warranty terms and conditions. Also consider that any after-market products do not go through the same quality checks as your vehicle which means that they often become the weakest link in your system.

Equipment can make one's life a lot more comfortable. In some cases equipment could even be crucial for survival. But, equipment comes at a price. The price for equipment is paid in extra weight, more space taken up, adding to the bulk of your vehicle if fitted outside and, of course, money.

Extra weight increases your vehicle's fuel consumption and stopping distance, and especially when carried on the roof-rack can make your vehicle significantly more unstable. Extra weight can also take your vehicle or trailer closer to – or over – its legal weight limit.

Additional equipment taking up more space inside could make your vehicle cramped, or could force you to leave behind other equipment you actually want to take with you.

Equipment mounted outside your vehicle – especially bulky equipment – increases its aerodynamic drag and therefore fuel consumption. This means more of your trip budget will go towards fuel, and less towards the activities you have in mind. With increased fuel consumption, you'll also need to watch the distances between refuelling points more carefully than before.

If you don't want to waste money on equipment, don't buy anything you're not 100% sure you will use again. You can consider borrowing or renting equipment until you're sure that you really can't do another trip without it. You will learn what works for you as you become more experienced.

Additional advantages and disadvantages specific to particular equipment:

Packing systems

Advantages: Packing systems make it easier and quicker to get to out-of-reach items otherwise packed far behind or deep underneath other luggage.

Disadvantages: Packing systems usually become permanent fixtures and occupy their space permanently. For the same amount of luggage, the total weight carried by your vehicle is increased by the weight of your packing system itself. Because they're built with straight lines and square corners, they usually also leave odd spaces around them that are more difficult to utilise effectively. Some people complain of noisy rattling from their packing systems.

Suggestion: If you're considering buying a packing system, look for one that has a deck covered in non-slip material with tie-down points for securely transporting your luggage stored on top.

Roof-racks

Advantages: Roof-racks make it possible to carry awkward, dirty or dangerous items outside of the vehicle cabin. People typically use them to transport items like camping equipment, firewood or gas cyliders.

Disadvantages: Items are more difficult to reach on a roof-rack and can increase your vehicle's fuel consumption. Many types of roof-racks significantly add to wind noise while travelling. The sturdier types may not be able to flex as much as your vehicle on very uneven terrain and could damage your vehicle's roof or its pillars, especially when mounted too rigidly. Any items on the roof-rack, but especially heavy ones like a second spare wheel or toolbox, raise your vehicle's centre of gravity and

Rooftop tents are convenient and quick and easy to open. A hard-shell cover cannot be damaged by low-hanging branches. (Lindy Lourens)

reduce handling stability.

Suggestion: Any gap between the front of your roof-rack and the roof of your vehicle can snag low-hanging branches. If this becomes a problem, consider fitting branch deflector cables.

Rooftop tents vs. ground tents

A rooftop tent is the easiest way to sleep off the ground. This is helpful when your campsite is uneven, overgrown or water-logged or the soil too soft to anchor a tent. In these circumstances a ground tent would be less than ideal. Especially in wilderness areas, many people also prefer rooftop tents for putting some distance between themselves and wild animals lurking around at night. However, this is a false sense of security.

Rooftop tents are quick and easy to open. However, you need to close your rooftop tent every time you want to use your vehicle. Ground tents can be left behind in your campsite but the non-pop-up types take longer to erect than rooftop tents.

There can be a significant cost difference between entry-level ground tents and rooftop tents – a budget two person dome tent is far cheaper than the cheapest rooftop tent. If your vehicle doesn't yet have a roof-rack or luggage bars, it will add to the cost of fitting a rooftop tent.

Ground tents come in a greater variety of sizes for larger groups while most rooftop tents cater for only two people. Very few cater for up to four,

and those tend to become heavy and bulky.

Being fitted to the vehicle, rooftop tents can withstand wind speeds for which ground tents might need to be anchored.

The canvas covers most rooftop tents are fitted with, can get damaged by low-hanging branches, as can ground tents packed on the roof-rack. To resolve this problem, you can consider getting a hard-shell rooftop tent or a luggage carrier for your ground tent.

Together with a roof-rack, a rooftop tent can increase your vehicle's fuel consumption by as much as 10%. However, much the same applies to a bulky ground tent transported on the roof-rack.

Off-road trailers and off-road caravans

Advantages: These can be life-savers for larger families. Off-road trailers and caravans provide additional packing space and also offer more flexibility. For instance, you can store your clothing, camping gear and groceries in the trailer or caravan, leaving only recovery gear and the picnic basket in your vehicle. You can even fit your rooftop tent (or an additional one) to some trailers. This way you can leave your whole camp behind when going on day-trips.

Disadvantages: When towing, your vehicle will be more unstable, especially in cross-winds. Before departing, make sure you are familiar and com-

Off-road trailers provide extra packing space and in this case also a rooftop tent. (Johann Groenewald)

fortable with your vehicle's handling when towing.

A trailer or caravan increases the combined weight of your vehicle, which increases fuel consumption, makes overtaking and manoeuvring in tight off-road situations more difficult and will also increase braking distance. Make very sure that when laden, your trailer/caravan + vehicle combination complies with legislated weight limits. Individual and combined weight limits are determined by: your vehicle's specifications, your trailer's or caravan's specifications as well as your driver's licence!

Suggestion: In addition to other factors to consider when buying a trailer or caravan, the ideal is to buy one with the same track width and tyres as your vehicle. The matching track width minimises drag off-road and matching the wheels and tyres means you have more swapping options in case of punctures.

Awnings

Advantages: Awnings provide shelter against sun and rain. They can make an exposed campsite pleasant – or at least bearable – and can also provide impromptu protection against rain and sun for roadside stops like lunch breaks or even repairs. Most available awnings are fairly easy to set up and stow away.

Disadvantages: Depending on their size and construction, awnings can be bulky and heavy. A heavier type can upset your vehicle's levelling unless balanced by a similar weight on the opposite side. Exposed awnings or those fitted with fabric covers are susceptible to damage from low-hanging branches. When an awning protrudes from the front of the vehicle, branches can also snag between the awning and roof-rack or the roof of the car.

Suggestion: To prevent the awning from getting damaged by branches, fit one with a metal cover. Correctly fitted branch deflector cables will help prevent the front of the awning snagging branches.

Camp showers

For the utmost in quick-and-clean simplicity, some people wash up from a basin.

To carry and set up a camp shower is considered a luxury. If you will be camping at sites with facilities you do not need to take one along. About 62% of the campsites in Botswana do have shower facilities.

Advantages: Camp showers are the easiest way to wash long hair and otherwise offer an enjoyable way of cleaning up after a hard day out. Various types are available – the most basic ones consist of a suspended water container with shower head. Many types include a water pump, there are models that also provide warm water and some come with their own collapsible enclosures; you could also buy the bits and pieces separately. Some of the basic suspended showers are made of black plastic so that it can also warm your shower water when put in the sun.

Disadvantages: Showers can be cumbersome to set up, especially the more complex ones that provide hot water and a collapsible enclosure. These will be less than ideal when you break camp every day, but are great when staying over for a few days. Showers can waste precious drinking water if you're not careful.

Suggestion: If you'll be on the move daily and will mostly be using secluded or private campsites, you could make do without an enclosure. You can also warm your water on the fire if you have a fire bucket, or in hot weather you can even get by without warmed water altogether.

Inverters

Advantages: A 220 V inverter makes it unnecessary to take along a 12 V power supply for every one of your electronic accessories – simply plug their 220 V adapters into the inverter.

Disadvantages: Being dependent on an inverter to power or charge your accessories, introduces an additional potential point of failure. Quality and reliability vary widely, so pay some attention to back-up plans. The more powerful inverters also have significant 'stand-by' consumption – the power used when the inverter is on but not powering equipment.

Suggestion: Make sure your inverter is securely mounted, with enough ventilation to prevent heat build-up and protection against dust. The latter is especially important with inverters that have internal cooling fans.

Mobile fridges/freezers

Advantages: Mobile fridges/freezers make it possible to be self-sufficient in terms of perishables for extended periods of time, or to keep drinks cool.

Disadvantages: They are generally fairly bulky. Construction materials have improved but many still tend to be quite heavy. However, the most common complaint in overlanding communities is that fridges/freezers drain battery power. With a mobile fridge/freezer your battery will need regular monitoring and when standing over for a couple of days, you'll probably need to start the engine for a few minutes every day.

Suggestion: If your fridge doesn't have a freezer compartment, create one on top yourself by laying a news-paper sealed in a plastic bag across the frozen goods. If you're catering for a larger group, instead of buying a large dual fridge/freezer or two separate units, you can save money by rotating ice packs between your freezer and cooler box. To minimise the power consumption of your mobile fridge/freezer, open it as little as possible and keep it well insulated. Ensure there is enough ventilation space around the fridge/freezer (especially around its ventilation outlet). Where possible, cover up windows against the sun; when stationary, keep your vehicle in the shade as much as possible and open some vents and windows for ventilation. Try to buy a dual 12 V/220 V freezer and use its 220 V inlet wherever you find a supply.

Most fridge/freezers are fairly bulky and take up a lot of packing space, but they allow you to be self-sufficient in terms of perishables. (Billy Boshoff)

Dual battery systems

Advantages: With a dual battery system, your mobile freezer can run off its own dedicated battery. This way the vehicle's starter battery will not be drained. Any other 12 V accessories like camp lights, inverters, electrical compressors, etc. can also be moved to the auxiliary battery.

Disadvantages: Although dual battery systems are quite simple in operation, they do add to the complexity of your vehicle's electrical system, and failures – although not common – are not unknown. Conventional systems need to have the auxiliary battery close to the starter battery to prevent cable power loss. More advanced systems are available that provide the convenience of having the batteries further apart, but they cost more and cannot charge the auxiliary battery as quickly as conventional systems. What many people also don't realise is that battery capacity is like a bank loan. Even if you increase your battery capacity (loan), your sustainable power consumption (spending) is still limited by your alternator power (income). Most

Solar panels which are not fixed onto your vehicle permanently need to be moved each time you pitch and break camp. (Billy Boshoff)

batteries will not fully recover their charge on a trip once drained; vehicle alternators simply weren't made to recondition batteries. Therefore, although dual battery systems do protect your vehicle's starter battery, they aren't a blank cheque for unlimited power usage.

Suggestion: Look for a dual battery system that has at least a low-voltage alarm, and preferably also a so-called bridge function, with which you can connect your starter and auxiliary batteries together in emergencies. This is useful for winching or for when the starter battery is flat.

Solar panels

Advantages: If you carefully manage your power consumption, with the right solar panel and enough sunshine you could run your freezer almost indefinitely. With a good regulator working in tandem with the alternator, a solar panel can even help keep your auxiliary battery better charged than the alternator on its own. As electricity sources independent of the vehicle, solar panels could also have some emergency use like charging a flat starter battery.

Disadvantages: The more powerful panels are bulky and fragile and need to be carefully mounted out of harm's way. The more robust panels are less powerful. Solar panels either take up space permanently (usually on the roof-rack), or need to be moved each time you pitch and break camp. Shade or overcast weather signifi-

cantly reduces the output of most solar panels.

Suggestion: A good solar panel regulator integrates with your dual battery system in such a way that the solar panel operates in tandem with the vehicle's alternator, without requiring you to remember or do anything.

Portable generators

If you planned on taking a generator along, we advise you to reconsider. This is way too much luxury, and the whole idea of camping is to get away from it all.

Rather leave this at home as you will be very unpopular in a campsite if you start up a generator. Most people go to remote areas to experience peace and quietness.

Most of the campsites at lodges or in towns will have electricity which means you can recharge your electronic equipment when you stay over at one of these. In Botswana 17% of all campsites do have electricity.

Long-range fuel tanks

Advantages: Long-range fuel tanks enable your vehicle to carry more fuel and travel further before needing to refuel. Normally being fitted underneath the vehicle, long-range fuel tanks could actually improve a vehicle's centre of gravity, especially compared to jerry cans on the roof-rack. Also, you do not need to take along extra fuel containers or pipes and funnel to get the fuel from the containers into your tank.

Disadvantages: Once fitted, long-range fuel tanks contribute to the permanent weight of your vehicle. They increase the vulnerable area underneath your vehicle and, depending on shape, might even decrease its ground clearance. They also add complexity and more potential points of failure to your vehicle's fuel system. Some chassis mounted long-range fuel tanks may require a transfer fuel pump to transfer fuel to the main tank. Failure of this fuel pump is a very real potential problem resulting in an out-of-fuel situation while there is still plenty of fuel in the reserve tank.

Suggestion: Get a long-range tank of common construction that any competent welder could repair if need be during your trip. If a fuel transfer pump is used, purchase a spare one and make sure you know how to connect it. Have the tank fitted to your vehicle some time before leaving on your trip to ensure through normal daily use that there are no leaks or problems with the installation.

Water tanks

Advantages: Water tanks make it possible to get rid of the scores of bottles and little containers you would otherwise have carried for extended expeditions. Usually they also make it possible to carry more water for longer distances between replenishment stops. Like long-range fuel tanks, chassis-mounted water tanks are better for the vehicle's centre of gravity than containers on the roof-

rack or inside the vehicle.

Disadvantages: Once fitted, water tanks contribute to the permanent weight of your vehicle. They increase the vulnerable area underneath your vehicle and, depending on shape, might also decrease its ground clearance.

It may also be difficult to clean a fitted tank which means that you have to use purification tablets which affects the taste of the water (and your coffee).

Suggestion: Get a simple water tank that could be easily repaired if it starts leaking during a trip. You could also just buy water in 5 ℓ containers in major towns and this way keep your drinking water separate.

Customised suspension

Advantages: Stiffer springs and/or shock absorbers may make your vehicle more stable when carrying a heavy load. Longer and/or softer springs may provide your vehicle with more articulation and traction on uneven terrain.

Disadvantages: Stiffer springs or shock absorbers can limit articulation and therefore traction on uneven terrain. Longer and/or softer springs may make your vehicle more unstable, especially at speed or on uneven terrain. Longer springs will also require you to fit longer shock absorbers.

Myth number one: "A suspension upgrade increases your vehicle's ground clearance". Of course a suspension upgrade can increase a vehicle's ground clearance slightly, but it is not simply a matter of changing springs and shock absorbers, which is not recommended for overland travel.

Myth number two: "A suspension upgrade increases your vehicle's load-carrying capacity". No matter what, that value on your vehicle's specification plate is fixed (unless you somehow manage to re-licence your vehicle).

Suggestion: From the advantages and disadvantages above you can see how these factors can work against one another. That is the one problem. The other one is that there does not seem to be many – if any – actual technical experts in the aftermarket suspension industry; experts who are trained and skilled enough to calculate what a potential suspension change would do to your vehicle. Most dealers will just sell you a standard 'lift kit'. If you load and use your vehicle within the manufacturer's recommendations, your vehicle's suspension will normally be fine.

Differential locks

Advantages: Differential locks can help traction on uneven terrain, thereby making it possible to get out of a tight spot on your own.

Disadvantages: Differential locks add to the so-called unsprung weight of the modified axle. This can cause a form of instability – known as trammelling – on corrugated surfaces which can be very dangerous. They also add to the complexity and potential points of failure in your vehicle's drivetrain. Unless de-activated when turning, differential locks increase the vehicle's turning circle and can accelerate tyre and transmission wear as well as damage to the road surface. Under certain circumstances they can suddenly transfer all engine power to a single wheel. Unless the vehicle is driven with the limitations of differential locks in mind, this can cause a catastrophe in a situation where otherwise only wheel spin would have resulted.

Suggestion: Many modern four-wheel-drive vehicles are factory-fitted with some form of traction control. If you own such a vehicle, you may not need the additional cost and complexities of a differential lock, especially if you don't foresee driving really gruelling terrain very regularly.

Snorkels

Advantages: By raising your vehicle's air intake, snorkels help keep it clearer of water and dust. This makes the air filter last longer and also makes water crossings safer for the engine.

Disadvantages: Snorkels are fitted to the outside of the vehicle, usually to the side or along the front edge of the windscreen, and are therefore exposed to potential damage from low-hanging branches. Despite being fitted with intake grids, snorkels still collect leaves and twigs which find their way to the vehicle's air cleaner which needs to be inspected and cleaned regularly.

Suggestion: To help reduce the amount of leaves and twigs collected, you can turn the snorkel's intake towards the back, although some people believe this reduces the snorkel's intake efficiency, especially at speed.

Sand/mud tracks

Advantages: These provide extra traction or better footing for recovering the vehicle from ditches, sand or mud. Two types are available: a rigid type usually called sand tracks, and a roll-up type usually made from linked rubber segments and called mud tracks. Which one is the better, depends on how you think and work. For instance, both can be used to cross sharp ditches – sand tracks could be laid across a ditch, while rolled-up mud tracks would be used to fill the ditch.

Disadvantages: Both can get very dirty from work, especially in mud, and they need to be stored in your vehicle or trailer.

Suggestion: Before stowing your muddy sand or mud tracks in your vehicle, cover them in empty firewood bags. If you don't have any, use black plastic bags (which you should always have with you in wilderness areas). Carefully consider which terrain you will drive before adding this extra weight to your vehicle.

If you are shipping your vehicle from abroad, you can have it kitted out locally. There are a number of 4x4 Fitment Centres in Botswana (Gaborone and Maun). Don't go to the first shop and start buying, shop around because prices, quality and service vary a lot.

PACKING YOUR VEHICLE

Pack only the things you absolutely need. NEED, not want or desire or which might come in handy. If you still run out of space, you need to re-think either your planning or packing, otherwise you're looking at getting a bigger vehicle or a (bigger) trailer.

Pack the heaviest items in the bottom and between the vehicle's axles. This optimises your vehicle's stability and handling with its load. Keep as little as possible on the roof; it is best not to have anything on the roof. If you have to pack on top, rather keep heavy items inside your vehicle and light stuff on the roof.

You may have to compromise to be able to fit recovery equipment. These are typically heavy, but you don't want to bury it right at the bottom if there is a good likelihood of needing it. Try being creative – perhaps you can pack it at the bottom in such a way that you can slide it in and out as needed.

CAMPING CHECKLIST

Self-drive travellers have different overnight options. They can choose to stay in full board or self-catering accommodation, or to camp. Campers have the option of travelling with and staying in a mobile home or campervan, or to camp the old-fashioned way. Well, not really the old-fashioned way, because nowadays there are so many gadgets and such a variety of equipment available in the outdoor shops. You can decide which of these things you want to take along to add some convenience to your camping, but there are some basic things that you will need for shelter and preparing your food. Here are some must-haves:

For camping

- Tent with built-in ground sheet and mosquito net (if you're not using a rooftop tent)
- Gazebo with ground sheet is convenient if you use a rooftop tent
- Hammer and spade
- Stretcher or inflatable/foam mattress
- Sleeping bag
- Sheets
- Pillow
- Folding table
- Camp chairs
- 12 V DC LED lights (preferably LED that draws low current from your vehicle battery)
- Clothes-line and pegs
- Dustpan and brush
- Wash-basin and toiletries
- Bag for carrying your towels, toiletries and clothes to the ablution block

- Cooler box or small refrigerator
- Water bottles filled with water from home (at least enough for the first day's drinking)
- Swiss army knife or Leatherman
- Picnic blanket
- Toilet paper
- Universal size plug
- Torch (a headlamp works best).

For cooking

- Braai equipment like grid, triangle, tongs, gloves, matches and fire lighters
- Gas cylinder and cooker head with spare rubber seals, key and nozzles
- Cast iron pot, frying pan, pot and kettle
- Plates and salad bowl
- Mugs and glasses
- Cutlery and can opener
- Chopping board, sharp knife and bread knife
- Egg lifter and grater
- Paper towel, tinfoil, jiffy bags (for leftovers) and refuse bags
- Washing-up bowl, dishcloths, scourers and detergents.

Technical hardware

- 220 V AC extension lead
- Extender plug
- 220 V AC battery chargers (for deep cycle batteries while at a place with electricity)
- Inverter
- Notebook with MapSource, T4A maps and photo programs installed to download tracks and photos
- External storage device to backup tracks and photos.

COMMUNICATION

When you travel, you would want to stay in contact with the outside world and/or your travel companions if you travel in a group. Nowadays there are mainly three ways of staying in touch: by cellular phone, satellite phone or two-way radio. Few travellers make use of the public phones that are still found all over Botswana.

TWO-WAY RADIO

If you want to stay in contact with other vehicles in your group, two-way radios are the most effective way. The best range will be found with VHF and UHF mobile (fixed) radios, with external antennas. These, however, require commercial radio licences. Bear in mind that licenses issued by the Independent Communications Authority of SA (ICASA) are only valid for the Republic of South Africa, and have no standing in neighbouring countries.

Two-way radios are a good way of staying in touch with other vehicles when you travel in a group. (Willie Solomon)

There has been a directive from Botswana Telecommunications department that prohibits the use of VHF radios when travelling in Botswana as it interferes with their own frequencies. Your VHF radio may be confiscated and you will be fined if you use it.

29 MHz radios, which are also good for staying in contact with a group, have a shorter span but can overcome obstacles like hills much better than VHF. They are very popular among 4x4 travellers and are allowed in Botswana. You have to apply for a visitor's license, which is difficult to get, unless you work through a communications company in Botswana. Licensed hand-held radios can be used for the above frequencies as well, but, unless they are connected to an external antenna, range will be severely limited. They have limited battery life, and an external power source should be considered. They are good enough for general convoy communication if the convoy is short. There is not much of a price difference between these hand-held radios versus the mobile (fixed) radios used by radio hams, but they have advantages like enabling you to stay in contact with the campsite when on walks in the surrounding area.

Licence-free hand-held radios can also be used, and are much more affordable than the radios mentioned above. Licence-free radios cannot operate on the licensed frequencies and vice versa. Their range is a lot shorter and they are unsuitable for convoy work, unless the vehicles are close to one another, e.g. on slow trails. The radios' ranges can be extended by connecting them to external antennas. There are many models available; not all have antenna connectors for external antennas which might be a consideration when purchasing a radio. These radios are ideal for around-camp and hiking, if that is all you need.

Many 4x4 and radio clubs will be happy to assist with detailed questions.

CELL PHONE

The Botswana mobile networks are well developed and you will have cell phone coverage in and near most towns and main routes. The two main cell phone operators are Mascom and Orange and the use of a European mobile phone is no problem. Remember the international dialling code (+267) if you want to phone local (Botswana) numbers from your cell phone.

It is, however, very expensive to make and receive calls on your cell phone once you have crossed the border. As data roaming is even more expensive, it is best to switch off the data connection of your smartphone before you cross the border.

If you organise with your own service provider to have your phone on SMS roaming, you can send and receive SMSs, but not calls. This will enable you to use your own cell phone number for messages, which will cost you much less than making or receiving calls. You will also have all your contacts' details, and should you need data connection for an emergency (like doing internet banking), you can turn your data connection on again.

The cheapest way to use your cell phone is to buy a SIM card with pay-as-you-go airtime as soon as you arrive in the country. You can buy it over the counter at almost any shop without any hassles. Let your friends and family know what your temporary number is as soon as you have swapped SIM cards.

If you want to download data to your own number, you can use wireless internet at establishments that offer it; otherwise, you would be wise to buy yourself a local 3G card with a bundle package. If you don't do that, you can end up with a hefty cell phone account when you get home.

Airtime (for phone calls) can usually be bought at any little shop but data bundles are not that readily available at the corner cafes – you may want to stock up on data bundles while you are in a city/town.

On most smartphones, replacing your SIM card with a local one changes all your settings. Although it is possible to download and change your settings back manually, you might want to consider putting the SIM card into an old phone. People find that the reception of the older phones is generally better and the batteries last longer than those of the smartphones. You can still keep all your data at hand on your smartphone.

SATELLITE PHONE

A satellite phone is a must when you travel alone into remote areas. As they provide wider coverage than cellular phones, that might be the only way to call for help in case of an accident or breakdown. Waiting for a car to pass by might take several days.

Under normal circumstances satellite phones work well, but there is no guarantee that they will work everywhere. Reception can be adversely affected by cloud and tree cover if your satellite phone is not of a good quality. It is therefore worth your while to invest in a good quality satellite phone. Airtime for satellite phones is more expensive than airtime for cellular phones, but you will only use it in case of an emergency.

If you do not have a satellite phone, consider renting one. Many vehicle rental companies also rent out satellite phones. See our section on vehicle rental companies on page 94.

Inmarsat in Johannesburg, South Africa, specialises in renting satellite phones. You can contact them at:
Tel: +27 11 794 9050
Email: info@ast-sa.co.za
Web: www.satcomms.com

BORDER POST
RED TAPE

Botswana is considered to be part of 'Africa Lite' which means that travellers won't suffer under the typical African bureaucracy. You will find that most Botswana border posts are efficiently run, albeit less sophisticated than for instance South Africa and Namibia. Be courteous and you will receive a warm welcome.

Make sure you have all the necessary paper work and you should not have any trouble.

Remember that border officials often differ in how strictly they apply regulations. This means that you may get by with them bending a rule nine out of ten times, but the tenth time you may get an official who does apply the rules strictly. Be prepared for the strict official.

The border post at Twee Rivieren/Two Rivers at the Kgalagadi Transfrontier Park. (Karin Theron)

BORDER POST CROSSINGS BETWEEN
BOTSWANA AND NEIGHOURING COUNTRIES

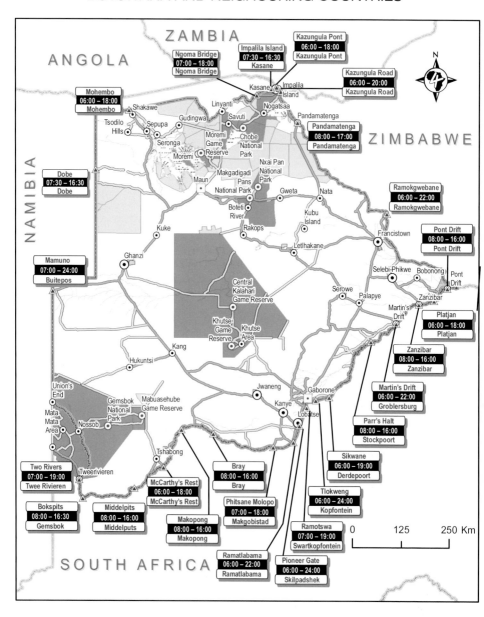

You can travel Botswana for a maximum of 90 days per year, whereafter you will have to apply at the Ministry of Home Affairs for permission to extend your stay.

DOCUMENTS REQUIRED

When you travel by car, make sure that you have the following documents at hand:

- Original vehicle registration papers (a certified copy is acceptable). People whose vehicles are still being financed by the bank, will not have the original vehicle registration documents. They would therefore use the vehicle license papers (where the renewal disk is cut out annually), or a copy of the vehicle registration papers. Have them signed by a Commissioner of Oaths.
- If you are not the registered owner of the vehicle that you are driving (e.g. it is still being financed by the bank or you are driving a friend's vehicle), you must have a letter from the financial institution or friend giving you authorization to take the vehicle across the border. This letter must stipulate dates that you are allowed to take the vehicle out of the country and be signed by a Commissioner of Oaths.

- If you are not the registered owner of the vehicle, you must have an affidavit from the police, giving you authorization from the owner/financial institution to take the vehicle abroad.
- A Carnet de Passage en Douane

(CPD) is the international customs document which covers the temporary admission of a motor vehicle and is compulsory only for vehicles coming from a country outside the Southern African Common Customs Area (Botswana, Lesotho, South Africa, Swaziland and Namibia).

A Police Clearance Certificate is not required if you are on holiday with your own vehicle, but if you enter with a work permit, you must have one.

Keep all your official documents together in a plastic envelope. Print your vehicle details (like license number and make) in large letter type and put that, together with your registration paper, back to front in the envelope so that it is readable through the envelope. If you have a trailer, put its detail to be visible if you turn the envelope around. Whenever you are asked for your vehicle or trailer details, you just hold your handy envelope against the window for the official to read.

The basic procedure for crossing a Botswana border by land is as follows:

1. The driver and all passengers must present themselves to immigration first to get their passports stamped. Always check that your passport has been stamped according to the correct dates of your stay and have it amended immediately if necessary.
2. Each passport holder older than 16 in your group will be required to fill in an Arrival/Departure form

(ask for the blue form), so take a pen with you.

3. At immigration the driver must ask for the vehicle register and complete the details. Have all the required vehicle documents ready. The driver will receive a gate pass.

4. Proceed to customs. Here the driver needs to pay the following border charges and get the stamp on the gate pass:
   - Motor Vehicle Insurance for a powered vehicle is valid for a period of three months: BWP 50. (Not applicable to trailers.)
   - National Road Fund (NRF) is valid for a period of 12 months: BWP 50. (This is applicable to cars and trailers.)
   - Road Permit for vehicles up to 3500 kg (RTP): Single entry is BWP 50; Return entry is BWP 90. (Not applicable to trailers.) If you are planning to go to Namibia/Zambia through Botswana and again return through Botswana, ask for a multi entry permit – it will save you some money. (2013 Charges).

5. Declare all your valuables at customs. Have a list of all your cameras and electronic equipment with serial numbers and values ready; it will be much easier to complete the forms.

Make sure you declare all your equipment at all the border posts; otherwise you might be liable for paying import duty when you arrive back in your home country.

6. You can now proceed to the border gate. Have your gate pass (signed by both the customs and immigration departments) together with your passports ready for inspection. If your gate pass is not stamped, you will be sent back to the border post for the additional stamp!

Not all Botswana border posts are equipped to accept payments and issue receipts for all the vehicle fees. Don't worry too much about that. If you are stopped anywhere and asked for the receipts, the official will check your passport to see at which border you crossed and will pardon you if that particular border is not equipped to take payments.

CUSTOMS

It is illegal to have any of the following prohibited goods in your possession:

- Narcotic, habit-forming drugs and related substances in any form.
- Military firearms, ammunition and explosives.
- Indecent and obscene material such as pornographic books, magazines, films, videos, DVDs and software.

Botswana is a tourist friendly country and allows visitors to take personal items like binoculars, cameras, clothing, jewellery, etc. into the country without having to pay customs duty. There are, however, restrictions on the duty free quantities of the following consumables:

Cigarettes – 200
Tobacco – 250 g
Spirits or other alcoholic beverages – 1 ℓ
Eau de Toilet – 250 ml

Cigars – 20
Wine – 2 ℓ
Perfume – 50 ml

Other than your personal items, travellers can take new or used goods to the value of not more than the equivalent of 3 000 South African rand duty free into Botswana.

When passing through Customs, you are required to declare all goods in your possession on a baggage declaration document, called Form J, to a customs official on duty.

Botswana has limitations to the quantity of food for personal use that you can take into the country:

Products	Maximum Quantity
Red meat, goat/lamb	25 kg per family
Poultry meat	5 kg per person
Tinned poultry meat	20 kg per person
Eggs	36 eggs per person
Fresh milk	2 ℓ per person
Maize and maize products	25 kg per person
Wheat	25 kg per person
Pulses (beans, peas, lentils)	25 kg per person
Sorghum and sorghum products	25 kg per person
Cabbage	1 bag per person
Onions	1 bag per person
Potatoes	1 bag per person
Oranges	1 bag per person
Tomatoes	1 box per person
Rape	2 kg per person
Spinach	2 kg per person
Bread loaves	6 per week

When you return to South Africa, you are not allowed to take fuel in containers through the border without paying import duty. Empty the fuel containers into your vehicle before crossing the border.

A SPECIAL NOTE ON MEAT, FRUIT AND VEGETABLES

The regulations on importing meat, meat products, fruit and vegetables change frequently because they are based on disease outbreaks in the region. Unfortunately there is not yet an official website that can give you the latest update on these regulations; it is therefore best to speak to people who recently visited the country. We suggest that you ask on a trustworthy travel forum (see www.4x4community.co.za, www.overland.co.za or www.tracks4africa.co.za/community) for an update, rather than relying on the personal experience of just one person.

Because foot-and-mouth disease was detected in South Africa during 2011 and 2012, the import of all cloven hoof animals (including game) from all provinces of South Africa, was banned. That means that you are currently not allowed to take any RAW meat or animal products like unpasteurised milk and cheese from South Africa into Botswana. Veterinary staff at the border will ensure that such products are confiscated and destroyed.

Botswana has good quality meat at good prices, so you might as well buy your meat there. Any Spar, Pick n Pay or Choppies have a good selection of fresh meat, as do many local butcheries. When there is an outbreak of foot-and-mouth disease, you are still allowed to take in fish and usually also chicken.

See more information about foot-and-mouth disease on page 75.

Because of the outbreak of avian flu (bird flu) among ostriches in South Africa in April 2011, some veterinary inspectors may currently confiscate chicken meat.

The Botswana Gazette reported on 17 August 2011 that, due to the outbreak of asian fruit fly (Bactrocera invadens) in the Limpopo region of South Africa, fruit and vegetables like tomatoes, citrus, mango, cashew nuts, papaya, guava, green pepper, water melons, squash, pumpkins, butternuts, bananas, avocado, patty pan, cucumber, baby marrow and several wild host plants will be restricted.

You can phone the Chief Plant Protection Officer on +267 392 8745 or +267 392 8786 for the latest update on fruit and vegetable restrictions.

VISAS

Nationals from the countries listed below are NOT required to obtain a visa when travelling to Botswana: All Commonwealth countries (except for Bangladesh, Ghana, India, Nigeria,

Pakistan and Sri Lanka), Argentina, Austria, Belgium, Brazil, Bulgaria, Chile, Czech Republic, Costa Rica, Croatia, Denmark, Dominican Republic, Estonia, Federal Republic of Germany, Finland, France, Greece, Holy See, Iceland, Israel, Italy, Japan, Latvia, Liechtenstein, Luxembourg, Mexico, Monaco, Netherlands, Norway and colonies, Paraguay, Peru, Poland, Portugal, Republic of Ireland, Romania, Russian Federation San Marino, Slovak Republic, Slovenia, South Korea, Spain, Sweden, Switzerland, United States of America, Uruguay, Venezuela and Zimbabwe.

NB: All countries that are not listed require visas for entry into Botswana. See the official Botswana Tourism website (www.botswanatourism.org) for more information about applying for a visa.

BORDER POSTS

Some border posts accept credit cards, but you cannot count on that as they might be offline. It is always best to have Pula with you (and make sure you have change) as the posts do not always accept foreign currency.

BOTSWANA/ SOUTH AFRICA BORDER

Borders across the Limpopo River can sometimes be closed during the rainy season. When in doubt, phone them to confirm if they are open.

Two Rivers/Twee Rivieren:
07:00 – 19:00
Tel: +267 653 0228.

This border crossing can only be used by tourists crossing the Kgalagadi Transfrontier Park and staying in the park for two nights.

Bokspits/Gemsbok:
08:00 – 16:30 Tel: +267 73 002 892.

There is no actual border control. Immigration is handled by the Bokspits Police Station. You will need to report at the Bokspits Police Station when you drive through the town. You will find it on the T4A GPS map.

Middlepits/Middelputs:
08:00 – 16:00
Tel: +267 653 0060.
McCarthy's Rest:
06:00 – 18:00
Tel: +267 653 0056.
Makopong:
08:00 – 16:00
Tel: +267 653 0063.
Bray:
08:00 – 16:00
Tel: +267 653 0068.
Phitsane Molopo/Makgobistad:
07:00 – 18:00
Tel: +267 548 7204.
Ramatlabama: 06:00 – 22:00
Tel: +267 54 86296.
Pioneer Gate/Skilpadshek:
06:00 – 24:00
Tel: +267 533 3992.
Ramotswa/Swartkopfontein:
07:00 – 19:00
Tel: +267 539 0344.

Tlokweng/Kopfontein:
06:00 – 24:00
Tel: +267 317 0800.

Sikwane/Derdepoort:
06:00 – 19:00 Tel: +267 570 0000.

Parr's Halt/Stockpoort:
08:00 – 16:00 Tel: +267 494 0007.

Martin's Drift/Groblersburg:
06:00 – 22:00 Tel: +267 491 5907.

Zanzibar: 08:00 – 16:00
Tel: +267 263 0012.

Platjan: 06:00 – 18:00
Tel: +267 264 6333.

Pont Drift: 08:00 – 16:00
Tel: +267 264 5260.

**BOTSWANA/
ZIMBABWE BORDER**

Kazungula Road: 06:00 – 20:00
Tel: +267 625 1303.

Ramokgwebane: 06:00 – 22:00
Tel: +267 248 9266.

Pandamatenga: 08:00 – 17:00
Tel: +267 623 2025/29.

**BOTSWANA/
ZAMBIA BORDER**

Kazungula Pont:
06:00 – 18:00 Tel: +267 625 0420.

**BOTSWANA/
NAMIBIA BORDER**

Mohembo: 06:00 – 18:00
Tel: +267 687 5505.

Ngoma Bridge: 07:00 – 18:00
Tel: +267 620 0050.

Kazungula Pont: 06:00 – 18:00
Tel: +267 625 0420.

Dobe: 07:30 – 16:30
No telephone Botswana side.
Tel. on Namibian side:
+264(0)67 243 328.

Mamuno/Buitepos: 07:00 – 24:00
Tel: +267 659 2013.

Kasane/Impalila Island:
07:30 – 16:30
Tel: +267 625 0252.

This border post and crossing is for people only – there is no vehicle access to Impalila Island from Kasane and lodge guests need to leave their vehicles in Kasane. There is secure parking in the grounds of the immigration office, and guests are transported from there to Namibian Immigration, which is on Impalila Island, by small boats. The boat trip takes about 15 minutes. At the end of their stay on Impalila Island, the guests are brought back by boat and re-enter Botswana at the same office in Kasane. There is also an air-strip on Impalila Island for access by air.

INTERNATIONAL AIRPORTS

The only international airports are in Gaborone and Maun, but there are regular regional flights to Kasane and Francistown airports from neighbouring countries.

VETERINARY FENCES AND FOOT-AND-MOUTH DISEASE

In Southern Africa the control of foot-and-mouth disease is aided by restricting the movement of animals through veterinary fences, as well as through banning the import of raw meat and animal products like unpasteurised milk and cheese of cloven hoofed animals. Import restrictions and veterinary fences are actually two forms of the same thing – animal disease control. The only difference is that import restrictions apply to international border posts between countries and veterinary fences apply to disease control within a particular affected country. Basically the same rules apply for both measures.

The aim of state veterinarians when putting up veterinary fences in the 1960s was to protect cattle against foot-and-mouth disease infections from buffalo. However, in the past 50 years, the number of diseases which potentially affect cattle and which now have to be considered as veterinary control problems has increased. The current veterinary fences are thus about more than just controlling foot-and-mouth disease.

Photo: Johann Groenewald

Buffalo, like these in Chobe, often are carriers of foot-and-mouth disease. (Peter Levey)

WHAT IS FOOT-AND-MOUTH DISEASE?

Foot-and-mouth disease or hoof-and-mouth disease (Aphtae epizooticae) is an infectious and sometimes fatal viral disease that affects cloven-hoofed animals like African buffalo, antelope, impala, springbok, sheep, goats and domestic cattle. The virus is highly variable, which limits the effectiveness of vaccination.

The virus causes a high fever for two or three days, followed by blisters inside the mouth and on the feet that may rupture and cause lameness. Adult animals may suffer weight loss from which they do not recover for several months, as well as swelling in the testicles of mature males, and in cows milk production can decline significantly. Though most animals eventually recover from foot-and-mouth disease, the disease can lead to myocarditis (inflammation of the heart muscle) and death, especially in new born animals. Some infected animals remain asymptomatic, but they nonetheless carry foot-and-mouth disease and can transmit it to others.

Foot-and-mouth disease is a severe plague in animal farming, since it is highly infectious and can be spread by close contact with infected animals as well as over a long distance. Furthermore, it can be spread through contact with contaminated meat and animal products, farming equipment, vehicles, clothing and skin of animal handlers, animal feed, and by domestic and wild predators. Its containment demands considerable efforts in vaccination, strict monitoring, export bans for meat and other animal products, quarantine, and occasionally the elimination of millions of animals.

Hedgehogs and elephants may develop mild symptoms of foot-and-mouth disease, but are resistant to the disease and do not pass it on to other animals of the same species. Just as humans may spread the disease by carrying the virus on their clothes and bodies, animals that are not susceptible to the disease may also aid in spreading it.

Humans can be infected with foot-and-mouth disease through contact with infected animals, but this is extremely rare. The disease is not to be confused with Hand, foot and mouth disease (HFMD) which is usually caused by a Coxsackie virus and often seen in toddlers. Because foot-and-mouth disease rarely infects humans but spreads rapidly among animals, it is a much greater threat to the agriculture industry than to human health.

Foot-and-mouth disease is not unique to Africa, but has been reported in countries like the United States, United Kingdom, Taiwan,

China, Japan, Korea and Bulgaria. *(Source: Wikipedia)*

IMPORT RESTRICTIONS

The conditions for importing meat into Botswana vary according to where the meat comes from. Imports of products for own consumption are the result of bilateral agreements and are subject to change depending on the prevailing animal health situation. Travellers are urged to check with the local Directorates of VeterinaryServices what the current regulations are.

You can contact Dr. Letlhogile Modisa, Director of Veterinary Services at Tel: +267 368 9000 or e-mail: lmodisa@gov.bw.

Some people do not take this prohibition seriously and try to hide their meat. However, you should be polite to your host country as something like foot-and-mouth disease can bring the whole meat industry of a region to its knees. The minute foot-and-mouth disease is detected, all exports are suspended, and that includes exports to the EU which is a

Local cattle farmers are often adversely affected by foot-and-mouth disease. (Ruud Kampf)

THE NORTH OF BOTSWANA IS CONSIDERED FOOT-AND-MOUTH-DISEASE INFECTED AREA

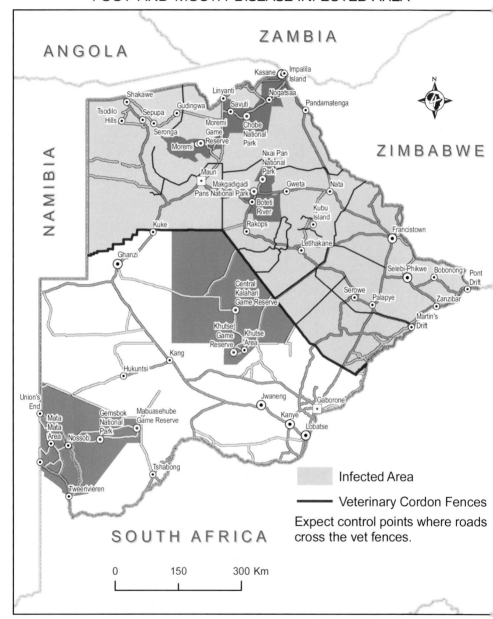

At some veterinary checkpoints you may be asked to drive your vehicle through a dip with disinfecting solution. (Hannelie Bester)

massive market for Botswana. Be a responsible visitor and respect your host country's regulations.

VETERINARY FENCES

Veterinary cordon fences are physical fences demarcating control zones in accordance with the guidelines of the International Animal Health Authority. These fences are referred to as vet fences and they are indicated with red lines on T4A's GPS maps. The movement of raw meat and animal products, including unpasteurised milk, are allowed into but not out of an area classified as an infected zone.

Often visitors feel that their vacuum packed or deep frozen meat poses a minimal disease risk, but unfortunately the logistics of having every possible permutation of the rules in a form that can be understood by the vet fence guards, is quite impossible. Therefore you should rather not try to take raw meat in any form past a vet fence checkpoint.

In Botswana vet fence restrictions basically allow you to move meat from south to north and from east to west. However, you cannot move meat from north to south and from west to east past the vet lines as the northern regions are classified as foot-and-mouth infected zones.

The vast majority of veterinary fences and the gates allowing access are static; therefore some checkpoints have been in operation at the same places for years. However, temporary veterinary gates are erected when it is possible to contain a foot-and-mouth disease outbreak within a smaller area, thus preventing it from spreading through the entire sector. This occurs quite often in Botswana on the western side of the pan handle. The temporary gates operate similar to police road blocks; sometimes they are in operation, but more often not. It all depends on the veterinary health in the area at a specific point in time.

At some of these checkpoints you may be asked to drive your vehicle through a dip filled with a disinfecting solution and you and your passengers will also have to exit the vehicle and walk on a mat impregnated with the solution to disinfect your shoes (the ones you are wearing plus extras) as it is said that the disease is also carried by the urine and faeces of infected animals.

It is best to have shoes and cool boxes/fridges readily accessible as a nothing-to-hide attitude makes life so much easier. Keep all shoes in a box so that you won't need to unpack your luggage to find them at a control point. It also prevents the disinfectant from covering other gear.

Because of vet fences you are not allowed to take meat from Maun to Nxai Pan, Makgadigadi, Nata or Ghanzi. You can however take meat from Maun to Tsodillo Hills, Moremi, Chobe or Savuti.

If you need to travel in the 'right' direction past vet fences with meat, e.g. from Ghanzi north to Maun, you should declare the meat and show your till slip indicating where you bought the meat. The official is then supposed to issue you with a permit. However, because of the human factor this system doesn't always work out well.

If you are polite and courteous to the officials at these vet check points you will very seldom encounter any problems.

Cattle crossing the road at Bobonong. (Peter Levey)

HEALTH

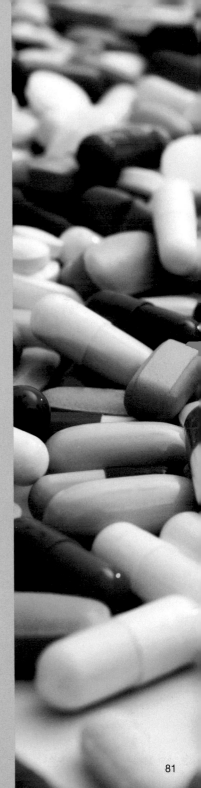

Travelling anywhere into Africa poses some health risks. You should consult a medical practitioner at your local travel clinic about all the possible risks, inoculations and vaccinations needed. Having said this, driving probably still is the biggest risk to health when travelling southern Africa!

With the courtesy of *Travelsafe Clinics*, we offer you some information on health issues for your overland trip to Botswana. You can contact
Dr. Izak Joubert of the clinic at doctor@travelsafeclinic.co.za or 0860 100072 (South Africa), +27 21 851 7643.

For some health risks you can take precaution and for others not. Malaria is the most obvious health issue when you travel to Botswana. However, hepatitis A, cholera, typhoid and diarrhoea can occur where water is not 100% safe. You should also be aware of the risk of heat exhaustion or heat stroke.

Hepatitis B is transmitted like the AIDS virus which means that if you have to undergo dental or medical procedures while in Botswana, you are at the same risk as anywhere in Africa.

The bush traveller may be exposed to tick-bite fever, rabies, bilharzia and other infections or parasitic diseases. Then there also are the risks of snake bites and scorpion stings which could be lethal.

PhotoSearch

BURNS

Second-degree burns are quite common when camping because you often make and cook over a fire. These burns are painful and usually accompanied by swelling and blisters. First degree and second degree burns that are fewer than 7 cm in diameter or totalling less than 5% of the body surface area are generally considered minor burns.

These types of burns usually heal quickly with minimal care. The only exceptions to this are burns in critical areas of the face, or burns that go around the whole circumference of a limb or finger, which need specialist care.

Prevention:

The most important thing is to prevent burns – whether it is an open fire or gas flame. Keep children and flammables away from open flames, especially cooking oil. Do not start fires with petrol or diesel.

Treatment:

The most important immediate treatment is to rapidly cool the area because heat below the surface can continue to cause tissue damage after the burn has occurred. Pouring on cold water or holding it under a running tap is recommended.

Every camper should have a few packets of sterile trauma hydrogel burn dressings in their First Aid Kit. These are designed to cool and protect burns. The hydrogel has a longer term cooling and soothing effect and the dressing instantly shields and protects the wound against further contamination and infection. Fluid loss is kept to a minimum, and so the potential for shock is reduced.

Dressings should cover the whole of the burn area. The non-adhesive moist gel impedes bonding of the dressing to the wound and thereby facilitates easy removal of the dressing. You should take the dressing off within a day and apply antiseptic ointment to prevent infection.

If you have to clean the burn area/blisters, do so with a sterile saline solution. To make a sterile saline solution, mix 10 ml salt in 1ℓ of water, boil the solution for a minute and let it cool down. Do not use an antiseptic liquid like Savlon or Dettol as it can cause chemical burns if not used in the correct dilution.

Take a pain reliever if needed.

MALARIA

Malaria is found in all areas of Botswana, except for the Southern Kalahari Desert. Therefore the biggest part of Botswana is a high risk malaria area for which you need to take prophylaxis. Even in winter when it is cooler and the risk less, there is still a lot of water around which acts as breeding ground for mosquitoes.

Most doctors will advise you not to take toddlers under the age of five into a malaria risk area. You can take some kind of precaution like spraying the children with mosquito repellents and keeping them inside mosquito nets in the afternoon and at night, but it still is a gamble and the risks are high. Remember, adults have about 10 times more blood in their bodies which means that if they do get infected, they have so much more time than a toddler before their condition gets serious.

Malanil and Malarone have paediatric versions for children of 11 kg and more, and the dosage is determined by their weight. Ask your travel clinic for more information. Malarone is extremely effective in preventing malaria and have few side effects, but can be expensive. You still need to take anti-biting precautions even if taking preventive drugs, as the drugs do not fully eliminate the risk.

Prevention:

There are measures you can take to limit mosquito bites. Mosquitoes feed mainly between dusk and dawn. Female mosquitoes will take a blood meal just before laying their eggs, which happen at night. It is therefore important that repellents are used between dusk and dawn. Use a repellent that contains DEET or a natural repellent such as lemon and eucalyptus.

While clothing alone will not protect you against mosquito bites, it can help limit bites when used together with other preventative measures. Clothing that covers the body, like long sleeves and long trousers tucked into socks, will lower the risk of being bitten. While mosquitoes are able to bite through many materials, canvas mosquito boots and thick denim jeans will make it more difficult for the mosquitoes.

Clothing that has been impregnated with permethrin will also help repel mosquitoes. Such clothing, along with impregnated wrist and ankle bands, lower the risk of mosquito bites. If you are reluctant to impregnate everyday clothing, impregnated netting worn over your clothing will prevent contact between the chemicals and skin. Most travel clinics stock sprays for clothing and nets.

Research suggests that mosquitoes are attracted by sweat and dark colours; keeping clothes (especially socks) clean and wearing light colours or white clothing, might also help prevent being bitten.

While air conditioning helps to keep mosquitoes away due to the lower temperature, it is important that it is left on all day and that the windows are closed.

Using a mosquito net in an area where there is malaria, is a good idea. Ideally, the net should be impregnated with permethrin at least every six months or when it is washed. If bed nets do not reach the floor, they should be tucked under mattresses.

Note that no precautionary measures are 100% effective.

Symptoms:

Anyone experiencing flu-like symptoms shortly after returning from a malaria area, must immediately consult a doctor and mention the visit to the malaria area. Make sure that the clinic you attend can do a reliable malaria test, either a blood slide with a microscope or one of the newer RDT (rapid diagnostic tests) dipstick tests on a drop of blood. The RDTs are often better than the microscope tests because they do not rely on how experienced the microscopist is.

Other symptoms of malaria include body pain, diarrhoea and vomiting. The usual incubation period for malaria is 14 days, but it can take as little as a week to manifest itself, or as long as two months in some cases.

HEPATITIS A

This is a viral infection of the liver which is generally transmitted by food and water. Outbreaks have been linked to contaminated water.

Prevention:

Although the water quality in Botswana is high, it is safest to treat any drinking water or to drink bottled water. Ensure that the bottles are sealed when you buy it. Don't drink anything with ice, since you cannot be sure of the source from which the ice was made.

Symptoms:

Patients usually become jaundiced, nauseous, vomit and experience joint pain that may last up to 12 weeks. It can be effectively prevented by two injections, six months apart, to give permanent immunity. (Another option is a combination vaccine against hepatitis A and hepatitis B – a series of three injections).

HEPATITIS B

This is a viral infection of the liver which is contracted in the same way as the AIDS virus. You don't know beforehand if you might need to undergo dental or medical procedures while you travel.

Prevention:

Three doses of vaccine constitute the complete series of immunisation. The first two doses are usually given one month apart with the third dose about six months later. A further booster every five years is recommended.

Symptoms:

Most people remain healthy without any symptoms while they fight off the virus. Some will not even know they have been infected. However, until the virus has been cleared, they can remain infectious.

If there are any symptoms, they will develop on average 60 to 90 days after exposure to the virus. Symptoms of hepatitis B include flu-like symptoms such as tiredness, general aches and pains, headaches and a high temperature. Further symptoms are loss of appetite and weight loss, feeling sick, being sick, diarrhoea, pain in your upper right-hand side as well as yellowing of the skin and eyes. Symptoms will usually pass within one to three months.

However, hepatitis B is said to be chronic when you have been infected for longer than six months. The symptoms are usually much milder and tend to come and go. In many cases, people with chronic hepatitis B infection will not experience any noticeable symptoms.

Symptoms of chronic hepatitis B may include feeling tired all the time, loss of appetite, feeling sick, abdominal pain, muscle and joint pains and itchy skin. This disease may eventually lead to liver cancer.

TRAVELLER'S DIARRHOEA

The reasoning "What is good for the local people, cannot be bad", is only partially correct. The local population may have developed resistance or tolerance to a number of harmful components in their food, such as parasites or other infectious agents.

Infections are the most important food related hazards. They relate mainly to the contamination of food by parasites, but also bacteria or viruses of human origin present in human excreta. These can contaminate food through dirty hands or the water used in food preparation which has

been soiled by sewage or leakages from latrines. Human excreta used as fertiliser can carry dangerous parasites or germs.

Improper hygiene of food and water leads to traveller's diarrhoea. Many of these infectious agents can be destroyed by heating, but some are found on the surface of foodstuffs such as fruit and vegetables which we do not want to cook. Meat and fish may contain parasites which undergo a biologic cycle ending in the animal. However, the intensive heat of frying, baking or stewing largely destroys these parasites.

Bacteria are responsible for 50% to 80% of cases of traveller's diarrhoea. E. coli will be the most likely cause.

Prevention:

If you prepare your own food while you travel, you limit the risk of diarrhoea substantially. Also, rather buy your food from a trusted supermarket than a street vendor or open-air market. The saying "Cook it, peel it or leave it!" carries considerable wisdom when you buy from the street markets. A solution of 10 drops of unscented bleach per 1 ℓ water can be used to rinse all veggies and/or fruit that will be consumed raw. Treat non-bottled water with chlorine iodine or silver based purifiers, or boil it.

Symptoms:

Diarrhoea causes profuse watery stools which can lead to dehydration.

RABIES

No animal bite should be ignored! Since the disease is invariably fatal once symptoms appear, post-exposure treatment is based on the principle of inducing immunity before the virus gains access to the nervous system. Victims must get treatment without delay.

Prevention:

Overland travellers should consider pre-exposure immunisation (three injections within one month) as there are many domestic dogs roaming around Botswana. Wild animals like bats, jackals, foxes, skunks, mongooses, meerkats and monkeys can also carry rabies. Be very suspicious if these animals behave as if they are tame.

Symptoms:

Rabies is a fatal disease contracted by virus-laden saliva after a bite from a rabid animal. The disease progresses

One must be very suspicious of tame meerkats as they can be carriers of rabies. (Karin Theron)

to paresis or paralysis. Spasms of muscles on attempts to swallow will lead to a fear of water (hydrophobia). Delirium and convulsions follow. After two to ten days, death results (often due to respiratory paralysis).

CHOLERA

The mode of transmission is primarily through ingestion of water contaminated with faeces or vomit of infected people or, to a lesser extent, faeces of carriers. It is often associated with flooding, poor water supplies and/or poor sanitation.

Prevention:

Cholera can be prevented by an oral vaccine dissolved in water. Its effectiveness is from six months to two years. You can avoid cholera by only drinking bottled water, especially in areas where you are not 100% sure of the water source.

Symptoms:

Cholera is caused by bacteria and will usually cause profuse watery stools and vomiting. Rapid dehydration may follow which may lead to the patient's death within a few hours.

TYPHOID

This is a systemic bacterial disease, contracted when food or water contaminated with faeces or urine of an infected person or carrier is ingested.

Prevention:

Inoculation with a typhoid injection is advised if you are travelling to remote areas where you are not 100% sure of the water source and are not able to take enough bottled water. The inoculation provides immunity for three years.

Symptoms:

It may cause fever, headache and constipation (more common than diarrhoea). Intestinal haemorrhage or perforation may occur in untreated cases, which can lead to the death of the infected person.

YELLOW FEVER

You do not need a yellow fever certificate for Botswana. However, if you cross over to Zambia or Angola, you will need one.

Yellow fever is endemic in the tropics of Africa and America and is a much bigger problem in Africa than in America. It is a virus transmitted by a mosquito which flourishes in human habitations, especially under slum conditions. It is prevalent in the large urban informal settlements in tropical Africa.

Prevention:

A single inoculation provides excellent immunity in over 95% of recipients, providing long-lasting immunity that will probably last a lifetime. International travel regulations, however, demand that boosters be administered every 10 years. The risk of infection can be minimised by taking general measures to prevent or reduce mosquito bites, as one would do for malaria.

 Keep your inoculation certificate in your passport.

Symptoms:

The time between being infected with yellow fever and the start of symptoms is usually three to six days. This is known as the incubation period.

The symptoms of yellow fever usually appear in two stages. The initial symptoms (the acute first stage) can include a high temperature, headache, shivers, nausea and vomiting, aching muscles, backache and loss of appetite. Symptoms usually improve after three or four days.

After the initial symptoms of yellow fever, about 15% of people go on to develop more severe symptoms. The symptoms of the toxic second phase can include a recurrent high temperature, abdominal pain, vomiting, a yellow tinge to the skin and whites of the eyes that is caused by liver damage, kidney failure, bleeding from the mouth, nose, eyes or stomach; you can also have blood in your vomit or stools.

Half of the people who have the second toxic phase of symptoms, die within 10 to 14 days. The other half recover with no major organ damage and are immune from the disease for life. Overall, this means that around seven or eight people out of every 100 who develop yellow fever, will die from it.

TICK-BITE FEVER

Tick-bite fever is transmitted by a hard tick. It has been shown that at all stages of development, the common dog tick (larva, nymph and adult) is infective, and there is hereditary transmission of the disease to succeeding generations through the tick eggs. (This is believed to continue indefinitely).

Prevention:

No vaccine is presently licensed for public use. This disease requires specific antibiotics for treatment. You should inspect yourself and your clothing for ticks at the end of each day, especially if you are camping in or walking through bush. Prompt removal of ticks can prevent some infections.

Symptoms:

Tick-bite fever is characterised by a primary sore (often having a blackish centre), swollen lymph nodes and, in most cases, intermittent fever lasting 10 to 14 days. The incubation period for this disease is about seven days. There is a sudden onset with significant malaise, deep muscle pain, severe headache and conjunctivitis. A rash, appearing on the hands and feet on about the third day, soon includes the palms and soles and spreads rapidly to most of the body. Bleeding underneath the skin is common. Blood tests may frequently be negative in the early stages – the diagnosis may therefore be missed if tests are not repeated! The rash on the palms and soles is also a hot clue.

BILHARZIA

This is a blood fluke infection with adult male and female worms living over a life-span of many years in certain veins of the infected person. The infection is acquired from contact with water containing free-swimming larval forms which have developed inside snails.

Prevention:

The only prevention is to avoid swimming in contaminated lakes and rivers. If you are not 100% sure that a lake or river is bilharzia free, rather abstain from swimming. (You should in any case be very cautious of crocodiles and hippos!)

Symptoms:

Severe liver complications and bladder cancer may result with chronic infections.

If you suspect that you might have been in contact with contaminated water, go for a bilharzia test at a pathologist when you return home.

SCORPIONS

The majority of scorpions are harmless to humans, although their sting is extremely painful and will require painkilling treatment.
Scorpions prefer rocky areas and mostly come out at night, apparently more so when the wind blows.

Prevention:

Campers are advised to always wear closed shoes after dusk. Outdoor lights attract insects and thus the scorpions that feed on insects. Yellow outdoor lighting is less attractive to insects and is recommended in areas where scorpions are prevalent.

It is always a good idea to check for scorpion holes during daytime so that you know before nightfall if there might be any around. A scorpion hole is easy to recognise. The burrow entrances are usually situated in open ground and look like oval shaped smallish holes.

A compound in the exoskeleton of scorpions refracts ultraviolet light in the visible spectrum and causes them to fluoresce or glow. The fluorescence is thought to serve as an ultraviolet sensitivity mechanism, perhaps allowing the scorpion to avoid damaging light levels. Because the exoskeleton glows in UV light, it is very easy to find scorpions at night using a torch with UV LEDs. If you use a UV torch and walk around your campsite at night, you have an excellent chance of finding scorpions. Depending on the UV output of the torch you will be able to find scorpions from a distance of one to ten meters. The scorpions will have a greenish glow and will be easy to spot against the dark background of the ground. The scorpions do not seem to suffer any ill effect of the UV light and do not react to the UV light at all.

(Reference: www.wildlifephotography.nl)

Boomslang. iStockphoto

Symptoms:

Moderate to more serious poisoning through scorpion sting causes malaise, sweating, heart palpitations, rise in blood pressure, salivation, nausea, vomiting and diarrhoea. Hyper acute (typically allergic) reactions include blurring of consciousness, unconsciousness, convulsions, fall in blood pressure, shock and even death.

Treatment:

Pain at the site of a scorpion sting can sometimes be limited with an ice cube, but strong painkillers might be needed. In the case of more marked symptoms, treatment must be given as for snake bites, and the patient must receive medical treatment as quickly as possible.

SNAKES

Fatalities from snake bites are quite rare and the vast majority of snakes are actually not venomous. Less than 10% of bites ever need anti-venom. Venomous snakes will often avoid humans, and if they bite they rarely inject their full venom load. In Botswana the most deadly snakes are black mambas, puff adders, boomslang and Cape cobra.

Prevention:

Be very careful and on the lookout for snakes whenever you are in the bush. It is best to wear boots when you are out in the field and shake them out in the morning before putting them on.

Symptoms:

Depending on the species of snake, there are five types of venom that have been identified. Each venom acts differently inside the body of the victim:

Cobras and mambas have neuro-toxic venom that attacks the central nervous system. It starts affecting movement, breathing, swallowing, speech and sight.

Boomslang has haematoxic venom that affects the blood by using up the clotting factors so that it no longer coagulates. This leads to extensive blood loss into the tissues.

Cape Cobra. iStockphoto

Black Mamba (Above), Puff Adder (Below). iStockphoto

Puff adders have cytotoxic venom that attacks the body cells or tissues. The bite is extremely painful with much swelling and the victim experiences marked symptoms of shock.

(Reference: http://goafrica.about.com)

Treatment:

Anybody bitten by a poisonous snake must get professional medical treatment as quickly as possible. Wash the bite with plain water and tightly bandage the limb. Note that a bandage is not the same as a tourniquet, which should never be used.

Keep the victim as still as possible to help keep the venom from entering the system. If a snake spits on you, rinse the affected area as soon as possible with clean water or milk.

Only if there is NO risk of the photographer getting bitten in the process, photos can be taken of the snake for identification purposes. This will aid the doctor/hospital in treating the bite.

SLEEPING SICKNESS

African trypanosomiasis (generally known as sleeping sickness) is a parasitic disease transmitted by tsetse fly. Apparently no new cases were reported in Botswana for decades, so it is currently not seen as a threat to visitors. There is no vaccine available for sleeping sickness.

HEAT EXHAUSTION OR HEAT STROKE

An adult should normally drink four to six litres of water or other fluids (including what is in foods) per day. High temperatures can easily double this requirement. Loss of water and salt from the body causes heat exhaustion and ultimately heat stroke.

Prevention:

Make sure that you always have enough water with you and take special precaution when you travel into remote areas. Make sure that your water intake is enough, especially when it is hot.

Symptoms:

Heat stroke occurs when the body can no longer sweat to cool itself while the body temperature is rising. Heat stroke presents with a temperature of greater than 40,6 °C in combination with vomiting, confusion and a fast pulse.

Treatment:

People suffering from heat stroke must be cooled in the shade with water poured on them, after which they must slowly start drinking water.

MEDICAL INSURANCE

You have to ensure that your own medical insurance have you well covered during your overland trip, otherwise take out extra travel insurance. Make sure that your insurance includes medical evacuation.

Medical evacuation insurance does not include search and rescue.

FIRST AID KIT

When you travel you should always have a well-kitted first aid kit. Apart from special needs like chronic medication for adults and paediatric medicine and a thermometer if you travel with children, there are a few basic things that should be in every first aid kit. If you already have a first aid kit for travelling, don't forget that medicine have a limited lifetime. Check 'use by' dates, and ask your pharmacist for advice to ensure the contents of your kit remain effective and safe to use.

If you are travelling into remote areas, you are strongly advised to do a course in first aid before you leave.

Your first aid kit should contain at least the following, but you can add medicine according to your travel party's personal needs:

1 x Quicklot trauma pack
2 x Plastic SP Joints Stabilisers
2 x Dressings
3 x Bandages
2 x Gauze swabs
1 x Triangular bandages
2 x Conforming bandages
Cotton wool
2 x Gauze
1 x Sterile dressing
1 x Sterile dressing pad
2 x Eye pads
1 x Sterile eye pad
1 x Eyebath

1 x Eye patch
2 x Big sterile trauma hydrogel burn dressing
1 x Small sterile trauma hydrogel burn dressing
1 x Roll clear Elastoplast
6 x Plasters
Respirator mouthpiece
6 x Rehydrate packets
Antiseptic ointment (e.g. BactrobanR)
Antiseptic solution
Antacid for heartburn and stomach acid
Antihistamines
Laxatives
Imodium for mild diarrhoea
A broad spectrum antibiotic
Painkillers with aspirin or paracetamol and anti-inflammatories

Skin-disinfecting agent or antiseptic wipes
Water purification tablets
Gloves, scissors, tweezers and safety-pins
Having your own syringes, sterile needles and possibly scalpels will help if you have to undergo treatment at a place where you doubt the hygiene.

INDEMNITY: *This information is NOT intended as a complete list of all the risks encountered in Botswana. Consultation with a qualified doctor at a travel clinic is recommended. Travel-safe Clinic and Tracks4Africa are not responsible for any infection/illness resulting from the use of this information.*

When you travel, you should always have a first aid kit. (Karin Theron)

PITFALLS TO RENTING A 4x4 WITH CAMPING EQUIPMENT

(By Robbie Becker from Maun Self Drive 4x4. Visit them at www.maunselfdrive4x4.com.)

It is possible to fly to Botswana and rent a 4WD vehicle, fully equipped for camping. There are many trustworthy companies with lots of experience offering this service and for some people this is a really good option. You can rest assured that the rental companies in Botswana compare to the best in the world.

It is advisable to make accommodation reservations prior to committing to hire a 4WD. Since Botswana has privatised DWNP campsites, it has become increasingly difficult to reserve your first choice of itinerary, unless you do this well in advance. For specific itineraries during high season, you have to book up to eleven months in advance. There are just a few booking agencies that are knowledgeable about routes, campsites and accommodation and have a close relationship with the privatised campsite operators.

It is possible to rent a 4x4 with camping equipment in Botswana. (Billy Boshoff)

Once your itinerary is fixed, look for recommendations on rental companies on the internet. You will often find personal recommendations on some Africa forums like www.4x4community.co.za, www. overland.co.za or www.tracks4africa.co.za/community, or you can start a new thread on one of these forums and ask for advice.

You should also search the internet for reviews on specific companies that you are interested in getting a quote from. Remember, not finding any reviews is not necessarily a negative sign. Most people tend to only comment about bad rentals or experiences.

When comparing rates, check for the terms and conditions on insurance, applicable taxes and extra charges. Going with what appears to be the cheapest quote often is not what it appears to be. Unlimited mileage seems to be the standard practice.

INSURANCE

Normally vehicle insurance does not cover the loss of personal items. Check the insurance in your rental contract, and be aware of the following fine print:
1. You can choose to pay zero excess, reduced excess or full excess in the event of loss of or damage to the vehicle. This influences your daily rental rate.
2. You might still be held responsible for damage to tyres, windscreen, glass, head lamps and paintwork.

3. Most rental companies have conditions on negligence and driving after dark.
4. Underbody and clutch damage might not be covered in your insurance.
5. Make sure your insurance covers tow in.

Ask about backup vehicles in case of breakdown or recovery. You would not want to be stuck for several days waiting for a replacement vehicle or recovery.

EXTRA CHARGES

You might be charged extra for the following:
1. Transfer to and from the airport.
2. Cleaning the vehicle on return.
3. Refuelling on return.
4. Additional driver.
5. Cross-border fees.
6. Some companies charge a once off contract or administration fee.

When renting a 4WD through an international rental company, make sure you specify that you want a 4x4 vehicle. Some rental companies will advertise a 4x4 or similar vehicle and you might end up with something like a SUV which may not be suitable for off-road driving.

For reasons of fuel economy, it is recommended to hire a 4WD with a diesel engine. A diesel engine also has better low end torque for driving in thick sand.

If you rent a vehicle with camping

equipment, ask for the equipment list in advance. Not all vehicles are kitted out the same way. If you are travelling during winter, make sure enough warm bedding is included.

It is essential that you make sure exactly what is included in your contract and what not before you rent a vehicle. Then, carefully check that you got what you expected when you receive the vehicle. It is difficult when you've just arrived and you cannot wait for the adventure to begin, but time spent checking the vehicle is time well spent.

Check that the vehicle has all the equipment you signed for and that it functions properly. Check for bad electrical connections if you rent a fridge/freezer.

It is important that the vehicle has good quality off-road tyres and that you have at least one, but preferably two, spare tyres of good quality if you intend travelling off-road. Your vehicle should be kitted with an electric compressor and pressure gauge so you can adjust tyre pressure as needed. When pumping high tyre pressures, make sure you do not overheat the compressor but give it short breaks to cool down. Make sure there is a jack and that the wheel spanner fits the nuts. Also, make sure emergency triangles are supplied. If a tyre repair kit is not included, ask for one or buy one yourself before leaving for remote areas. Even if you don't know how to use it,

someone passing by might be able to help.

Check the basic toolset which normally comes with the vehicle. Ask if they supply a spare fan belt and if not, what must be done if you have a breakage. Make sure that spare fuses are supplied and the vehicle is kitted with a fire extinguisher.

If you don't have any experience in off-road driving, you should only rent through a company that offers you 4WD driving instructions.

Vehicle maintenance is critical to the operation of a 4x4 hire company. This is the primary source of problems that develop with companies that turn around their vehicles without a proper preventative maintenance program. A company should schedule a few days at least between vehicle hire. If you discover that the maintenance work has not been done, ask for another vehicle.

Many routes involve long distances and/or a considerable number of days of game driving. Long range tanks are advisable over carrying too many jerry cans on a roof-rack. Besides the danger aspect, it raises the centre of gravity and with a rooftop tent you will exceed the recommended rooftop mass.

If you are driving in areas with water like Moremi or the Khwai River area, it is important to get up to date information on water hazard conditions

A water crossing in the Khwai River area. (Hannelie Bester)

and suggested routes. Otherwise you may land in trouble and find yourself requiring a vehicle recovery or, worse yet, in need of a replacement vehicle.

If you are driving into remote areas where traffic is infrequent, you should consider renting a satellite phone. An essential piece of equipment is a GPS with a good off-road map like the latest version of Tracks4Africa. Most companies that rent vehicles also rent these.

When you collect the vehicle, check for any damage on the paint and bumper, for windscreen cracks as well as for dents or pitting. Note any damage on the form that you have to sign and take photographs of the damage to cover yourself. Ask the rental company about their policy on fair wear and tear and the type of damage for which they charge clients. Make sure what their policy on disputes is.

Finally, make sure you have the list of emergency contact numbers of the company you are renting from. If you intend crossing a border with the vehicle, make sure you have a letter of authorization from the vehicle renting company and a certified copy of the vehicle registration papers as well as the police clearance for that specific vehicle.

Do not travel too far on the first day as you might suffer from jetlag or tiredness. Also, anything that turns out bad during the first day/night shakedown is quicker put right if you don't have a long trek back to the rental company.

See a list of companies in Botswana that rent out 4WD and camping vehicles on page 324. Tracks4Africa does not recommend these companies, but merely list them for your convenience. We cannot be held responsible for any poor service rendered by these rental companies.

We would appreciate feedback, good or bad, on the rental companies that you have used so that we can advise fellow travellers.

ADD MORE FLAVOUR TO YOUR HOLIDAY

Activities like river cruising, quad biking, hot air ballooning, horse riding and taking scenic flights, to name but a few, can really enrich your travel experience. By aeroplane, boat, hot air balloon, mountain bike, donkey, mokoro, on horseback or on foot, you will see Botswana very different from when you travel by vehicle.

If you know beforehand what kind of tour services are offered at which destinations, you can plan your holiday so much better to make the most of each day and destination.

There are many tour operators in Botswana that offer a wide variety of services, ranging from adventure activities to city tours. For your convenience we list a number of these operators. Tracks4Africa does not recommend these operators and can in no way be held responsible for poor service rendered by any of them.

You should search the internet for reviews on specific companies that you are interested in getting a quote from. Remember, not finding any reviews is not necessarily a negative sign. Most people tend to only comment about bad services or experiences. *See list of tour operators on page 324*

Flying over the Okavango Delta is really spectacular. (Lindy Lourens)

DON'T GO WITHOUT...

- A Garmin GPS that enables you to read the Tracks4Africa maps.
- Paper maps and all available information regarding the planned area to be visited.
- A good guide book will give you a lot of extra information on the region as well as practical advice that will make life much easier.
- Books on animals, birds, fauna and flora and/or trees of the region. Botswana is renowned for its natural capital and you will enjoy the region so much more if you can recognise the different animals, birds, reptiles, plants and trees.
- Download and print all available information on the destinations while planning the trip, and take it with you.
- Camera and/or video camera. Remember to take extra batteries and your chargers. Ensure you have enough charged batteries and data cards for the cameras.
- Notebook with external storage to store and backup photos and videos.
- Adaptor for power points. Botswana uses the 15 A version of the BS 546 plug.
- Binoculars.
- Insect repellent.
- A spade and toilet paper.
- Sunglasses and hat.
- Suntan lotion.
- Headlamp and/or torch with spare batteries.
- Laundry bag.
- Old towel or bathroom mat for stepping out of the bath or shower.
- Buff (for sale at outdoor shops) for keeping your head and neck warm in winter and protecting it against mosquitos in summer. It also helps if you have a bad hair day.
- Long socks will help keep you warm in winter and protect your legs against mosquitos in summer.
- Wool cap and gloves if you travel in winter because Botswana can get quite cold at night.
- Ephemeris info (see http://en.wikipedia.org/wiki/Ephemeris) of the destinations to be visited to help plan your days around sunrise/sunset, moon rise/moonset.

CENTRAL KALAHARI

The Central Kalahari Game Reserve is beautiful after good rains. (Lindy Lourens)

The Central Kalahari region includes the Central Kalahari Game Reserve and the surrounding area. The beauty of this area with its open plains, deceptive salt pans (they appear full of water until one gets to the edge) and riverbeds lie in the remoteness.

After the rains this dry area blooms and is visited by migratory gemsbok, springbok, wildebeest, ostrich and giraffe, followed by the Kalahari's famous black-mane lions, cheetah and hyena. Deception Valley is especially beautiful after rains.

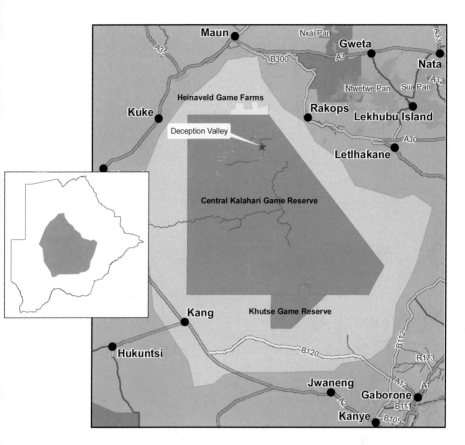

You should be self-sufficient and an experienced overlander if you want to visit this region. The undeveloped, unfenced and rustic campsites are best accessed by 4x4, especially since the Kalahari is most enticing when it is most difficult to travel.

The Central Kalahari Game Reserve was established in 1961. Originally home to the Bushmen (San people), this beautiful reserve comprises of open plains, salt pans and ancient riverbeds. It is said to be the second largest game reserve in the world; it covers an area of 52,800 km².

Khutse Game Reserve borders the south of the Central Kalahari Game Reserve and there are no fences separating the two reserves. Khutse was established in 1971 and covers an area of 2,500 km².

The **Heinaveld Game Farms** is a huge private conservation area adjacent to the northern border of the Central Kalahari Game Reserve. It offers luxury accommodation as well as camping facilities.

CENTRAL KALAHARI GAME RESERVE

The Central Kalahari Game Reserve was established in 196 and is said to be the second largest game reserve in the world. Originally home the Bushmen (San people), this beautiful reserve comprises open plains, salt par and ancient riverbeds. After the rains this dry area blooms and is visited by migrato gemsbok, springbok, ostrich, giraffe and herds of wildebeest, followed by the Kala hari's famous black-mane lions, cheetah and hyena. This is the ultimate in remot destinations, therefore you should be self-sufficient and an experienced overland er if you want to visit this region. The undeveloped and rustic campsites are be accessed by 4x4, especially since the Kalahari is most enticing when it is most di ficult to travel.

TRAVELLER DESCRIPTION:

There are a number of camps to choose from in the Central Kalahari Game Reserve Booking and pre-payment is essential for all of them, but reserve entry en vehicl fees can be paid at the gates. Bigfoot Safaris operates 41 campsites and the Depart ment of Wildlife and National Parks (DWNP) the rest. Borehole water is availabl but visitors are encouraged to bring their own drinking water. Water is only availabl at Matswere Gate and Xade Camp, so you have to fill extra containers with wate for your own campsite. This is one of the few reserves where visitors are allowed t collect wood from the bush. Night drives are prohibited.

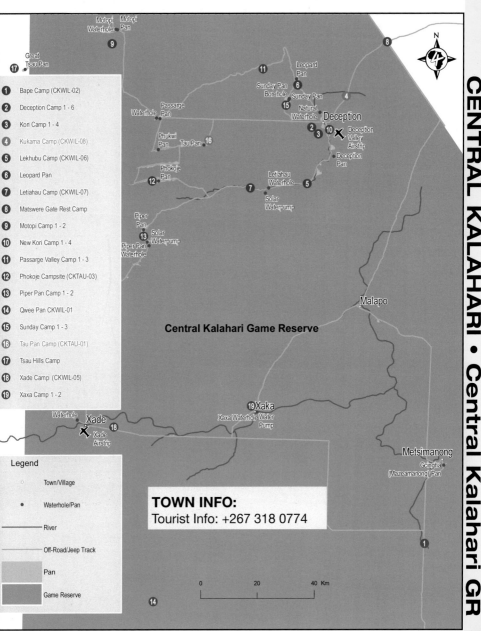

1 Bape Camp (CKWIL-02)

2 Deception Camp 1 - 6

3 Kori Camp 1 - 4

4 Kukama Camp (CKWIL-08)

5 Lekhubu Camp (CKWIL-06)

6 Leopard Pan

7 Letiahau Camp (CKWIL-07)

8 Matswere Gate Rest Camp

9 Motopi Camp 1 - 2

10 New Kori Camp 1 - 4

11 Passarge Valley Camp 1 - 3

12 Phokoje Campsite (CKTAU-03)

13 Piper Pan Camp 1 - 2

14 Qwee Pan CKWIL-01

15 Sunday Camp 1 - 3

16 Tau Pan Camp (CKTAU-01)

17 Tsau Hills Camp

18 Xade Camp (CKWIL-05)

19 Xaxa Camp 1 - 2

Central Kalahari Game Reserve

Legend

○ Town/Village

• Waterhole/Pan

── River

── Off-Road/Jeep Track

▭ Pan

▭ Game Reserve

TOWN INFO:
Tourist Info: +267 318 0774

0   20   40 Km

TRAVEL TIP: Visitors must be totally self-sufficient as the reserve is very undeveloped.

CENTRAL KALAHARI GAME RESERVE

Bape Camp (CKWIL-02) — 1

Park Camp   w179307
BWP 30.00 to 120.00 pp (2013)
111km or 5h32min NW of Khutse South Gate (4WD)

Tel: +267 318 0774, Fax: +267 318 0775
dwnp@gov.bw
www.mewt.gov.bw

The camp is still undeveloped and is only used as an overnight stop so that visitors do not drive in the park at night. Campers should be totally self-sufficient as there are no facilities.

Facilities:
Activities:

Deception Camp 1 - 6 — 2

Park Camp   w17932C
BWP 30.00 pp (2013)
40.2km or 1h56min SW of Matswere Gate (4WD)

Tel: +267 318 0774, Fax: +267 318 0775
DWNP@gov.bw
www.mewt.gov.bw

Six campsites are spread out along the track from Deception Valley to Sunday Pan. Each site is set among trees and is very private. Facilities are very basic; a pit (long drop) toilet, bucket shower and braai area.

Facilities:
Activities:

Kori Camp 1 - 4 — 3

Park Camp   w150664
BWP 30.00 pp (2013)
42.2km or 2h07min SSW of Matswere Gate (4WD)

Tel: +267 318 0774, Fax: +267 318 0775
dwnp@gov.bw

Four campsites are well spread out and situated along a side track in Deception Valley. Each site is in an area under small Acacia trees and is very private.

Facilities:
Activities:

Kukama Camp (CKWIL-08) — 4

Tented Camp   w192465
BWP 160.00 pp (2013)
25km or 1h10min SSW of Matswere Gate (4WD)

Tel: +267 39 533 60, Fax: +267 39 533 60,
Cell: +267 73 5555 73
reception@bigfoottours.co.bw, www.bigfoottours.co.bw

Bookings for Kukama are done through Big Foot Safaris but park and vehicle entry fees are still paid to the Department of Wildlife. You need to bring your own drinking water.

Facilities:
Activities:

Lekhubu Camp (CKWIL-06) — 5

Tour Operator Camp   w150222
BWP 75.00 to 200.00 pp (2013)
64km or 3h06min SSW of Matswere Gate (4WD)

Tel: +267 395 3360, Fax: +267 395 3360,
Cell: +267 73 55 5573
reservations@bigfoottours.co.bw, www.bigfoottours.co.bw

This campsite is just off the main track between Deception Valley and Piper Pan. It is situated in a small clump of Acacia trees on a small rise. You can book through Bigfoot Safaris.

Facilities:
Activities:

Leopard Pan — 6

Park Camp   w15031C
BWP 30.00 pp (2013)
54.2km or 2h35min SW of Matswere Gate (4WD)

Tel: +267 31 807 74
DWNP@gov.bw
www.mewt.gov.bw

The campsite at Leopard Pan is exposed. Facilities are a long drop toilet, bucket shower and braai area.

Facilities:
Activities:

etiahau Camp (CKWIL-07) 7

Park Camp w150084
BWP 75.00 to 200.00 pp (2013)
?4km or 4h01min SW of Matswere Gate (4WD)

el: +267 395 3360, Fax: +267 395 3360,
Cell: +267 73 55 5573
eservations@bigfoottours.co.bw, www.bigfoottours.co.bw

his campsite is situated a short distance from the track
etween Deception Valley and Piper Pan. Two areas have
een used, both under Acacia trees on a small hill. The
amp is unfenced and there are no facilities.

acilities:

ctivities:

Matswere Gate Rest Camp 8

Park Camp w189303
BWP 30.00 pu (2012)
46km or 01h11min WSW of Rakops (4WD)

(We were unable to confirm the information for this listing. Please use at your own discretion). The camp near
Matswere Gate is under-developed. There are no facilities,
and water is available, but far from the camping site.

Activities:

Motopi Camp 1 - 2 9

Park Camp w192461
BWP 75.00 to 200.00 pp (2013)
6.5km or 3h21min SE of CKGR Tsau Gate (4WD)

el: +267 395 3360, Fax: +267 395 3360,
Cell: +267 72 24 3567
eservations@bigfoottours.co.bw

n the north of the CKGR two campsites are situated far
part, near Motopi Pan. Facilities are very basic; a pit
ong drop) toilet, bucket shower and braai area. These
ampsites are operated by Bigfoot Safaris.

acilities:

ctivities:

New Kori Camp 1 - 4 10

Park Camp w211011
BWP 30.00 pp (2011)
43km or 2h10min SSW of Matswere Gate

Tel: +267 318 0774, Fax: +267 318 0775
dwnp.parrogabs@gov.bw

(We were unable to confirm the information for this listing.
Please use at your own discretion). This undeveloped
public camping site must be booked in advance. Visitors
need to be self-sufficient.

Facilities:

Activities:

assarge Valley Camp 1 - 3 11

Park Camp w149900
BWP 75.00 to 200.00 pp (2013)
?2km or 4h00min SW of Matswere Gate (4WD)

el: +267 39 533 60, Fax: +267 395 3360,
Cell: +267 73 555 573
eservations@bigfoottours.co.bw, www.bigfoottours.co.bw

hree campsites are situated near Passarge Pan. These
ites are very isolated and facilities are limited. Each site
as a pit (long drop) toilet, bucket shower and braai area.
hese sites are run by Bigfoot Safaris.

acilities:

ctivities:

Phokoje Campsite (CKTAU-03) 12

Park Camp w152044
BWP 30.00 pp (2013)
124km or 05h57min SW of Matswere Gate (4WD)

Tel: +267 318 0774, Fax: +267 318 0775
DWNP@gov.bw

Phokoje Campsite has basic facilities that include a fire pit,
toilet and shower. You need to bring your own water.

Languages: English

Facilities:

Activities:

CENTRAL KALAHARI GAME RESERVE

Piper Pan Camp 1 - 2 — 13

Park Camp — w150665
BWP 75.00 to 200.00 pp (2013)
131km or 6h43min SW of Matswere Gate (4WD)

Tel: +267 395 3360, Fax: +267 395 3360,
Cell: +267 73 5555 73
reservations@bigfoottours.co.bw, www.bigfoottours.co.bw

Piper Pan Camp 1 is set under a couple of the tallest trees in the area on the verge of Piper Pan while Camp 2 is a bit further away. Facilities are a pit (long drop) toilet, bucket shower and braai area.

Facilities:
Activities:

Qwee Pan CKWIL-01 — 14

Park Camp — w22671

Central Kalahari Game Reserve, SSE of Xade Gate

We don't have any detailed information available on this listing because we were unable to contact them. However, it has been visited by our Tracks4Africa community of travellers.

Sunday Camp 1 - 3 — 15

Park Camp — w150313
BWP 75.00 to 200.00 pp (2013)
56.2km or 2h43min SW of Matswere Gate (4WD)

Tel: +267 395 3360, Fax: +267 395 3360,
Cell: +267 73 55 5573
reservations@bigfoottours.co.bw, www.bigfoottours.co.bw

Campsite 1 is situated on the west of Sunday Pan in a small Acacia grove and campsites 2 and 3 on the east of the pan, overlooking a waterhole. Facilities are a long drop toilet, bucket shower and braai area.

Facilities:
Activities:

Tau Pan Camp (CKTAU-01) — 16

Tented Camp — w15121
USD 440.00 to 520.00 pp (2013)
84km or 4h36min SW of Matswere Gate (4WD)

Tel: +267 683 0095, Fax: +267 686 1457
reservations@kwando.co.bw
www.kwando.co.za

The camp at Tau Pan opened in March 2009 and offers eight comfortable, thatched en-suite tents. Each tent has an outside shower, a fan and private viewing deck. Guests can relax in the dining room, lounge or library.

Facilities:
Activities:

Tsau Hills Camp — 17

Park Camp — w195857

139km or 03h26min ENE of Dekar

We don't have any detailed information available on this listing because we were unable to contact them. However, it has been visited by our Tracks4Africa community of travellers.

Xade Camp (CKWIL-05) — 18

Park Camp — w15149
BWP 30.00 pp (2013)
35km or 1h40min SE of Xade Gate (4WD)

Tel: +267 318 0774, Fax: +267 318 0775
dwnp@gov.bw
www.mewt.gov.bw

Xade is a great stop-over while travelling from Matswere Gate through the Park to Khutse Gate. It is also the only place in the Park where you can fill up your water tanks. This undeveloped campsite has limited facilities.

Facilities:
Activities:

Xaxa Camp 1 - 2 19

Park Camp w192464
BWP 30.00 pp (2013)
89.8km or 4h30min E of Xade Gate (4WD)

Tel: +267 318 0774, Fax: +267 318 0775
dwnp@gov.bw
www.mewt.gov.bw

Xaxa Camp is located on very thick sand and has no
facilities. Two sites, situated opposite the waterhole, are
available.

Facilities:

Activities:

Photo: Lindy Lourens

KANG

KANG Post Office

- SEND AND RECEIVE LETTERS, PARCELS AND CASH
- ACCESS INTERNET, PHOTOCOPY AND FAX DOCUMENTS
- BUY STATIONERY

Bo w o

Kang is situated in the Kalahari Desert and lies on the Trans-Kalahari Highwa' between Ghanzi in the north and Sekoma in the south. The route via Ghanzi take' one to the Namibian border, whilst that to Sekoma leads to Gaborone, the capita of Botswana. Kang is about halfway between Windhoek and Johannesburg o the Trans-Kalahari Highway and is a good pit-stop on the A2 between Ghanzi an Lobatse.

TRAVELLER DESCRIPTION:
Kang provides access to the Kgalagadi Transfrontier Park in the south-west and the Central Kalahari Game Reserve in the north-east. You can refuel and replenish stocks in Kang.

TRAVEL INFO:
There is no private doctor or hospital in Kang, but you can visit the clinic for medical help. Their number is +267 651 7021. For serious injuries or sickness you will be taken to the hospital in Hukuntsi.

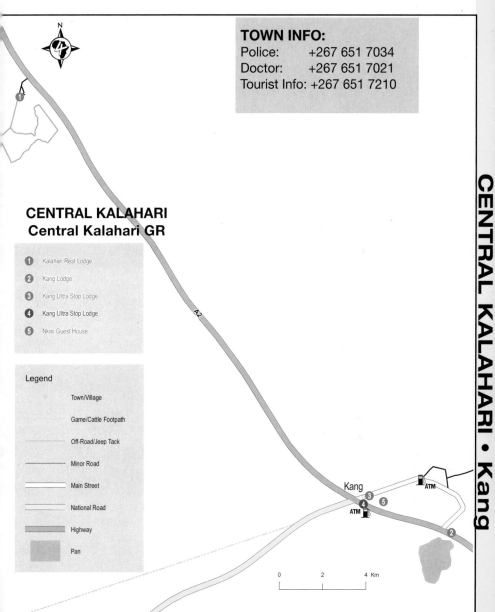

TOWN INFO:
Police: +267 651 7034
Doctor: +267 651 7021
Tourist Info: +267 651 7210

CENTRAL KALAHARI
Central Kalahari GR

1. Kalahari Rest Lodge
2. Kang Lodge
3. Kang Ultra Stop Lodge
4. Kang Ultra Stop Lodge
5. Nkisi Guest House

Legend

○	Town/Village
	Game/Cattle Footpath
	Off-Road/Jeep Track
	Minor Road
	Main Street
	National Road
	Highway
	Pan

Kang

TRAVEL TIP: There is an ATM at the Cash and Carry shop.

KANG

Kalahari Rest Lodge — 1

Lodge   w179202
BWP 475.00 to 660.00 pu (2012)
26km or 20min NW of Kang

Cell: +267 72 386 548
bmhe@it.bw
www.kalaharirest.com

The lodge offers en-suite chalets as well as camping facilities. Each campsite has its own bathroom, dishwashing facility and a 220V power point. The bar is open to all guests.

Facilities:

Activities:

Kang Lodge — 2

Lodge   w150945
BWP 510.00 to 560.00 pu (2012)
5km or 6min ESE of Kang

Tel: +267 651 8050, Fax: +267 651 8049
kanglodge@gmail.com

The lodge, situated next to the Trans Kalahari Highway, is the perfect stopover after a long journey. They offer chalets with en-suite bathrooms and air conditioning. No camping.

Languages: English

Facilities:

Kang Ultra Stop Lodge — 3

Lodge   w179348
BWP 250.00 to 560.00 pu (2012)
Trans Kalahari Highway, in Kang

Tel: +267 651 7294, Fax: +267 651 7294
ultrastopkang@yahoo.com
www.kangultrastop.com

The lodge is situated at the Ultra Fuel Stop. It offers comfortable, en-suite budget accommodation. Rooms are air-conditioned and have satellite television and coffee/tea making facilities. Guests can relax at the bar.

Facilities:

Activities:

Kang Ultra Stop Lodge — 4

Lodge Camp   w256087
BWP 40.00 pp (2012)
Trans Kalahari Highway, in Kang

Tel: +267 651 7294, Fax: +267 651 7294
ultrastopkang@yahoo.com
www.kangultrastop.com

The lodge, conveniently situated at the Ultra Fuel Stop, also has a camping area. Campers are welcome to use the lodge facilities and bar.

Facilities:

Activities:

Nkisi Guest House — 5

Guest House   w179207
BWP 560.00 to 720.00 pu (2012)
2km or 3min E of Kang

Tel: +267 65 173 74, Fax: +267 6517 389
nkisiguesthouse@yahoo.com
www.nkisiguesthouse.com

The guest house offers a variety of en-suite rooms, ranging from single or double to family size. The restaurant is open from 07:00 to 21:00 and the guest house will happily pack you a snack box for the road.

Facilities:

Activities:

Photo: Lorraine du Toit

KHUTSE GAME RESERVE

ENING HOURS
- 18:30hrs (Apr - Sept)
) - 19:00hrs (Oct - Mar)
JOY YOUR STAY

KHUTSE

Photo: Willie Solomon

Khutse Game Reserve borders the Central Kalahari Game Reserve. Khutse was established in 1971 and covers an area of 2,500 km² in Bakwena tribal land. It has undulating bush savanna and pans overgrown with grass. Many herbivores thrive on this grass, which in turn attract predators. Khutse is a protected area with minimum development, except for the areas that have been made camp-sites. The wilderness atmosphere has been carefully preserved, offering a sense of timelessness and isolation. All camps are unfenced allowing animals entry into the camp grounds, so be alert.

TRAVELLER DESCRIPTION:
Campsites are mainly concentrated in an area between Khutse I and Khutse II Pans, but more isolated individual camps are to be found at Moreswe Pan in the south-western area of the reserve. Further isolated sites are Maharushele, Molose, and Khanke. Camping is also possible at Khutse South Gate Rest Camp which has a nearby airstrip. Visitors to Khutse should be completely self-sufficient as the camp-sites have very basic facilities like a longdrop, bucket shower and a fire pit. There is no drinking water and visitors must take out their own litter. All campsites must be pre-booked through Bigfoot Safaris; reserve and vehicle entry fees can be paid at the gates.

TRAVEL INFO:
There are some private lodges just outside the Game Reserve.

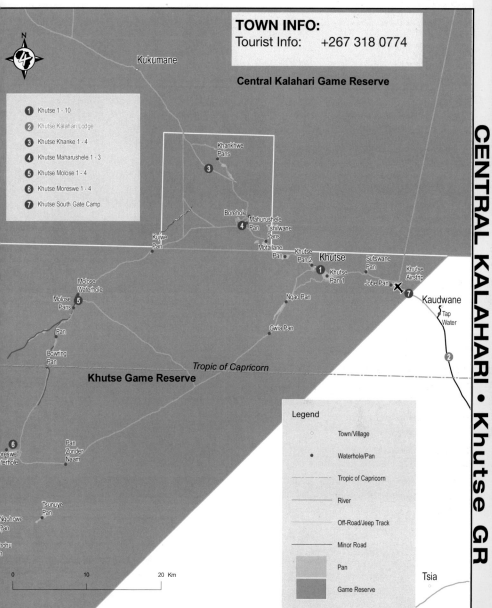

TOWN INFO:
Tourist Info: +267 318 0774

Central Kalahari Game Reserve

Kukumane

N

1 Khutse 1 - 10
2 Khutse Kalahari Lodge
3 Khutse Khanke 1 - 4
4 Khutse Maharushele 1 - 3
5 Khutse Molose 1 - 4
6 Khutse Moreswe 1 - 4
7 Khutse South Gate Camp

Khankhwe Pans

3

Borehole
Mahurushele Pan
Tshilwane Pans

Kutiwe Pan

Motailane Pan

Khutse Pan 2

Khutse

Khutse Pan 1

1

Sutswane Pan

Khutse Airstrip

Jobe Pan

X

7

Kaudwane

Tap Water

Molose Waterhole

Molose Pans

5

Ngao Pan

Pan

Gwia Pan

Bowring Pan

Tropic of Capricorn

Khutse Game Reserve

2

6
reswe terhole

Pan Zonder Naam

Tsunuye Pan

Ngohowe Pan

ohu

Legend

○	Town/Village
●	Waterhole/Pan
- - -	Tropic of Capricorn
——	River
——	Off-Road/Jeep Track
——	Minor Road
▨	Pan
▨	Game Reserve

Tsia

0   10   20 Km

KHUTSE GAME RESERVE

Khutse 1 - 10   1

Park Camp   w179140
BWP 75.00 to 200.00 pp (2013)
14km or 1h05min NW of Khutse South Gate (4WD)

Tel: +267 395 3360, Fax: +267 395 3360,
Cell: +267 73 55 5573
reservations@bigfoottours.co.bw

Ten campsites are situated between Khutse I and Khutse II Pans. Facilities are very basic; a pit (long drop) toilet, bucket shower and braai area. These campsites are operated by Bigfoot Safaris.

Facilities:
Activities:

Khutse Kalahari Lodge   2

Lodge   w179327
BWP 980.00 to 1250.00 pp (2012)
11km or 21min SE of Khutse South Gate (4WD)

Tel: +267 31 871 63, Fax: +267 390 8501,
Cell: +267 71 972 900, reservations@khutsekalaharilodge.com, www.khutsekalaharilodge.com

Accommodation is offered just outside the Game Reserve in en-suite rondavels. The main lodge area has an elevated deck which allows spectacular views of the surrounding bush. Pre-booking is essential. Credit cards only accepted at their office in town.

Facilities:
Activities:

Khutse Khanke 1 - 4   3

Park Camp   w179358
BWP 75.00 to 200.00 pp (2013)
38km or 2h38min NW of Khutse South Gate (4WD)

Tel: +267 395 3360, Fax: +267 395 3360,
Cell: +267 73 55 5573
reservations@bigfoottours.co.bw, www.bigfoottours.co.bw

There are four campsites near Khanke Pan. Facilities are very basic; a pit (long drop) toilet, bucket shower and braai area. These campsites are operated by Bigfoot Safaris.

Facilities:
Activities:

Khutse Maharushele 1 - 3   4

Park Camp   w150171
BWP 75.00 to 200.00 pp (2013)
28km or 1hr42min NW of Khutse South Gate (4WD)

Tel: +267 395 3360, Fax: +267 395 3360,
Cell: +267 73 55 5573
reservations@bigfoottours.co.bw, www.bigfoottours.co.bw

Three campsites are situated close to Maharushele Pan. Facilities are very basic; a pit (long drop) toilet, bucket shower and braai area. These campsites are operated by Bigfoot Safaris.

Facilities: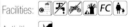
Activities:

Khutse Molose 1 - 4   5

Park Camp   w179355
BWP 75.00 to 200.00 pp (2013)
53km or 2h55min W of Khutse South Gate (4WD)

Tel: +267 395 3360, Fax: +267 395 3360,
Cell: +267 73 55 5573
reservations@bigfoottours.co.bw, www.bigfoottours.co.bw

There are four campsites situated near Molose Pan. Facilities are very basic; a pit (long drop) toilet, bucket shower and braai area. These campsites are operated by Bigfoot Safaris.

Facilities:
Activities:

Khutse Moreswe 1 - 4   6

Park Camp   w150054
BWP 75.00 to 200.00 pp (2013)
76km or 5h47min SW of Khutse South Gate (4WD)

Tel: +267 395 3360, Fax: +267 395 3360,
Cell: +267 73 55 5573
reservations@bigfoottours.co.bw, www.bigfoottours.co.bw

Four campsites are situated around Moreswe Pan. Facilities are very basic; a pit (long drop) toilet, bucket shower and braai area. These campsites are operated by Bigfoot Safaris.

Facilities:
Activities:

hutse South Gate Camp — 7

ark Camp — w151040

WP 75.00 to 200.00 pp (2013)

ocated at Khutse South Gate (4WD)

el: +267 395 3360, Fax: +267 395 3360,

ell: +267 73 5555 73

eservations@bigfoottours.co.bw, www.bigfoottours.co.bw

hutse South Gate Camp cannot be pre-booked as these re emergency campsites only. Facilities are a long drop ilet, bucket shower and braai area. There is no running ater.

acilities:

ctivities:

hoto: Karin Theron

CHOBE/KASANE

Elephants coming down to the waterhole to drink at the Senyati Safari Camp near Kasane. (Hannelie Bester)

The Chobe National Park is the biggest attraction of the Chobe/ Kasane region. It is one of the largest parks in Botswana and the landscape varie from lush floodplains, dense Mopane forests and savanna to grasslands. You ca expect to see a wonderful wealth of game including giraffe, elephant, zebra, hippo potamus, buffalo, warthog, lion, hyena, jackal, bat-eared fox, cheetah, wild dog anc

Elephant Graveyard

**Impalila
Island** **Kasane**

Chobe Flood Plains

A33

Lesoma Memorial

Linyanti

Nogatsaa Tchinga

Kwando Reserve

Linyanti

Nogatsaa

Gudingwa

Bushmen Rock Art

Savuti

Chobe National Park

Maun

A3

A33

A33

a huge variety of antelope. Chobe is notorious for its huge elephant population.

The landscape and animals vary from the central part of the park to the Chobe Flood Plains, Linyanti, Savuti and Nogatsaa sections of the park. You need a 4WD to drive in Chobe. Camps are unfenced, so you need to be alert for wild animals. You are not allowed to collect fire wood in the park; therefore you must bring enough wood with you.

Linyanti, which is a very popular part of the park, is on the delta which forms the border between Botswana and Namibia. The only campsite in Linyanti is run by the SKL (Savute Khwai Linyanti Concession) and a tented camp was erected recently.

Bushmen rock art can be seen at a historical site in Savuti. A visit to the elephant graveyard on the Chobe Flood Plains offers an eerie experience.

Animal migrations from the adjacent Moremi Game Reserve are one of the highlights of Chobe. Chobe is one of the few places on earth where you will find the rare Puku antelope and the endemic Chobe bushbuck.

Game viewing is best during the drier months when the animals come down to drink at the river or permanent waterholes within the park. One of the great pleasures of Chobe is that you can view game from a boat on the Chobe River. You have a choice between camping or lodge accommodation in the park.

A beautiful viewpoint from Kasane. (Peter Levey)

A mokoro is the best mode of transport to get by in the Kasai Channel. (Willie Solomon)

You would be wise to make your reservations well in advance. It is best to phone the Department of Wildlife and National Parks (DWNP) in the mornings for reservations; you will battle to get hold of them after 15:00. Camping fees can only be paid at the main gates. If you don't plan on entering at one of the main gates you have to prepay at one of the DWNP offices. You have to show your official receipt (which is also your entry permit) at the gate. Park entry and vehicle fees can be paid at all gates.

Outside the park

Many of the wilderness areas in this region are managed by community trusts who usually partner with photo or hunting tour operators as a means of raising funds for community development.

The Kwando Reserve is quite a big conservation area run under conces-sion by Kwando Safaris, who operates various camps on the Kwando River.

Kasane is the main town of this region and is a tourist hub. From Kasane you can visit Impalila Island on Namibian territory or do day trips to the Victoria Falls of Zimbabwe. Kasane also offers boat trips for game viewing on the Chobe River and many visitors find this a highlight of their tour. It is quite spectacular to see so many different animals and birds in such a short time and it is very enjoyable to sail on a large boat with a top deck from where one has a 360 degrees view.

Close to Kasane the Lesoma Memorial was erected in remembrance of the 15 Botswana Defence Force Soldiers who were killed when the civil war in Rhodesia (now Zimbabwe) spilt over into Botswana.

CHOBE / KASANE

119

CHOBE NATIONAL PARK

The Chobe National Park is one of the largest parks o Botswana. Nogatsaa and Tchinga in the northern section of the park are probably the most under-utilised game areas of the park. Camps were closed to the public a few years ago. Nogatsaa has a cluster of clay-bottomed pans that hold water well into winter. Often they hold the only water for miles around during the dry season. The Savuti Marsh is still evidence of a large inland lake that dried up long ago. Today the Marsh is fed by the erratic Savuti Channel which is currently flowing. In January 2010 it reached the Savuti Marsh for the first time since 1982. As a result of this variable flow, there are hundreds of dead trees along the channel's bank. As the bigger Savut region is also covered with extensive savannahs and rolling grasslands, this section of the Chobe National Park is rich in bird life and especially during the rainy season it is a wildlife haven as animals move in to feed on the lush new grass. They are then followed by predators.

TRAVELLER DESCRIPTION:
Overlanders often travel through the Nogatsaa area en-route from Kasane to Savuti. You can either use the western route via the Chobe Riverfront, or the eastern route through the Nogatsaa Pans. During the wet season you are recommended to rather use the western route via the Chobe Riverfront as you can easily get stuck in the clay soils found around the pans. However, birding can be particularly good around the pans at that time of the year. You can fly or drive into Savuti, although the roads are especially challenging and muddy during the rainy season.

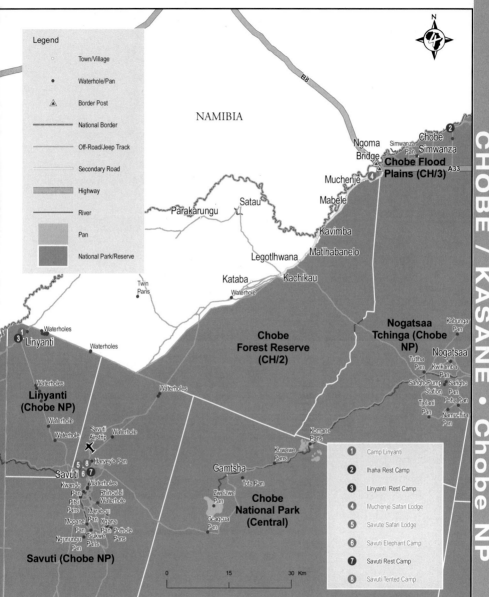

Legend

- ○ Town/Village
- • Waterhole/Pan
- ▲ Border Post
- ▬ National Border
- — Off-Road/Jeep Track
- — Secondary Road
- ▬ Highway
- ─ River
- ▨ Pan
- ▨ National Park/Reserve

NAMIBIA

B8

Ngoma Bridge
Simwanza Pan
Chobe
Simwanza
Chobe Flood Plains (CH/3)
A33

Muchenje
Mabele

Satau
Kavimba
Parakarungu
Matlhabanelo
Legotlhwana
Kataba
Kachikau
Waterhole

Twin Pans

Waterholes
Linyanti
Waterholes

Chobe
Forest Reserve
(CH/2)

Nogatsaa
Tchinga (Chobe
NP)
Kabunga Pan
Nogatsaa
Tutlha Pan
Kwikamba Pan
Sangho Pump Station
Sangho Pan
Poha Pan
Tjelani Pan
Namuchira Pan

Waterholes
Linyanti
(Chobe NP)

Waterholes
Waterhole

Waterhole
Savuti Airstrip
Waterhole
✕ Harvey's Pan
Komane Pans

Kowawe Pans

Savuti
Kwando Pan
Waterholes
Rhinovlei Waterhole
Pitsi Pans
Marabou Pan
Mopane Pan
Xgana Pan
Pothole Pans
Ngunungu Pan
Tsukwe Pans

Gamtsha
Tola Pan
Zwelzwe Pan
Ceagcua Pan

Chobe
National Park
(Central)

Savuti (Chobe NP)

0   15   30 Km

1 Camp Linyanti
2 Ihaha Rest Camp
3 Linyanti Rest Camp
4 Muchenje Safari Lodge
5 Savute Safari Lodge
6 Savuti Elephant Camp
7 Savuti Rest Camp
8 Savuti Tented Camp

TRAVEL INFO:

Chobe National Park is a Malaria risk area, especially during the rainy season. There is no petrol, diesel or food supply available anywhere in the park.

TRAVEL TIP: To enter the Chobe National Park you need a 4WD vehicle.

CHOBE NATIONAL PARK

Camp Linyanti — 1

Tented Camp   w256088
USD 415.00 to 500.00 pp (2012)
39km or 01h52min NNW of Savuti (4WD)

Tel: +267 68 653 65, Fax: +267 686 5367
sklcamps@botsnet.bw
www.sklcamps.com

The water camp offers five intimate and charming round shaped beige canvas tents in beautiful surroundings. Open sky showers. Overlooks the great Linyanti River.

Facilities:
Activities:

Ihaha Rest Camp — 2

Park Camp   w150087
BWP 100.00 to 260.00 pp (2012)
43km or 1h15min W of Chobe Sedudu Gate (4WD)

Tel: +267 686 1448, Fax: +267 686 1448,
Cell: +267 71 308 283
kwalatesafari@gmail.com

Situated in the middle of Chobe National Park, the camp has ten sites with own braai areas close to the river. Solar panels are used for hot water and lights. There are two clean ablution blocks.

Facilities:
Activities:

Linyanti Rest Camp — 3

Park Camp   w179287
ZAR 50.00 pp (2013)
40km or 01h48min NNW of Savuti Camp (4WD)

Tel: +267 686 5365, Fax: +267 686 5367
reservations@sklcamps.co.bw
www.sklcamps.com

Five campsites each has their own water point and braai area. The camp is secluded and has flush toilets. Reservations are made through Mapula Lodge in Maun. You have to drive through very deep sand to reach this camp.

Languages: English

Facilities: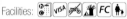
Activities:

Muchenje Safari Lodge — 4

Lodge   w179228
USD 375.00 to 595.00 pp (2013)
60km or 01h21min WSW of Kasane

Tel: +267 62 000 13, Fax: +267 62 00 016,
Cell: +27(0)72 170 8879
info@muchenje.com, www.muchenje.com

The lodge offers accommodation in eleven thatched chalets, each with en-suite bathroom and private veranda. Guests can make use of the library or relax at the bar. Airport transfer services available.

Facilities:
Activities:

Savute Safari Lodge — 5

Game/Safari Lodge   w150946
USD 476.00 to 856.00 pp (2013)
No self-drive access (4WD)

Tel: +267 686 1559, Fax: +267 686 0037
info@desertdelta.com
www.desertdelta.com

Twelve en-suite chalets each has a private viewing deck on top of the lodge's expansive deck. Visit the nearby ancient San rock art. No children under 6 years. Every year the camp closes for a few weeks for maintenance.

Languages: English

Facilities:
Activities:

Savuti Elephant Camp — 6

Tented Camp   w179197
USD 680.00 to 1430.00 pp (2013)
Savuti, Chobe NP (4WD)

Tel: +27(0)21 483 1600, Fax: +27(0)11 481 6065
safaris@orient-express.com
www.savuteelephantcamp.com

The camp, situated in the heart of the Chobe National Park, offers accommodation in twelve en-suite luxury tents on raised wooden decks. The camp overlooks the Savuti Channel.

Facilities:
Activities:

Savuti Rest Camp 7

Park Camp   w179201
ZAR 60.00 to 250.00 pp (2012)
Savuti, Chobe NP (4WD)

Tel: +267 686 5366, Fax: +267 686 5367
reservations@sklcamps.co.bw
www.sklcamps.com

Most of the ten campsites are under big Acacia trees. Sites 1 to 4 overlook the Savuti Channel. There is an ablution facility with flush toilets and running water and all sites have a dustbin and fire pit.

Facilities: 🚻 VISA ✂ 🏕 FC 👥

Activities: 🥾

Savuti Tented Camp 8

Tented Camp   w256092
USD 415.00 to 500.00 pp (2012)
Savuti, Chobe NP (4WD)

Tel: +267 68 653 65, Fax: +267 686 5367
sklcamps@botsnet.bw
www.sklcamps.com

Five Meru-style tents on platforms overlook Savuti Channel. The tents are spacious with en-suite facilities as well as an outside shower. Activities include game drives twice a day. Transfer to and from the airstrip.

Facilities: 🛏 🍴 VISA ✂ ✗ 👥

Activities: 🥾 🚙

Photo: Lindy Lourens

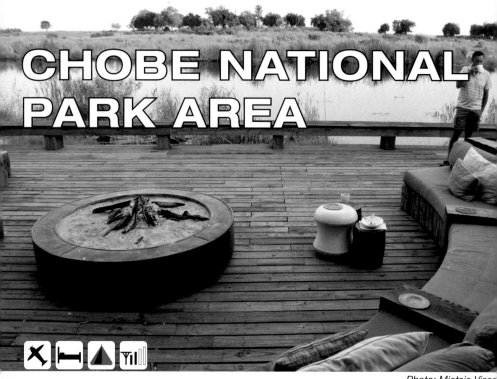

CHOBE NATIONAL PARK AREA

Photo: Mietsie Visse

The area west of the Chobe National Park and north of the Moremi Game Reserve caters mainly for upmarket fly-in tourists. This is a vast and remote conservation area that is run mostly by local communities or under concession by tour operators. It includes the Selinda Private Game Reserve, Kwara Reserve, Kwando Reserve and the Linyanti Wildlife Reserve. Special features of this area are the Linyanti River, Savuti Channel and the Selinda Spillway.

This area has a wonderful diversity of habitat that makes it a haven for wildlife. There are open grasslands and waterholes along the Savuti Channel and the Linyanti River as well as Mopane and Leadwood forests inland.

TRAVELLER DESCRIPTION:

This remote area mainly offers luxury tented accommodation. There are a number of airstrips that provide fly-in access to these upmarket lodges. Self-drive access is either not possible or not allowed. Note that despite there being a track marked on the maps from Seronga towards the Linyanti, this is not a practical route to use. Firstly, neither private self-drive vehicles nor mobile operators are allowed to drive through the private concessions between Linyanti and the Okavango. Secondly, even with a GPS navigation would be a complete nightmare, and the hunters in the centre of the concessions wouldn't be at all welcoming.

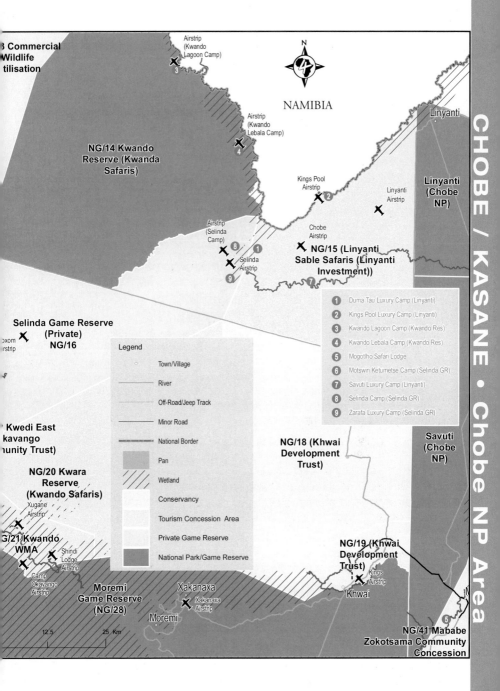

CHOBE NATIONAL PARK AREA

Duma Tau Luxury Camp (Linyanti)   1

Tented Camp   w151540
USD 868.00 to 1333.00 pp (2013)
No self-drive access

Tel: +27(0)21 702 7500, Fax: +27(0)21 701 0765
enquiry@wilderness.co.za
www.wilderness-safaris.com

Each tent has an en-suite bathroom as well as outdoor shower and views over the lagoon. Join the evening camp-fires or night drives. Among the many activities offered is game viewing by motor boat. Pre-booking required.

Facilities:

Activities:

Kings Pool Luxury Camp (Linyanti)   2

Tented Camp   w17919
USD 1194.00 to 1986.00 pp (2013)
No self-drive access

Tel: +27(0)21 702 7500, Fax: +27(0)21 701 0765
enquiry@wilderness.co.za
www.wilderness-safaris.com

The camp is located close to Kings Pool and the Linyanti River. Accommodation is offered in luxury tents that are thatched and have en-suite bathrooms. Enjoy dinner around the campfire in the boma. Pre-booking is essential

Facilities:

Activities:

Kwando Lagoon Camp (Kwando Res)   3

Tented Camp   w195805
USD 550.00 to 1063.00 pp (2013)
No self-drive access

Tel: +267 686 1449, Fax: +267 68 61457,
Cell: +267 72 311 128
reservations@kwando.co.bw, www.kwando.co.za

The camp on the Kwando River was rebuilt in 2011. Accommodation is available in tents raised on a platform, with en-suite bathrooms. Activities include fly fishing and boat cruises. Vehicles to rent. Pre-booking required.

Facilities:

Activities:

Kwando Lebala Camp (Kwando Res)   4

Tented Camp   w19580
USD 550.00 to 1063.00 pp (2013)
No self-drive access

Tel: +267 68 614 49, Fax: +267 68 61457,
Cell: +267 72 311 128
reservations@kwando.co.bw, www.kwando.co.za

The camp offers accommodation in comfortable tents, each with en-suite bathroom, outside shower, private deck and foyer. The camp is run by Kwando Safaris who requires pre-booking.

Facilities: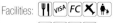

Activities:

Mogotlho Safari Lodge   5

Tented Camp   w195932
BWP 600.00 to 2950.00 pp (2013)
114km or 03h18min NE of Maun (4WD)

Tel: +267 686 5788, Fax: +267 686 5787
mankwe@info.bw
www.mankwe.com

Mogotlho Safari Lodge is situated on the bank of the Khwai River and offers luxury en-suite tented accommodation. Rates are fully inclusive of meals and transfers to Maun. Pre-booking is required.

Facilities:

Activities:

Motswiri Ketumetse Camp (Selinda GR)   6

Tented Camp   w15153
USD 495.00 to 720.00 pp (2013)
No self-drive access

Tel: +267 686 0244, Fax: +267 686 0242
info@rawbotswana.co.bw
www.rawbotswana.com

This remote camp is situated in the Selinda Reserve between flood plains and thick forest. Accommodation is offered in large, en-suite Meru tents on raised decks overlooking the Selinda Spillway. Pre-booking required.

Languages: English

Facilities:

Activities:

avuti Luxury Camp (Linyanti)   7

nted Camp   w199777
5D 708.00 to 1218.00 pp (2013)
> self-drive access

l: +27(0)21 702 7500, Fax: +27(0)21 701 0765
quiry@wilderness.co.za
ww.wilderness-safaris.com

-suite tents are raised from the ground and are joined
th a wooden walkway. Hides provide good game viewing
d bird watching opportunities. Night drives also offered.
e-booking required.

cilities:

Selinda Camp (Selinda GR)   8

Tented Camp   w150242
USD 683.00 to 1099.00 pp (2012)
No self-drive access

Tel: +27(0)21 702 7500, Fax: +27(0)21 701 0765
enquiry@wilderness.co.za
www.wilderness-safaris.com

Accommodation offered in large Chobe-style tents, each
with en-suite bathroom, fans and mosquito nets. At night
guests can sit around the campfire. No children under the
age of 6 years. Pre-booking required.

Facilities:
Activities:

arafa Luxury Camp (Selinda GR)   9

nted Camp   w179357
5D 1149.00 to 1799.00 pp (2012)
> self-drive access

l: +27(0)21 702 7500, Fax: +267 86 671 6471
quiry@wilderness.co.za
ww.wilderness-safaris.com

ccommodation is offered in Meru-style tents built on a
ooden platform. Each tent has a private plunge pool and
spectacular view of the surrounding plain and wildlife. No
ildren under 8 years. Pre-booking is essential.

cilities:
tivities:

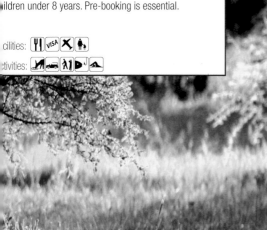

Photo: Lindy Lourens

IMPALILA ISLAND

Photo: Ichobezi Safari bo

Impalila Island is an 11 000 hectare patch of land bounded by th Chobe River, Zambezi River and the Kasai Channel. The island has about 800 inhab itants staying in 22 villages. The island, which is a conservancy, is very secluded an has limited facilities. Although Impalila Island is on Namibian territory, Kasane is th nearest town and therefore the logistic management of the lodges on the island run from Kasane.

TRAVELLER DESCRIPTION:
There are two lodges on the island. Ichingo Chobe River Lodge is on the Chobe side and Impalila Island Lodge on the Zambezi side. Guests have to leave their vehicles in safe parking at the Botswana Immigration Office in Kasane and are fetched by boat. The boat trip takes about 15 minutes and guests have to clear Namibia Immi gration on the island. The border post and crossing to Impalila Island is for people only, no vehicles are allowed. There are only a few vehicles on the island. Game viewing is done by boat along the Chobe River into the Chobe National Park and you can fish in the Chobe and Zambezi Rivers as well as in the Kasai Channel.

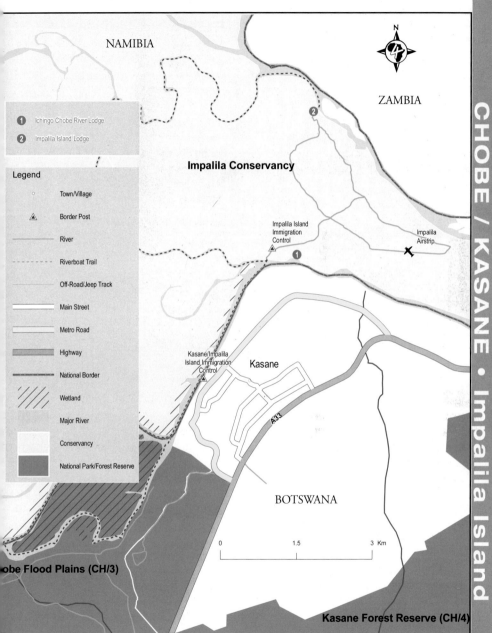

NAMIBIA

ZAMBIA

1 Ichingo Chobe River Lodge

2 Impalila Island Lodge

Impalila Conservancy

Legend

○	Town/Village
▲	Border Post
	River
	Riverboat Trail
	Off-Road/Jeep Track
	Main Street
	Metro Road
	Highway
	National Border
	Wetland
	Major River
	Conservancy
	National Park/Forest Reserve

Impalila Island
Immigration
Control

Impalila
Airstrip

Kasane/Impalila
Island Immigration
Control

Kasane

A33

BOTSWANA

obe Flood Plains (CH/3)

Kasane Forest Reserve (CH/4)

0   1.5   3 Km

TRAVEL TIP: Fishing and birding are excellent on the island.

IMPALILA ISLAND

Ichingo Chobe River Lodge 1

Tented Camp   w140528
ZAR 3000.00 to 4000.00 pp (2013)
No self-drive access

Fax: +27(0)866 185 220, Cell: +27(0)79 871 7603
ichingo@iafrica.com
www.ichobezi.co.za

The secluded lodge offers luxury rooms and outstanding cuisine. Guests will be collected from the Kasane Immigration office where they leave their vehicles and are transferred by boat to Impalila Island.

Languages: English

Facilities:

Activities:

Impalila Island Lodge 2

Lodge   w13998
USD 373.00 to 628.00 pp (2013)
No self-drive access

Tel: +27(0)11 781 1661, Fax: +264(0)86 766 9369,
Cell: +267 71 303 418
res2@africananthology.co.za

The en-suite chalets have views of Mambova Rapids. All meals included. Enjoy bird watching, river cruises and game viewing. Impalila Airstrip is closed during the rainy season. Transfer to and from Kasane Airport.

Languages: English, Afrikaans

Facilities:

Activities:

CHOBE / KASANE • Impalila Island

Photo: Ichingo Chobe River Lodge

KASANE

Kasane is an important tourist hub close to the border of Botswana, Zambia, Namibia and Zimbabwe. The town offers good shopping and other services to over land travellers and is a convenient gateway to the Chobe National Park. There are n fences between the reserve and the town and animals such as elephant and hipp can frequently be seen in and around Kasane. Kasane is situated on the banks of the Chobe River which is famous for its game viewing river boat cruises and bir watching.

TRAVELLER DESCRIPTION:
The town offers good shopping and other services to overland travellers and many people prefer to find cheaper accommodation in town when visiting the Chobe National Park. You will be able to find just about anything you need in Kasane and tyre repair services in the nearby Kazungula.

TRAVEL INFO:
Kasane has Engen and Shell garages. There are two private clinics. Phone the Chobe River Clinic (+267 625 1555) to get in touch with doctor Marios. The Meat Market has superb quality meat. If you want to order, you can phone +267 625 1222 or mail mfourie@botsnet.bw.

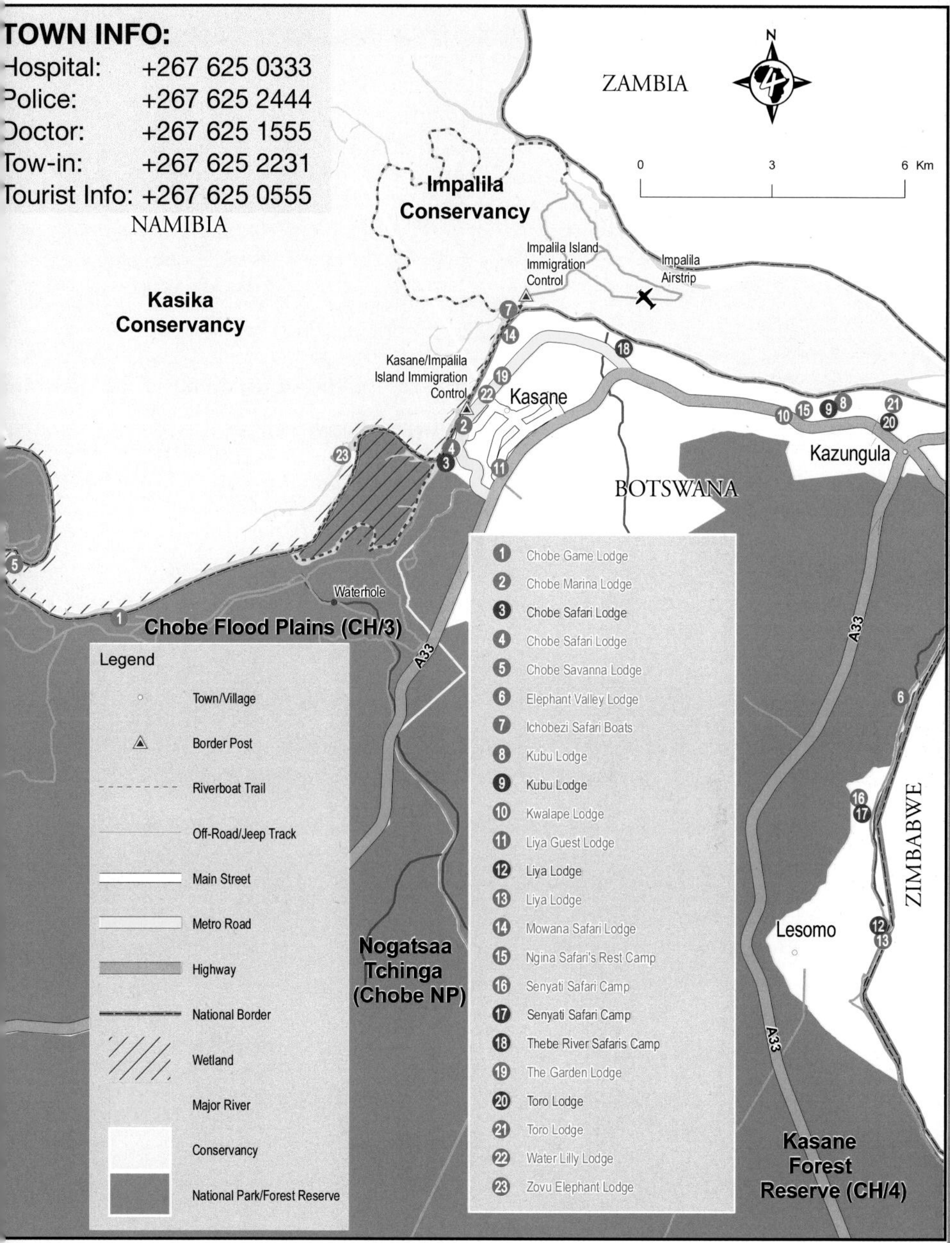

TOWN INFO:
Hospital: +267 625 0333
Police: +267 625 2444
Doctor: +267 625 1555
Tow-in: +267 625 2231
Tourist Info: +267 625 0555
NAMIBIA
ZAMBIA
BOTSWANA
ZIMBABWE
N
0 3 6 Km
Impalila Conservancy
Kasika Conservancy
Impalila Island Immigration Control
Impalila Airstrip
Kasane/Impalila Island Immigration Control
Kasane
Kazungula
Waterhole
Chobe Flood Plains (CH/3)
Nogatsaa Tchinga (Chobe NP)
Lesomo
Kasane Forest Reserve (CH/4)
A33
Legend
Town/Village
Border Post
Riverboat Trail
Off-Road/Jeep Track
Main Street
Metro Road
Highway
National Border
Wetland
Major River
Conservancy
National Park/Forest Reserve
1 Chobe Game Lodge
2 Chobe Marina Lodge
3 Chobe Safari Lodge
4 Chobe Safari Lodge
5 Chobe Savanna Lodge
6 Elephant Valley Lodge
7 Ichobezi Safari Boats
8 Kubu Lodge
9 Kubu Lodge
10 Kwalape Lodge
11 Liya Guest Lodge
12 Liya Lodge
13 Liya Lodge
14 Mowana Safari Lodge
15 Ngina Safari's Rest Camp
16 Senyati Safari Camp
17 Senyati Safari Camp
18 Thebe River Safaris Camp
19 The Garden Lodge
20 Toro Lodge
21 Toro Lodge
22 Water Lilly Lodge
23 Zovu Elephant Lodge

TRAVEL TIP: One of the must-do's for every tourist in Kasane is to take a late afternoon cruise on one of the boats along the Chobe River.

KASANE

Chobe Game Lodge   1

Game/Safari Lodge   w179252
USD 476.00 to 856.00 pp (2013)
15km or 35min WSW of Kasane (4WD)

Tel: +267 686 1559, Fax: +267 68 0037
info@desertdelta.com
www.desertdelta.com

The lodge offers accommodation in comfortable en-suite rooms. Among the many facilities at the lodge is a library, bar and cigar lounge. River boat cruises available. Pre-booking is essential.

Languages: English

Facilities:

Activities:

Chobe Marina Lodge   2

Lodge   w179340
USD 308.00 to 486.00 pp (2012)
President Avenue, Kasane (4WD)

Tel: +267 625 2221, Fax: +267 62 52 224
res1@chobemarinalodge.com
www.chobemarinalodge.com

Sixty fully equipped, air-conditioned, en-suite rooms available. Facilities include a health and beauty spa and a bar. Activities include sun downer cruises, bungee jumping and white water river rafting.

Facilities:

Activities:

Chobe Safari Lodge   3

Lodge Camp   w179273
BWP 60.00 to 75.00 pp (March 2013)
2km or 3min SSW of Kasane (4WD)

Tel: +267 625 0336, Fax: +267 625 0437
reservations@chobesafarilodge.com
www.chobesafarilodge.com

Chobe Safari Lodge, situated on the bank of Chobe River, offers camping facilities. Campsites are scattered in the riverine forest and share a clean ablution block. Campers have access to the lodge facilities.

Facilities:

Activities:

Chobe Safari Lodge   4

Lodge   w179345
BWP 975.00 to 1175.00 pu (March 2013)
1km or 2min SW of Kasane (4WD)

Tel: +267 625 0336, Fax: +267 625 0437
reservations@chobesafarilodge.com
www.chobesafarilodge.com

Accommodation offered in rooms or rondavels; all with views of the Chobe River. Rooms are en-suite and air-conditioned. Facilities include a cocktail bar, activity centre, health and beauty spa, and a craft shop.

Facilities:

Activities:

Chobe Savanna Lodge   5

Lodge   w198310
USD 385.00 to 580.00 pp (2013)
No self-drive access. Access by boat only

Tel: +267 686 1559, Fax: +267 686 0037
info@desertdelta.com
www.desertdelta.com

Thatched en-suite chalets have air conditioning, mini bars and ceiling fans. Relax at the bar or visit a remote village. The lodge closes for about three months each year for maintenance, therefore pre-booking is essential.

Languages: English

Facilities:

Activities:

Elephant Valley Lodge   6

Tented Camp   w151212
USD 280.00 to 480.00 pp (2013)
18km or 22min ESE of Kasane (4WD)

Tel: +27(0)11 781 1661, Fax: +27(0)11 781 7129
sherryl@africananthology.co.za
www.evlodge.com

The lodge offers accommodation in luxury Meru-style tents with en-suite shower and toilet as well as a fan. Enjoy river cruises along the Chobe River. The road to the lodge can get very sandy at certain times of the year.

Languages: English, Setswana

Facilities:

Activities:

chobezi Safari Boats 7

Houseboat w232873
ZAR 2850.00 to 4000.00 pp (2013)
No Self-drive access

Fax: +27(0)866 185 220, Cell: +27(0)79 871 7603
nfo@ichobezi.co.za
www.ichobezi.co.za

Enjoy a floating safari on the Chobe River. The boat has
four cabins, a lounge, bar, sun deck with splash pool and
open air dining area. Cell reception only available if the
boat is near Kasane.

Languages: English

Facilities:

Activities:

Kubu Lodge 8

Lodge w179299
USD 281.00 to 578.00 pu (2013)
10km or 12min E of Kasane

Tel: +267 62 50 312, Fax: +267 62 51 092,
Cell: +267 71 265 000
kubu@botsnet.bw, www.kubulodge.net

Thatched, en-suite chalets are equipped with ceiling fans,
mosquito nets and coffee/tea making facilities. Relax at
the bar or enjoy a cruise on the Chobe River. No children
under 4 years.

Facilities:

Activities:

Kubu Lodge 9

Lodge Camp w179382
USD 15.00 pp (2013)
9km or 12min E of Kasane

Tel: +267 625 0312, Fax: +267 625 1092,
Cell: +267 71 26 5000
kubu@botsnet.bw, www.kubulodge.net

The campsite is not grassed, but, depending on the season, large trees give shade. Each site has a braai area. The
camp has an ablution block, washing up basins, two power
points and lights. No caravans or motor homes.

Languages: English

Facilities:

Activities:

Kwalape Lodge 10

Lodge w235196
ZAR 188.00 to 1250.00 pu (2013)
8km or 10min E of Kasane

Tel: +267 625 1181, Fax: +267 625 1163,
Cell: +267 76 614 211
kwalape@africasafaricamps.com
www.kwalapesafarilodge.com

The lodge offers accommodation in en-suite chalets,
executive rooms and safari tents, sharing communal bathrooms. Campers are welcome. Airport transfers available
but pre-booking required. Languages: English

Facilities:

Activities:

Liya Guest Lodge 11

Lodge w179223
BWP 350.00 to 875.00 pu (2012)
Plateau Street, Kasane

Tel: +267 62 523 76, Fax: +267 625 1450,
Cell: +267 72 132 030
liyaglo@botsnet.bw

Liya Guest Lodge offers single, double and family rooms
with air conditioning and en-suite bathrooms. Among the
activities offered at the lodge are boat cruises and entertainment include traditional dances.

Languages: English, Setswana

Facilities:

Activities:

Liya Lodge 12

Lodge Camp w151870
BWP 83.00 to 93.00 pp (2012)
27km or 34min SE of Kasane

Tel: +267 625 2376, Fax: +267 625 1450,
Cell: +267 71 75 6903
liyaglo@botsnet.bw

Liya Lodge offers camping facilities. There is no electricity
at the campsite, but a generator does provide power for
a few hours each day. Guests can enjoy boating or bush
safaris.

Languages: English, Setswana

Facilities:

Activities:

KASANE

Liya Lodge — 13

Lodge — w152395
BWP 225.00 to 608.00 pu (2012)
27km or 31min SE of Kasane

Tel: +267 625 2376, Fax: +267 625 1450,
Cell: +267 71 756 903
liyaglo@botsnet.bw

The lodge is located at Lesoma Village and offers accommodation in chalets or pre-erected tents. Together with their camping facilities they can accommodate up to 100 people. Guests can enjoy boating or bush safaris.

Languages: English, Setswana

Facilities:

Activities:

Mowana Safari Lodge — 14

Lodge — w179362
USD 352.00 to 667.00 pu (2013)
3km or 4min NNE of Kasane

Tel: +267 62 50 300, Fax: +267 62 52 266
resmowana@cresta.co.bw
www.crestahotels.com

The lodge offers accommodation in air-conditioned rooms, each with en-suite bathroom, mini bar, mosquito net and coffee/tea making facility. Enjoy a river rafting trip or just relax at the comfortable lodge.

Languages: English

Facilities:

Activities:

Ngina Safari's Rest Camp — 15

Tented Camp — w151815
BWP 250.00 to 495.00 pu (2012)
9km or 12min E of Kasane (4WD)

Tel: +267 625 0882, Fax: +267 62 508 82,
Cell: +267 75 452 322
reservations@chobe-ngina.com, www.chobe-ngina.com

The rest camp is situated near Kasane and consists of pre-erected tents and basic ablution blocks, a toilet, shower and bath.

Languages: English

Facilities:

Activities:

Senyati Safari Camp — 16

Self-catering — w189268
BWP 435.00 to 870.00 pu (2013)
19km or 23min SE of Kasane

Fax: +267 31 85 505, Cell: +267 71 881 306
senyatisafaricamp@gmail.com
www.senyatisafaricamp.com

The camp in the Kasane Forest Reserve offers three en-suite, self-catering chalets that can each sleep four people. An executive family unit is also available. During the rainy season you need a 4WD to get to the camp.

Facilities:

Activities:

Senyati Safari Camp — 17

4WD Trail Camp — w223077
BWP 65.00 to 135.00 pp (2013)
19km or 23min SE of Kasane

Fax: +267 318 5505, Cell: +267 71 88 1306
senyatisafaricamp@gmail.com
www.senyatisafaricamp.com

The camp is situated in the Lesoma Valley of the Kasane Forest Reserve. Ten campsites each has their own thatched ablution block and kitchen facilities. During the rainy season you need a 4WD to get to the camp.

Facilities:

Activities:

Thebe River Safaris Camp — 18

Lodge Camp — w150276
BWP 95.00 pp (2013)
4km or 6min ENE of Kasane

Tel: +267 625 0575, Fax: +267 625 0314,
Cell: +267 625 1272
reservations@theberiversafaris.com
www.theberiversafaris.com

The spacious camp on the riverbank has a covered cooking area and two large communal ablution areas. A few pre-erected tents with twin beds are available. Campsites cannot be booked in advance.

Facilities:

Activities:

The Garden Lodge | 19

Lodge   w179142
USD 250.00 to 395.00 pp (April 2013)
Plot 714, President Avenue, Kasane

Tel: +267 625 0051, Fax: +267 71 30 150,
Cell: +267 71 304 150
reservations@oshaughnessys.org
www.thegardenlodge.com

Eight rooms are en-suite, air-conditioned and overlook the Chobe River from private verandas. Relax in the beautiful, lush garden or undertake game drives or boat cruises into the Chobe National Park.

Facilities: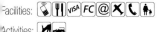

Activities:

Toro Lodge | 20

Lodge Camp   w179185
BWP 90.00 to 110.00 pu (2013)
11km or 14min E of Kasane

Tel: +267 625 2694, Fax: +267 625 2695,
Cell: +267 74 58 4254
torolodge@botsnet.bw, www.torolodge.co.bw

The camp, situated on the bank of the Chobe River, was constructed in 2002. Each of the 27 campsites has their own ablution facilities. Guests can relax at the bar.

Facilities:

Activities:

Toro Lodge | 21

Lodge   w179330
BWP 738.00 to 1103.00 pu (2013)
11km or 14min E of Kasane

Tel: +267 62 52 694, Fax: +267 62 52 695,
Cell: +267 72 111 283
torolodge@botsnet.bw, www.torolodge.co.bw

Toro Lodge, on the Chobe River, offers comfortable, air-conditioned chalets with en-suite bathrooms, television and coffee/tea making facilities. Enjoy boat trips on the Chobe River. Airport transfers available.

Facilities:

Activities:

Water Lily Lodge | 22

Lodge   w152002
BWP 695.00 pu (2013)
Plot 344 Kazungula Road, Kasane

Tel: +267 625 1775, Fax: +267 625 0759
waterlily@botsnet.bw

Water Lily Lodge offers comfortable en-suite air-conditioned rooms with DSTV. Relax at the bar or enjoy one of the many activities like boat cruises and bird watching.

Facilities:

Activities:

Zovu Elephant Lodge | 23

Lodge   w252901
ZAR 1100.00 to 1250.00 pp (2012)
No self-drive access

Cell: +267 71 318 210
bookings@zovuelephantlodge.com
www.zovuelephantlodge.com

The lodge offers accommodation in ten double en-suite rooms. Guests will be collected from the Kasane Immigration office where they park their vehicles and are transferred by boat to Impalila Island. Pre-booking is essential.

Languages: English, German

Facilities:

Activities:

Photo: Peter Levey

Beautiful rock formations near Bobonong. (Peter Levey)

Eastern Botswana, also known as the Tuli Block, consists mainly of privately owned game farms. They offer spectacular upmarket safari tourism with splendid game viewing and bird watching opportunities.

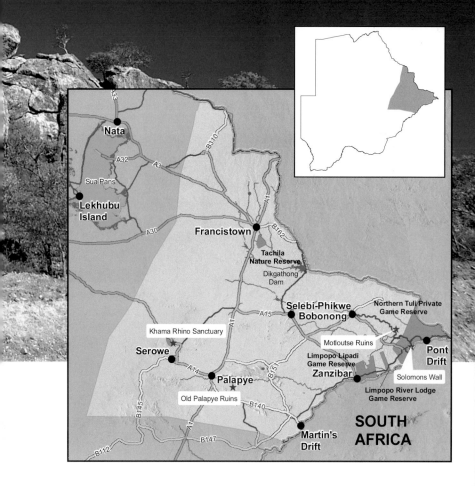

Animals are allowed to roam free between the Motloutse and Limpopo Rivers, thus creating a natural habitat for the animals of the Limpopo Lipadi Game Reserve, Limpopo River Lodge Game Reserve and the Northern Tuli Private Game Reserve. Solomon's Wall is a must see in the latter Game Reserve. These private reserves offer luxury lodging as well as camping accommodation and exciting safari experiences.

The Khama Rhino Sanctuary near Serowe and the Tachila Nature Reserve near Francistown are well worth a visit. The Khama Rhino Sanctuary Trust is a community based wildlife project, established in 1992 to assist in saving the vanishing rhino, restore an area formerly teeming with wildlife to its previous natural state and at the same time provide economic benefits to the local Batswana community through tourism and the sustainable use of natural resources.

Remains of ancient settlements relating to the Mapungubwe era (circa 1200-1270 AD) are dotted throughout the area; the most significant being the Motloutse Ruins.

The Bamangwato people, under Khama III, are widely believed to be the first people to have settled down near present-day Palapye. The settlement of Phalatswe, also called Old Palapye, was the capital of these

A White rhinoceros in the Khama Rhino Sanctuary. (Eric Champenois)

Camping near Serowe. (Peter Levey)

people in the early part of the 20th century. The ruins of Phalatswe still stand today, a few kilometres away from the town centre.

The rocky outcrops of the Tuli Block make this region unsuitable for agriculture. The villages east of Palapye are nestled in among the Lepokole and Tswapong Hills, which have a higher rainfall than the surrounding areas. These spectacular hills with beautiful gorges and waterfalls beg you to explore them.

Bridge over the Limpopo River at Zanzibar. (Wouter Brand)

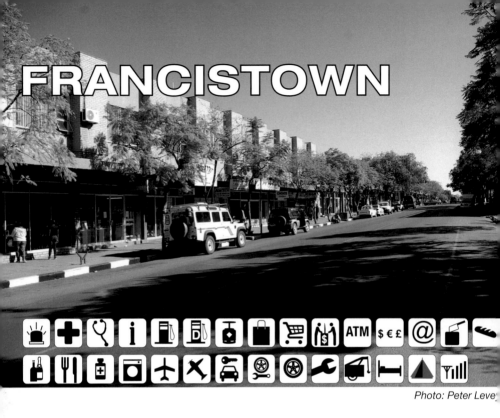

FRANCISTOWN

Francistown is also known as the capital of the north and is one of Botswana's oldest towns. It is Botswana's second largest town and a major transport hub as it is only 90 km from the Zimbabwean border. It is also en-route between Gaborone and the major tourist attractions such as Moremi and Chobe in the north.

TRAVELLER DESCRIPTION:
Visitors can expect a busy but organized town where you can stock-up on anything that you might need. The town has good shopping centres and services on offer. Comfortable lodging and camping is available.

TRAVEL INFO:
The contact number for another Police Station in town is +267 241 2231.

TRAVEL TIP: There are a couple of good camping sites on the outskirts of Francistown, most of which cater for overlanders.

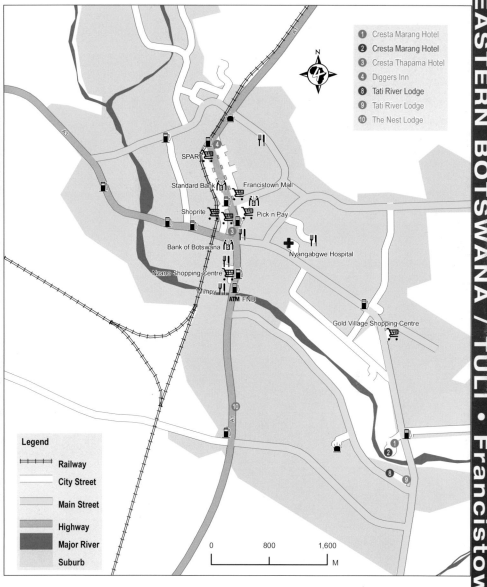

Legend

	Railway
	City Street
	Main Street
	Highway
	Major River
	Suburb

1 Cresta Marang Hotel
2 **Cresta Marang Hotel**
3 Cresta Thapama Hotel
4 Diggers Inn
8 **Tati River Lodge**
9 Tati River Lodge
10 The Nest Lodge

SPAR

Standard Bank   Francistown Mall

Shoprite   Pick n Pay

Bank of Botswana   Nyangabgwe Hospital

Nzano Shopping Centre

Wimpy

ATM FNB

Gold Village Shopping Centre

0   800   1,600   M

FRANCISTOWN

Cresta Marang Hotel — 1

Hotel   w179302
BWP 990.00 to 1168.00 pu (2013)
Old Gaborone Road, Francistown

Tel: +267 241 3991, Fax: +27(0)11 881 1232
resmarang@cresta.co.bw
www.crestahotels.com

Cresta Marang is a fully serviced hotel offering comfortable rooms, chalets and rondavels with en-suite bathrooms, coffee/tea making facilities and satellite television. The hotel also has a casino and a cocktail bar.

Languages: English

Facilities:

Activities:

Cresta Marang Hotel — 2

Holiday Resort Camp   w179311
BWP 75.00 pp (2013)
Old Gaborone Road, Francistown

Tel: +267 241 3991, Fax: +27(0)11 881 1232
resmarang@cresta.co.bw
www.crestahotels.com

Cresta Marang Hotel also offers grassed campsites and caravan spots. The camping area is close to the hotel and campers are welcome to use the hotel facilities.

Languages: English

Facilities:

Activities:

Cresta Thapama Hotel — 3

Hotel   w179213
BWP 1123.00 to 3653.00 pu (2012)
Blue Jack Street, Francistown

Tel: +267 241 3872, Fax: +267 241 3766
resthapama@cresta.co.bw
www.crestahotels.com

The hotel with casino offers en-suite and air-conditioned rooms, equipped with coffee/tea making facility, a television and mini bar. Facilities include a gymnasium and squash and tennis courts. Airport transfers available.

Facilities: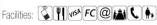

Activities:

Diggers Inn — 4

Hotel   w179128
BWP 505.00 to 1005.00 pu (2012)
Village Mall, Francistown

Tel: +267 244 0544, Fax: +267 244 0545
inn@diggersinn.co.bw

Diggers Inn Hotel offers a choice between luxury rooms, family rooms and executive rooms. All rooms are en-suite and air-conditioned and equipped with satellite television, coffee/tea making facilities and a mini bar.

Languages: English, Setswana

Facilities: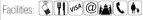

Activities:

Dumela Lodge — 5

Lodge   w242981
BWP 349.00 to 497.00 pp (2013)
6km or 15min N of Francistown

Tel: +267 240 3093, Fax: +267 24 173 13,
Cell: +267 79 200 867
dominic@dumelalodge.com, www.dumelalodge.com

This bush lodge offers accommodation in luxury tented chalets on raised timber decks. Chalets are en-suite and equipped with coffee/tea making facilities and television.

Languages: English

Facilities:

Activities:

Modumela Lodge — 6

Lodge   w195999
BWP 575.00 to 675.00 pu (2012)
66km or 01h03min NNE of Francistown

Fax: +271(0)29 960 556, Cell: +267 75 246 513
juneh@oaks.co.za

Primarily a 'Timeshare' Lodge with cabins and en-suite bathrooms. All cabins have fans, coffee/tea making facilities and a bar fridge. A fully-equipped kitchen is available if you want to cater for yourself. Prebooking is required.

Facilities:

Activities:

Modumela Lodge 7

Lodge Camp w249817
BWP 80.00 pp (2013)
66km or 01h03min NNE of Francistown (4WD)

Fax: +271(0)29 960 556, Cell: +267 75 246 513
uneh@oaks.co.za

This is a basic campsite at the lodge. Lapa structures from when it used to be a tented camp still provide shelter. Campers can make use of the facilities and enjoy the various activities offered by the lodge.

Languages: English

Facilities: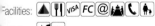

Activities:

Tati River Lodge 8

Lodge Camp w179212
BWP 75.00 pp (2012)
5km or 8min SE of Francistown

Tel: +267 240 6000, Fax: +267 240 6080
res@trl.co.bw
www.trl.co.bw

Tati River Lodge, situated on the Tati River bank, offers a campsite with clean ablution facilities. No fishing.

Languages: English

Facilities:

Activities:

Tati River Lodge 9

Lodge w179294
BWP 665.00 to 834.00 pp (2012)
5km or 8min SE of Francistown

Tel: +267 240 6000, Fax: +267 240 6080
res@trl.co.bw
www.trl.co.bw

Tati River Lodge is situated on the Tati River bank. Comfortable en-suite rooms are air-conditioned and have coffee/tea making facilities. Cellphone reception is limited to the main areas.

Languages: English

Facilities:

Activities:

The Nest Lodge 10

Motel w179385
BWP 450.00 pu (2012)
2km or 3min S of Francistown

Tel: +267 242 0100, Fax: +267 242 0101,
Cell: +267 74 221 632

The lodge offers comfortable en-suite rooms which are air-conditioned and well equipped. Safe and secure parking is available.

Facilities:

Activities:

Tshesebe Stop-Over Motel 11

Motel w200832
BWP 299.00 to 399.00 pp (2012)
54km or 48min N of Francistown

Tel: +267 24 884 55, Fax: +267 24 88 455
www.abcdafrica.com

The motel is well situated as a halfway stop between Botswana and Gauteng in South Africa. They offer basic rooms as well as executive suites.

Languages: English

Facilities:

Activities:

Wayside Ranch 12

Self-catering w245003
BWP 600.00 to 750.00 pu (2012)
21km or 23min NNE of Francistown (4WD)

Fax: +267 241 6327, Cell: +267 71 345 463
brahman@waysidebotswana.com
www.waysidebotswana.com

This family-owned ranch offers accommodation in spacious en-suite chalets that are equipped with DSTV, air-conditioning and coffee/tea making and braai facilities. Undercover parking is available. Book in advance.

Facilities:

Activities:

FRANCISTOWN

Woodlands Stop-Over · 13

Transit Camp · w179312
BWP 85.00 to 95.00 pp (2013)
18km or 22min NNW of Francistown

Tel: +267 244 0131, Fax: +267 244 0132,
Cell: +267 73 325 912
riverbend@botsnet.bw, www.woodlandscampingbots.com

The camp is on the original 'Hunters Road' that used to be the route travelled by hunters and explorers. Individual campsites are lawned and good ablution facilities are available.

Languages: English

Facilities:

Activities:

Photo: Woodlands Stop-Over

Woodlands Stop-Over · 14

Self-catering · w249820
BWP 370.00 to 1540.00 pu (2013)
18km or 22min NNW of Francistown

Tel: +267 244 0131, Fax: +267 244 0132,
Cell: +267 73 325 912
riverbend@botsnet.bw, www.woodlandscampingbots.com

The cottages at Woodlands nestle among the trees on the bank of the Tati River. Riverview rooms and campsite chalets are available. All chalets have coffee/tea making facilities.

Languages: English

Facilities:

Activities:

Photo: Woodlands Stop-Over

Photo: Hannelie Bester

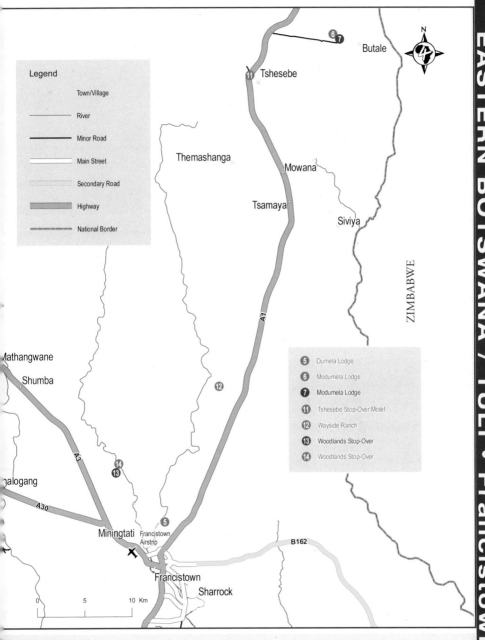

Legend

- ○ Town/Village
- River
- Minor Road
- Main Street
- Secondary Road
- Highway
- National Border

Butale

⑥⑦

⑪ Tshesebe

Themashanga

Mowana

Tsamaya

Siviya

ZIMBABWE

A1

Mathangwane

Shumba

⑫

⑤ Dumela Lodge
⑥ Modumela Lodge
⑦ Modumela Lodge
⑪ Tshesebe Stop-Over Motel
⑫ Wayside Ranch
⑬ Woodlands Stop-Over
⑭ Woodlands Stop-Over

A3

⑭
⑬

halogang

A30

Miningtati   Francistown
Airstrip

⑤

Francistown

Sharrock

B162

0   5   10 Km

TOWN INFO:

Hospital:	+267 241 1000	Police:	+267 241 5656
Doctor:	+267 241 3582	Tow-in:	+267 241 5860
Tourist Info:	+267 244 0113		

MARTIN'S DRIFT

Photo: Peter Levey

Martin's Drift is basically just a border crossing at the Limpopo River
Martin's Drift on the Botswana side lies on the B140 and is linked to Groblersbrug which lies on the N11 on the South African side. It is quite an important border crossing for South Africans.

TRAVELLER DESCRIPTION:
You should be able to refuel and buy something to eat at Martin's Drift. There is camping and accommodation available if you need to stay over.

TRAVEL INFO:
This border post is open from 06h00 – 22h00 and the telephone number is +267 494 0254. There is a Forex office at the nearby Kwa Nokeng Lodge.

TRAVEL TIP: The Caltex Garage shop is well-stocked but no meat is available. At times chicken is available, but the supply is not guaranteed.

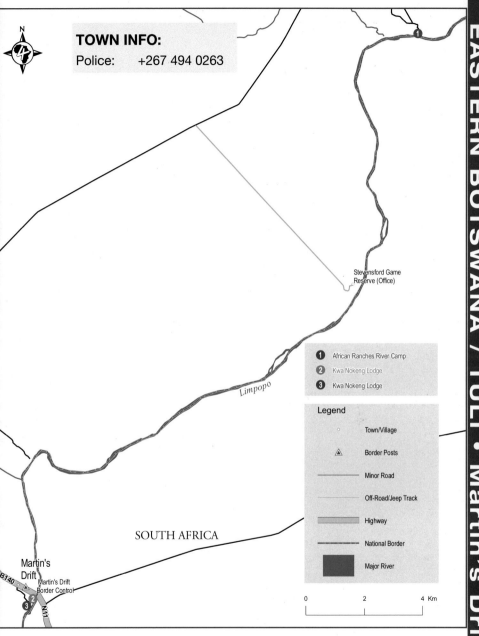

TOWN INFO:

Police: +267 494 0263

Stevensford Game
Reserve (Office)

1	African Ranches River Camp
2	Kwa Nokeng Lodge
3	Kwa Nokeng Lodge

Legend

∘	Town/Village
⚠	Border Posts
——	Minor Road
——	Off-Road/Jeep Track
▬	Highway
▬	National Border
▮	Major River

Limpopo

SOUTH AFRICA

Martin's
Drift

B140

Martin's Drift
Border Control

N11

0   2   4 Km

MARTIN'S DRIFT

African Ranches River Camp   1

4WD Trail Camp   w208183
ZAR 50.00 to 100.00 pp (2013)
36km or 51min NE of Martin's Drift

Fax: +27(0)86 714 7409, Cell: +27(0)82 269 0931
info@africanranches.com
www.africanranches.com

The camp, set on the Limpopo River, offers 12 campsites with clean ablutions. There is a communal braai area but no electricity at the camp. Bird watchers will enjoy the abundance of birds in the area.

Languages: English

Facilities:

Activities:

Kwa Nokeng Lodge   2

Lodge   w15069●
BWP 285.00 to 835.00 pu (2012)
1km or 2min SE of Martin's Drift

Tel: +267 491 5908, Fax: +267 491 5928,
Cell: +267 72 572 217
clinton@botsnet.bw, www.kwanokeng.com

The lodge offers self-catering cottages equipped with kitchenette, braai facility, en-suite bathroom, air conditioning and satellite television. Thatched bungalows, luxury tents and safari tents are also available.

Facilities:

Activities:

Kwa Nokeng Lodge   3

Lodge Camp   w150697
BWP 80.00 pp (2012)
1km or 2min SE of Martin's Drift

Tel: +267 491 5908, Fax: +267 491 5928,
Cell: +267 72 572 217
clinton@botsnet.bw, www.kwanokeng.com

The camp opposite Martin's Drift Border Post has campsites set out close to the lodge.

Facilities:

Activities:

Photo: Peter Leve

Travel Africa Informed

The **T4A AFRICA GUIDE,** (included on the T4A GPS Maps SD card), provides POI information and photos on your GPS unit.

Whilst travelling, find information on accommodation, activities, attractions, border crossings, where to buy airtime, the nearest mobile phone reception point and much more...

TRACKS 4 AFRICA

PALAPYE

Palapye is rapidly developing into one of Botswana's main financial, residential and educational hubs. The town's physical size has more than doubled since the 1990's. Palapye has a number of private and government schools and the newly built Botswana International University of Science & Technology (BIUST) commenced classes in August 2012. Also located at Palapye is the Morupule Colliery coal mine which supplies Morupule Power Station; Botswana's principal domestic source of electricity.

TRAVELLER DESCRIPTION:
Palapye has been a convenient stop-over for overlanders for many years as it is situated about halfway between Francistown and Gabarone and the town offers everything you might need. The area is known for upmarket safari tourism and the local tourist information centre will direct you to activities like game watching, hiking and birding.

TRAVEL INFO:
There are about five fuel stations in Palapye, as well as a Wimpy and Woolworths. The tow-in services are provided by Interlink Motors. The doctor's number will take you to the hospital. They will direct your call to a doctor.

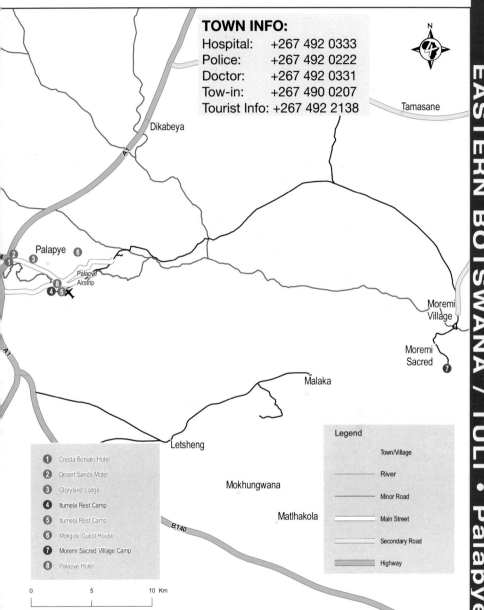

TOWN INFO:

Hospital:	+267 492 0333
Police:	+267 492 0222
Doctor:	+267 492 0331
Tow-in:	+267 490 0207
Tourist Info:	+267 492 2138

Dikabeya

Tamasane

Palapye

Palapye Airstrip

Moremi Village

Moremi Sacred

Malaka

Letsheng

Mokhungwana

Matlhakola

B140

Legend

○	Town/Village
	River
	Minor Road
	Main Street
	Secondary Road
	Highway

1 Cresta Botsalo Hotel
2 Desert Sands Motel
3 Gloryland Lodge
4 Itumela Rest Camp
5 Itumela Rest Camp
6 Mokgosi Guest House
7 Moremi Sacred Village Camp
8 Palapye Hotel

0   5   10 Km

TRAVEL TIP: Tourist attractions in the vicinity are the Khama Rhino Sanctuary, Tswapong Hills and Moremi Sacred Gorge. A visit to Old Palapye is also interesting as it is a multi-cultural site going back to the Middle Stone Age. This site is to be further developed to encourage tourism.

PALAPYE

Cresta Botsalo Hotel · 1

Hotel · w179122
BWP 1035.00 to 1210.00 pu (2013)
On Gaborone & Francistown Rd, Palapye

Tel: +267 492 0245, Fax: +267 492 0587
resbotsalo@cresta.co.bw
www.crestahotels.com

Cresta Botsalo Hotel offers en-suite rooms with air conditioning and satellite television. Facilities include a gymnasium and curio shop. Guests can enjoy activities like bird watching and game viewing.

Languages: English

Facilities:

Activities:

Desert Sands Motel · 2

Motel · w17912
BWP 534.00 to 730.00 pu (2012)
A1 Gaborone Francistown Highway, Palapye

Tel: +267 492 4400, Fax: +267 492 4361
Reservations@DesertSandsMotel.com
www.desertsandsmotel.com

The motel offers comfortable air-conditioned en-suite rooms, equipped with satellite television, mini bar and coffee/tea making facilities. There is a Wimpy nearby if you don't want to eat at their a la carte restaurant.

Facilities:

Activities:

Gloryland Lodge · 3

Lodge · w199795
BWP 290.00 to 495.00 pu (2012)
In Palapye

Tel: +267 492 4383, Fax: +267 492 4383,
Cell: +267 71 635 625

Gloryland Lodge has 23 en-suite rooms available. All rooms have air conditioning and satellite television. Single, double and executive rooms are available. Pre-booking required.

Facilities:

Activities:

Itumela Rest Camp · 4

Transit Camp · w15033
BWP 75.00 to 100.00 pp (2013)
6km or 9min ESE of Palapye

Fax: +267 492 0228, Cell: +267 71 80 6771
campitumela@gmail.com
www.campitumela.com

The separate campsites have individual braai areas but share two fully-equipped self-catering kitchens and three clean ablution blocks. This family-friendly camp offers a lot of games and activities. Excellent security.

Languages: English

Facilities:

Activities:

Itumela Rest Camp · 5

Self-catering · w249815
BWP 360.00 to 580.00 pu (2013)
6km or 9min ESE of Palapye

Fax: +267 492 0228, Cell: +267 71 80 6771
campitumela@gmail.com
www.campitumela.com

Itumela Rest Camp offers a choice of accommodation in dormitories, chalets, rooms or pre-erected tents. This family-friendly rest camp offers a lot of games and activities. Dinner buffets available. Excellent security.

Languages: English

Facilities:

Activities:

Mokgosi Guest House · 6

Guest House · w199793
BWP 450.00 pu (2012)
Extension 1, Palapye

Tel: +267 49 235 43, Fax: +267 71 267 897
MokgosiGuestHouse@gmail.com

Mokgosi Guest House offers accommodation in luxurious en-suite chalets which are air-conditioned and have satellite television. Breakfast, lunch and dinner are served at the guest house.

Languages: English

Facilities:

Activities:

<table>
<tr><td>

oremi Sacred Village Camp   7   (paw icon)

ommunity Camp   w208103

)km or 57min E of Palapye

e don't have any detailed information available on this
sting because we were unable to contact them. However,
has been visited by our Tracks4Africa community of
avellers. This is possibly a community camp.

</td><td>

Palapye Hotel   8

Hotel   w179225
BWP 330.00 to 470.00 pp (2012)
Next to Railway Station, Palapye

Tel: +267 49 202 77, Fax: +267 492 0568

Palapye Hotel offers 20 en-suite rooms, some of which
have air conditioning and have satellite television. Break-
fast included. Secure parking is available and pre-booking
is essential.

Facilities:

Activities:

</td></tr>
</table>

Photo: Peter Levey

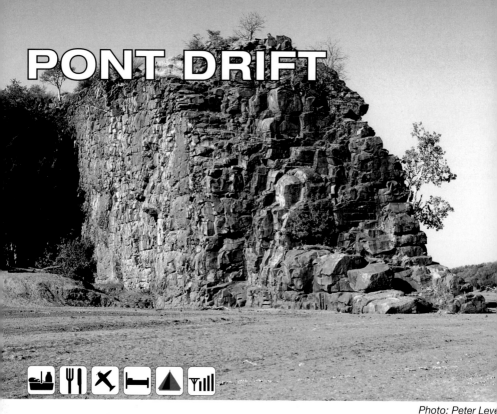

PONT DRIFT

Photo: Peter Leve

Coming from Messina in South Africa, this is a popular border crossing t Botswana's Tuli Block. The border post lies on the Limpopo River and has no faci ties. As soon as you cross the border, you are in the Northern Tuli Game Reserve.

TRAVELLER DESCRIPTION:
The 300 000 ha Northern Tuli Game Reserve is the collective name for severa privately-owned reserves such as Mashatu, Ntani and Tuli Game Reserves. The Mashatu Game Reserve reception is situated at the Pont Drift border post. This is a very quiet border post which has an unusual feature. When the Limpopo Rive is high and they close the road across the border, a cableway is used to transpor people across the river.

TRAVEL INFO:
The border control is open 08h00 -16h00 and the telephone number is +267 264 5260

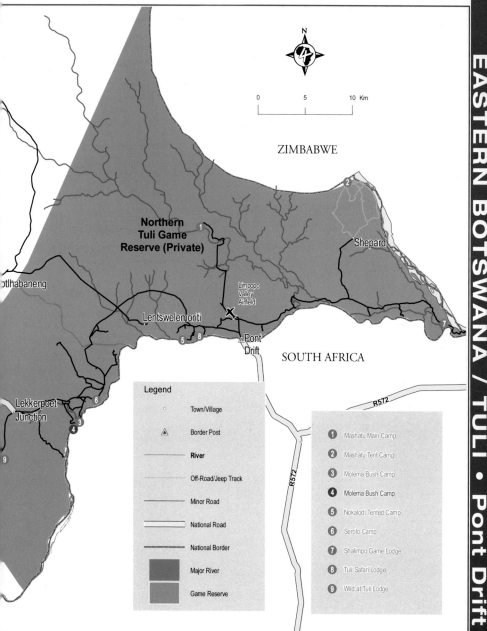

ZIMBABWE

**Northern
Tuli Game
Reserve (Private)**

Shepard

tlhabaneng

Limpopo
Valley
Airfield

Lentswelemoriti

Pont
Drift

SOUTH AFRICA

Lekkerpoet
Junction

R572

R572

Legend

○ Town/Village

⚠ Border Post

— **River**

— Off-Road/Jeep Track

— Minor Road

═ National Road

— National Border

■ Major River

■ Game Reserve

① Mashatu Main Camp

② Mashatu Tent Camp

③ Molema Bush Camp

④ Molema Bush Camp

⑤ Nokalodi Tented Camp

⑥ Serolo Camp

⑦ Shalimpo Game Lodge

⑧ Tuli Safari Lodge

⑨ Wild at Tuli Lodge

TRAVEL TIP: There is a Tuck Shop on the South African side of the border.

PONT DRIFT

Mashatu Main Camp — 1

Lodge   w195791
USD 440.00 to 660.00 pp (2013)
Tuli Game Reserve, 11km NW of Pont Drift (4WD)

Tel: +27(0)11 442 2267, Fax: +27(0)11 442 2318
mashatu@malamala.com
www.mashatu.com

Mashatu Main Camp offers accommodation in comfortable, en-suite rooms. Electricity is supplied from a generator and solar panels. Only prior arranged self-drive access allowed. Transfers to Limpopo Valley Airfield.

Facilities: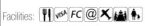
Activities:

Mashatu Tent Camp — 2

Tented Camp   w15120
USD 320.00 to 480.00 pp (2013)
31km or 01h30min NE of Pont Drift (4WD)

Tel: +27(0)11 442 2267, Fax: +27(0)11 442 2318
mashatu@malamala.com
www.mashatu.com

This camp in the Mashatu Game Reserve has eight spacious tents with private outdoor bathroom facilities. Tents are tucked under enormous trees, all connected via pathways. No children under 12. Pre-booking required.

Languages: English

Facilities:
Activities:

Molema Bush Camp — 3

Self-catering   w195786
BWP 280.00 to 305.00 pp (2013)
34km or 01h06min WSW of Pont Drift

Tel: +267 26 45 303, Fax: +267 26 453 44,
Cell: +267 72 403 690
info@tulilodge.com, www.molema.com

Twin or family size wooden chalets each have an en-suite bathroom, verandah and braai stand. Towels, bedding and daily housekeeping service provided. A fully-equipped kitchen and boma area are available for chalet guests.

Languages: English, Setswana

Facilities:
Activities:

Molema Bush Camp — 4

Lodge Camp   w19578
BWP 80.00 to 95.00 pp (2013)
34km or 01h06min WSW of Pont Drift

Tel: +267 26 45 303, Fax: +267 26 45 344,
Cell: +267 72 403 690
info@tulilodge.com, www.molema.com

Molema Bush Camp is situated on the Limpopo River. Each campsite has a private ablution and braai stand. The camp is unfenced. Fire wood for sale. You should be self-sufficient as there are no shops near Molema.

Languages: English, Setswana

Facilities:
Activities:

Nokalodi Tented Camp — 5

Tented Camp   w150739
BWP 350.00 to 450.00 pp (2013)
8km or 13min W of Pont Drift (4WD)

Tel: +267 26 453 03, Fax: +267 264 5344,
Cell: +267 74 841 993
info@tulilodge.com, www.tulilodge.com

Nokalodi is a self-catering tented camp on the Limpopo River. Twin or family size Meru-style safari tents each has an en-suite outdoor bathroom and patio. Towels, bedding and daily housekeeping services provided.

Languages: English, Setswana

Facilities:
Activities:

Serolo Camp — 6

Tented Camp   w19593
BWP 750.00 to 1050.00 pp (2012)
28km or 48min WSW of Pont Drift

Tel: +27(0)78 2911 460, Cell: +27(0)73 578 6475
info@tulitrails.com
www.tulitrails.com

This unfenced camp offers accommodation in tents with en-suite bathrooms. There are two fully-equipped kitchens but full catering is also available. No unaccompanied walking or driving is allowed. Pre-booking required.

Languages: English

Facilities:
Activities:

halimpo Game Lodge	7

elf-catering   w256093
AR 2600.00 pu (2012)
o self-drive access

el: +27(0)21 686 6056, Fax: +27(0)21 689 9795,
ell: +27(0)82 453 4936
pet@iafrica.com, www.shalimpo.co.za

he camp can accommodate groups of 8 people. It has a
ully equipped kitchen and a braai area. Book in advance
s a driver will meet you at the Pontdrift border and trans-
ort you to the lodge.

anguages: English

acilities:

ctivities:

Tuli Safari Lodge	8

Lodge   w179298
BWP 820.00 to 2030.00 pp (2013)
No self-drive access

Tel: +267 264 5303, Fax: +267 264 5344,
Cell: +267 74 841 993
info@tulilodge.com, www.tulilodge.com

Chalets are en-suite and air-conditioned and you can stay
on a full board, B&B or self-catering basis. Vehicles are left
at the border post. Pre-booking is essential.

Languages: English

Facilities:

Activities:

Vild at Tuli Lodge	9

odge   w230019
WP 595.00 to 960.00 pp (2013)
o self-drive access

ax: +27(0)86 649 1987, Cell: +267 72 113 688
di@wildattuli.com
www.wildattuli.com

his lodge on an island in the Limpopo River is reached by
hanging bridge. Accommodation is offered in en-suite
eru-style tents on a self-catering or full board basis.
re-booking required.

anguages: English

acilities:

ctivities:

Photo: Peter Levey

SELEBI-PHIKWE

Photo: Peter Levey

Selebi-Phikwe is a mining town which was originally divided into tw
villages on either side of the nickel and copper in the area. When the minerals wer
discovered, the area was developed into a mine with a township for the workers ar
eventually the two villages joined to form one. The town offers all essential amenitie
and facilities.

TRAVELLER DESCRIPTION:
Tourism in the nearby Lepokole Conservation Area is being promoted with the
development of camping facilities, nature walks and bird watching opportunities. Ir
the Lepokole Hills the ancestors of the San people left traces of their rock paintings
and, as the hills have a higher rainfall than the surrounding area, you can hike to
various gorges and explore waterfalls.

TRAVEL INFO:
The private doctor in town is Dr C.A. Chothia. The number of the Toyota dealer is
+267 261 0539.

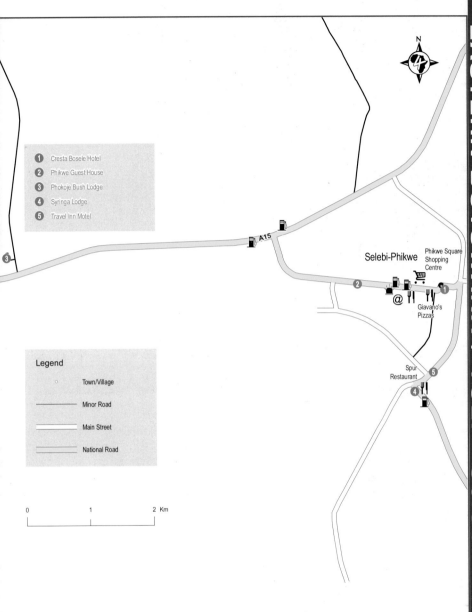

1 Cresta Bosele Hotel
2 Phikwe Guest House
3 Phokoje Bush Lodge
4 Syringa Lodge
5 Travel Inn Motel

A15

Selebi-Phikwe

Phikwe Square
Shopping
Centre

@

Giavano's
Pizzas

Spur
Restaurant

Legend

○ Town/Village

Minor Road

Main Street

National Road

0   1   2 Km

TOWN INFO:

Hospital: +267 261 0333
Doctor: +267 261 0202
Tourist Info: +267 261 1616

Police: +267 261 1997
Tow-in: +267 261 3411

SELEBI-PHIKWE

Cresta Bosele Hotel   1

Hotel   w179388
BWP 1046.00 to 1363.00 pu (2012)
Tshekedi Street, Selebi-Phikwe

Tel: +267 26 106 75, Fax: +267 261 1083
resbosele@cresta.co.bw
www.crestahotels.com

The hotel with spa offers en-suite rooms with air conditioning, satellite television, mini bar and coffee/tea making
facility. Guests can enjoy activities like boating, tennis or
golf. Pre-booking required.

Languages: English

Facilities: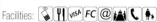

Activities:

Phikwe Guest House   2

Guest House   w219951
BWP 300.00 pu (2013)
Tshekedi Street, Selebi-Phikwe

Tel: +267 26 108 34

The guesthouse has limited facilities but offers comfortable and affordable rooms with either a double or 2 single
beds. It is conveniently situated close to a shopping mall.
Pre-booking is essential.

Facilities:

Phokoje Bush Lodge   3

Lodge   w179221
BWP 580.00 to 680.00 pu (2013)
7km or 11min W of Selebi-Phikwe

Tel: +267 26 015 96, Fax: +267 26 01 586
info@phokojebushlodge.com
www.phokojebushlodge.com

The lodge offers accommodation in en-suite thatched
chalets as well as en-suite rooms. Chalets and rooms are
air-conditioned and insect proof and have coffee/tea making facilities and DSTV.

Languages: English

Facilities:

Activities:

Syringa Lodge   4

Lodge   w179305
BWP 733.00 pu (2012)
2km or 3min SSW of Selebi-Phikwe

Tel: +267 26 104 44, Fax: +267 261 0450
resp@syringa.co.bw

Syringa Lodge offers comfortable rooms which are
air-conditioned and have en-suite bathrooms, satellite
television and coffee/tea making facilities. Safe and secure
private parking is available.

Facilities:

Activities:

Travel Inn Motel   5

Motel   w150800
BWP 385.00 to 498.00 pp (2012)
Plot 5165, Independence Road, Selebi-Phikwe

Tel: +267 26 229 99, Fax: +267 262 2998
travelinn@botsnet.bw

The motel offers self-catering rooms and can accommodate up to 32 people.

Languages: English

Facilities:

Activities:

Travel Africa Informed

- Namibia, Botswana, Mozambique & Malawi PAPER MAPS
- 1:1 000 000 scale
- Detailed coverage of tourist destinations
- Printed on tear and water resistant paper
- Travel times included

TRACKS4AFRICA

SEROWE

Photo: Peter Leve

Serowe is Botswana's fourth largest city and is regarded as the capital of the Central District and also of the Bamangwato people. The Ngwato dikgosi (chiefs) are buried here in a beautiful hillside cemetery and there are many other historical sites as well as a museum. The modern sector includes a major grain mill and a diamond cutting factory.

TRAVELLER DESCRIPTION:
Serowe lies west of the Gaborone-Francistown road and has a rich history. The main district hospital is in Serowe and apart from good medical services you will find everything that you need in this developing town. There are several excellent restaurants in Serowe town. It also provides all the services a traveller would require, from shopping to vehicle repairs.

TRAVEL INFO:
There is a Midas Spares, Battery Centre and Toyota in town, as well as a number of fuel stations. Sekgoma Memorial Hospital offers modern medical facilities with the latest technological equipment.

 TRAVEL TIP: The Spar in town sells good meat at good prices.

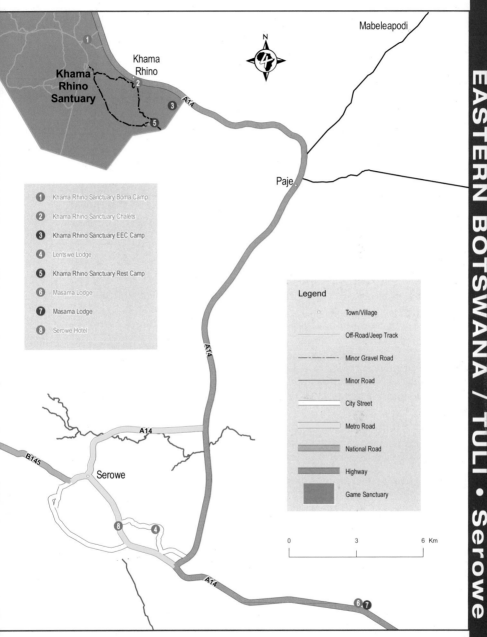

1 Khama Rhino Sanctuary Boma Camp

2 Khama Rhino Sanctuary Chalets

3 Khama Rhino Sanctuary EEC Camp

4 Lentswe Lodge

5 Khama Rhino Sanctuary Rest Camp

6 Masama Lodge

7 Masama Lodge

8 Serowe Hotel

Legend

○ Town/Village

Off-Road/Jeep Track

Minor Gravel Road

Minor Road

City Street

Metro Road

National Road

Highway

Game Sanctuary

0   3   6 Km

OWN INFO:

ospital:	+267 463 0333	Police:	+267 463 0222
octor:	+267 463 3502	Tow-in:	+267 71 68 3364

SEROWE

Khama Rhino Sanctuary Boma Camp 1 🐾

Self-catering   w151054
BWP 710.00 pu (March 2013)
33km or 27min N of Serowe

Tel: +267 463 0713, Fax: +267 463 5808,
Cell: +267 73 965 655, krst@khamarhinosanctuary.org.bw
www.khamarhinosanctuary.org.bw

Boma Camp is situated in the Khama Rhino Sanctuary, on
the edge of Serowe Pan. Chalets are fully equipped and
include bedding and towels. There is a craft shop. Support
this community based wildlife project.

Facilities:
Activities:

Khama Rhino Sanctuary Chalets 2 🐾

Self-catering   w249816
BWP 469.00 to 546.00 pu (March 2013)
28km or 20min N of Serowe

Tel: +267 463 0713, Fax: +267 463 5808,
Cell: +267 73 965 655, krst@khamarhinosanctuary.org.bw
www.khamarhinosanctuary.org.bw

Some chalets are near the entrance gate and others to
the south of Khama Rhino Sanctuary. The en-suite chalets
offer braai facilities and basic cooking equipment. Bedding
and towels included.

Facilities:
Activities:

Khama Rhino Sanctuary EEC Camp 3 🐾

Park Camp   w189286
BWP 50.00 to 67.00 pp (2012)
31km or 28min NNE of Serowe

Tel: +267 463 0713, Fax: +267 463 5808,
Cell: +267 73 965 655, krst@khamarhinosanctuary.org.bw
www.khamarhinosanctuary.org.bw

The camp at the Environmental Education Centre (EEC)
of Khama Rhino Sanctuary has clean ablution blocks.
Campers can use the facilities at the entrance gate to the
sanctuary. Support this community based wildlife project.

Facilities:
Activities:

Lentswe Lodge 4

Lodge   w179214
BWP 315.00 to 381.00 pu (2013)
4km or 8min ESE of Serowe

Tel: +267 46 343 33, Fax: +267 46 34 332,
Cell: +267 72 374 218
lentswereception@gmail.com

The lodge offers accommodation in en-suite rooms with
air conditioning and satellite television. Guests can visit the
nearby Khama Rhino Sanctuary. The landline is not reliable; rather use the cell number or email for bookings.

Languages: English

Facilities:
Activities:

Khama Rhino Sanctuary Rest Camp 5 🐾

Community Camp   w179352
BWP 50.00 to 67.00 pp (2013)
31km or 23min N of Serowe

Tel: +267 463 0713, Fax: +267 463 5808,
Cell: +267 73 965 655, krst@khamarhinosanctuary.org.bw
www.khamarhinosanctuary.org.bw

The camp is in the south of the Khama Rhino Sanctuary and has campsites and a few chalets. Each site has
a braai area and tap. There are two communal ablution
blocks. Support this community based wildlife project.

Facilities:
Activities:

Photo: Terry Purdo

Masama Lodge   6

.odge   w152179
BWP 395.00 pp (2012)
5km or 16min ESE of Serowe

Tel: +267 460 0703, Fax: +267 46 007 03,
Cell: +267 72 996 286
masamalodge@yahoo.com, www.masamalodge.com

Masama Lodge offers comfortable accommodation in
rooms furnished with double beds. Guests can tour the
royal cemetery, enjoy Tswana food and experience traditional Tswana life.

Languages: English, Setswana

Facilities:

Activities:

Masama Lodge   7

Lodge Camp   w223076
BWP 75.00 pp (2012)
15km or 16min ESE of Serowe

Tel: +267 46 00 703, Fax: +267 460 0703,
Cell: +267 72 996 286
masamalodge@yahoo.com, www.masamalodge.com

The lodge offers campsites with standard facilities. Campers can enjoy the lodge facilities and activities. Guests can
tour the royal cemetery, enjoy Tswana food and experience
traditional Tswana life.

Languages: English, Setswana

Facilities:

Activities:

Serowe Hotel   8

Hotel   w179342
BWP 585.00 to 785.00 pu (2012)
Main Road, Kgope Ward, Serowe

Tel: +267 463 0234, Fax: +267 463 0203,
Cell: +267 75 150 906
reservations@serowehotel.com, www.serowehotel.com

The hotel offers comfortable air-conditioned en-suite and
executive rooms. It also has a restaurant, pizza oven and
pool bar. Guests can enjoy bird watching or a visit to the
nearby museum or art gallery.

Languages: English

Facilities:

Activities:

Photo: Peter Levey

ZANZIBAR

Zanzibar is a small border crossing between South Africa and Botswana or the Limpopo River. It is situated 186 km east of Palapye and 96 km west of Alldays There is nothing but the border post and a lodge (Oasis Lodge) which also offers camping facilities and has a restaurant. It is situated between the border post and the entrance gate to the Limpopo Lipadi Game Reserve.

TRAVELLER DESCRIPTION:
The crossing is mainly used to gain entrance to the Limpopo Lipadi Game Reserve, a shareholder-owned, 32 500 hectare game reserve on the banks of the Limpopo River. Limited bookings from the public are accepted at their Limpopo-Lipadi River Camp.

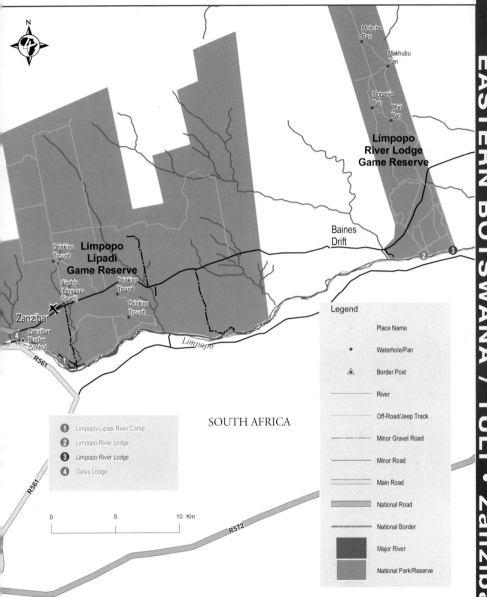

Mohobe
Pan

Makhubu
Pan

Mopanje
Pan

Phiri
Pan

**Limpopo
River Lodge
Game Reserve**

Baines
Drift

Drinking
Trough **Limpopo
Lipadi
Game Reserve**

Airstrip
(Limpopo
Lipadi)

Drinking
Trough

Drinking
Trough

Zanzibar

Zanzibar
Border
Control

R561

Limpopo

SOUTH AFRICA

① Limpopo-Lipadi River Camp
② Limpopo River Lodge
③ Limpopo River Lodge
④ Oasis Lodge

0   5   10 Km

R561

R572

Legend

○	Place Name
●	Waterhole/Pan
⚠	Border Post
——	River
——	Off-Road/Jeep Track
—·—·	Minor Gravel Road
——	Minor Road
═══	Main Road
▬▬	National Road
▬ ▬ ▬	National Border
▮	Major River
▮	National Park/Reserve

ZANZIBAR

Limpopo-Lipadi River Camp   1

Lodge   w204743
BWP 1600.00 to 2000.00 pp (2012)
No self-drive access

Fax: +27(0)12 349 2520, Cell: +267 72 479 048
enquiries@limpopo-lipadi.org

This shareholder-owned Limpopo-Lipadi Game Reserve recently opened for outside guests as well. Seven comfortable 2- or 3-bedroom chalets share a central braai area with boma, kitchen, dining area and bar. Catering is available on request.

Facilities:

Activities:

Limpopo River Lodge   2

Self-catering   w150654
BWP 343.00 to 383.00 pp (2013)
35km or 51min ENE of Zanzibar (4WD)

Cell: +267 72 106 098
janitas@montaguhomes.co.za
www.limpoporiverlodge.co.za

The lodge on the Limpopo River, in the Limpopo River Lodge Game Reserve, provides self-catering chalets and rondavels. Firewood must be purchased from the lodge as no collection of firewood is allowed. Pre-booking required.

Facilities:

Activities:

Limpopo River Lodge   3

Lodge Camp   w179170
BWP 118.00 to 208.00 pp (2013)
38km or 58min ENE of Zanzibar (4WD)

Cell: +267 72 10 6098
janitas@montaguhomes.co.za
www.limpoporiverlodge.co.za

The camp is situated away from the lodge on the Limpopo River, in the Limpopo River Lodge Game Reserve. There are 6 campsites with thatched ablutions. No drinking water or electricity. Wood is sold at the lodge. Pre-booking required.

Facilities:

Activities:

Oasis Lodge   4

Lodge   w208129
BWP 660.00 to 690.00 pp (2012)
At Zanzibar Border Post, Limpopo Lipadi GR

Fax: +267 72 646 220, Cell: +267 71 313 399
zanzibaroasis@gmail.com

The lodge, situated in the Limpopo-Lipadi Game Reserve, offers river chalets, rondavels, luxury or deluxe suites as well as VIP rooms. All rooms are en-suite and air-conditioned and have coffee/tea making facilities and DSTV.

Facilities:

Activities:

Photo: Frank Höppener

Photo: Frank Höppener

www.tracks4africa.co.za

EASTERN BOTSWANA / TULI • Zanzibar

HUNTER'S ROAD

Today the strip of land all along the Zimbabwean border of Botswana is known as Hunter's Road. Hunter's Road is the name given to a wagon road that was used extensively in the latter half of the 19th century to move trade goods from South Africa to the banks of the Zambezi River at Kazungula.

There is some dispute as to whether the current track is in fact the original Hunter's Road or just part of it. Today the road is a wide swath of ground right on the border that has been cleared of vegetation and doubles as a 4x4 track. In places it is very sandy, but it is quite manageable.

Hunter's Road consists of large sections of black cotton soil which, when wet, can cause vehicles to bog down completely. In addition the elephant tracks make big holes

Beautiful landscape near Pandamatenga. (Peter Levey)

in the soil which need to be negotiated with care. In the wet season this road needs to be tackled with care and preferably not alone.

It stretches from Kasane in the north to just north of Nata in the south. The off-road track along the border runs parallel to the A33 and passes through many hunting concessions, forest reserves and tribal trust land or villages.

Many of the wilderness areas in Botswana are now managed by community trusts, who usually partner with photo or hunting tour operators as a means of raising funds for community development. Tourism in this area is mostly run by local lodge owners and tour guides with concessions.

Although you may drive through the forest reserves and hunting concession areas, bush camping is not allowed. After heavy rains the road condition may not be good, therefore it is always best to inquire before you plan your trip.

PANDAMATENGA

Pandamatenga is a small border crossing town between Botswana and Zimbabwe, just north of the Hwange National Park and 100 km east of the Chobe National Park. It lies on the A33 that runs along the Botswana/Zimbabwe border from Nata to Kasane and consists mainly of a farming community.

TRAVELLER DESCRIPTION:
Pandamatenga is a good stop-over for weary travellers as you can choose between camping or lodge accommodation and you can get food supplies. Only basic food supplies are available.

TRAVEL INFO:
Doctors come to the government clinic on Thursdays but for serious cases it is best to go to the hospital in Kasane. The number for the clinic is +267 623 2008. Alternative numbers for the tow-in service are +267 71 820 863 or +267 623 2141. The border post is open between 08h00 and 17h00 and the telephone is +267 623 2025/29.

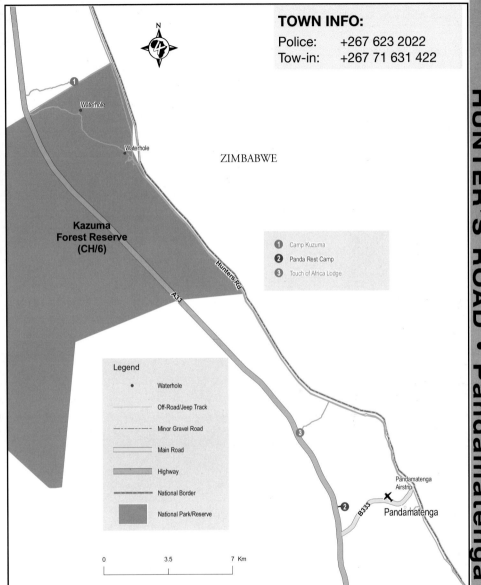

TOWN INFO:

Police: +267 623 2022
Tow-in: +267 71 631 422

ZIMBABWE

Kazuma
Forest Reserve
(CH/6)

Hunters Rd

A33

Waterhole

Waterhole

❶ Camp Kuzuma
❷ Panda Rest Camp
❸ Touch of Africa Lodge

Legend

• Waterhole

Off-Road/Jeep Track

Minor Gravel Road

Main Road

Highway

National Border

National Park/Reserve

Pandamatenga
Airstrip

Pandamatenga

B333

0   3.5   7 Km

TRAVEL TIP: Do not rely on diesel and petrol being available here as there have been reports of fuel shortages in the past. Although there is an ATM, it is not always working.

PANDAMATENGA

Camp Kuzuma   1

Lodge   w225480
USD 400.00 to 750.00 pp (2013)
84km or 01h05min SSE of Kasane (4WD)

Tel: +27(0)11 362 2748, Fax: +27(0)86 603 3733,
Cell: +27(0)83 705 5469
info@campkuzuma-bw.com, campkuzuma-bw.com

Safari tents are luxurious and en-suite. Private charters
and road transfers are available. Roads can become untra-
versable during the rainy season therefore pre-booking is
essential. No children under 12 years.

Languages: English

Facilities:

Activities:

Panda Rest Camp   2

Lodge Camp   w179144
BWP 40.00 pu (2011)
6km or 6min W of Pandamatenga

Cell: +267 71 725 434
pandarestcamp@yahoo.com

(We were unable to confirm the information for this listing.
Please use at your own discretion). Individual campsites
have their own electricity points and braai stands.

Facilities:

Activities:

Touch of Africa Lodge   3

Lodge   w179341
BWP 550.00 to 650.00 pu (2013)
10km or 9min WNW of Pandamatenga

Cell: +267 71 656 340
touchofafrica@botsnet.bw
www.touchofafrica.tv

The lodge is surrounded by bush, waterholes and sand
dunes. They offer accommodation in comfortable en-suite
chalets. Activities include safaris and night drives. Facilities
include a bar. Airport transfers available.

Languages: English, German, Afrikaans

Facilities:

Activities:

Photo: Peter Levey

Travel Africa Informed

KGALAGADI

Mabuasehube has a yellow flower carpet after good rains. (Lindy Lourens)

The Kgalagadi region is tucked away in the south-western corner of Botswana. The Kgalagadi Transfrontier Park forms the most significant part of this region.

There are a few interesting sites in the Kgalagadi to visit, like the grave of Hans Schwabe, a German geologist who died in 1958 when he wanted to prospect illegally

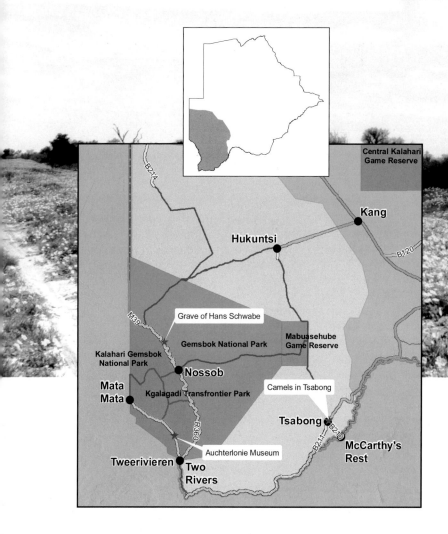

Central Kalahari
Game Reserve

Kang

B214

B120

Hukuntsi

M39

Grave of Hans Schwabe

Mabuasehube
Game Reserve

Gemsbok National Park

Kalahari Gemsbok
National Park

Nossob

Camels in Tsabong

Mata
Mata

Kgalagadi Transfrontier Park

R360

Tsabong

B241

B20

McCarthy's
Rest

Auchterlonie Museum

Tweerivieren

Two
Rivers

gally for diamonds in the Nossob River Valley. Another is the Auchterlonie Museum that depicts the way farmers used to live in this region before it was proclaimed a National Park.

The area north of the park towards Hukuntsi offers some remote areas for the adventurous and self-sufficient overlander. Some of the earliest travellers referred to this dry area as Thirstland, translated into Setswana as Kgalagadi.

Another attraction of this region is the camels that are used for patrol by the police in the Tsabong area.

Kgalagadi Transfrontier Park
(by Peter Derichs)

The park straddles the border between South Africa and Botswana and comprises of two adjoining national parks: Kalahari Gemsbok National Park in South Africa and Gemsbok National Park in Botswana, which includes the Mabuasehube Game Reserve. Approximately three-quarters of the park lie in Botswana and one-quarter in South Africa.

The park is situated in the Kalahari Desert, part of the arid savanna biome. Grasses dominate the dune fields and there are strands of trees, mainly Camel Thorn, Grey Camel Thorn and Swarthaak. The South African side of the park lies between the Auob and the Nossob Rivers, with extensive dune fields in between. The Botswana side stretches into the Kalahari dune fields interspersed with occasional clay pans.

In good rain years the grasses, especially the Kalahari Sour Grass, proliferate and cover the normally red sand dunes. When driving on the 4x4 tracks during this time it is advisable to have a mesh covering your radiator.

It is possible to do a combination of both parks. Tourists wishing to enter the park and traverse within the boundaries of the park and exit at the same point of entry are not required to do immigration control. However, if you want to exit at another point as your point of entry a two day stay in the park is compulsory.

On the South African side of the Kgalagadi there are both fenced and unfenced camps with chalets and camping facilities. On the Botswana side there are only basic camping facilities and all camps are unfenced.

There are two main roads in the park. The first leads from Twee Rivieren up the Auob River to Mata Mata. The second leads from Twee Rivieren up the Nossob River to the Nossob Camp to eventually reach a dead-end at the fence bordering Namibia.

The roads in the Kgalagadi Transfrontier Park are often a source of frustration for visitors. Firstly, although the roads are predominantly sand, corrugation builds up rapidly after they have been graded. These corrugations, although made of soft sand, are enough to shake and rattle every vehicle and its occupants for kilometres on end.

Secondly, after years and years of

grading, sections of the road have been lowered from the surrounding terrain and there are ridges of sand which have built up next to the road. This means that visitors travelling in sedan cars cannot see over these ridges for kilometres on end. To really enjoy all there is to see it is recomended that visitors use a vehicle with a high ground clearance such as a SUV or a 4x2 pick-up. Travelling on the Botswana side is not possible without a 4WD.

The two dry rivers, the Auob and the Nossob, have totally different characteristics. The Auob River is narrower with high calcrete cliffs and dunes on either side. The Nossob River is shallower and wider. Near the Namibian border it is difficult to discern where the banks of the Nossob riverbed are.

The combination of the dune environment and relatively ample water in the riverbeds makes it possible to sustain fairly large numbers of antelope and predators like lion, leopard, spotted and brown hyena and cheetah. There are no primates or warthogs in the park, but plenty of giraffe.

The park is also well-known for its large population of seasonal and permanent raptors. Owls are often seen. However, there is a variety of smaller animals like jackal, fox, mongoose, meerkat and ground squirrels that makes the Kgalagadi so fascinating.

Two Gemsbok near Twee Rivieren. (Karin Theron)

GEMSBOK NP
(Kgalagadi Transfrontier)

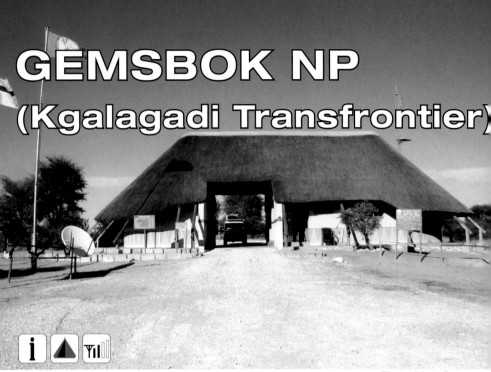

Photo:Johnn Groenewa

In 1999 Botswana and South Africa signed a treaty to form the first trans frontier peace park in Africa. The Gemsbok National Park in Botswana contribute the biggest section of the newly formed Kgalagadi Transfrontier Park. This protecte area is jointly managed by Botswana and South Africa as a single ecological unit, an gate receipts are shared. Tourist facilities, however, are still run autonomously.

TRAVELLER DESCRIPTION:
The Gemsbok National Park offers a taste of wild Africa. The only way to stay in this part of the Kgalagadi Transfrontier Park, is to camp. Camps are unfenced and offe only basic ablutions. Visitors need to be totally self-sufficient in terms of fuel, water wood and food.

TRAVEL INFO:
You are not allowed to collect firewood.

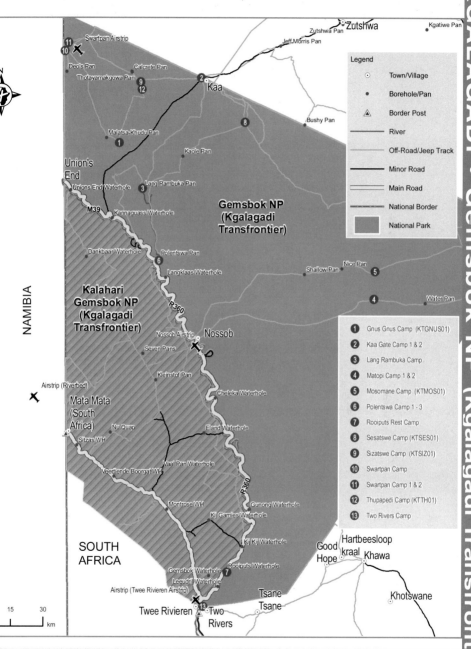

TOWN INFO:
Tourist Info: +267 318 0774

GEMSBOK NP (Kgalagadi Transfrontier)

Gnus Gnus Camp (KTGNUS01) — 1

Wilderness Camp — w150598
BWP 30.00 pp (2013)
66km or 3h08min SW of Kaa North Gate (4WD)

Tel: +267 318 0774, Fax: +267 318 0775
dwnp@gov.bw
www.mewt.gov.bw

The Gnus Gnus Camp is located near the Gnus Gnus Pan in the remote northern parts of the Kgalagadi. There are no facilities other than a braai pit. Booking and prepayment required.

Facilities:
Activities:

Kaa Gate Camp 1 & 2 — 2

Park Camp — w151107
BWP 30.00 pp (2013)
Located at Kaa North Gate (4WD)

Tel: +267 318 0774, Fax: +267 318 0775
dwnp@gov.bw
www.mewt.gov.bw

These two campsites at Kaa Gate have cold water showers and longdrop toilets. Booking and prepayment required.

Facilities:
Activities:

Lang Rambuka Camp — 3

Park Camp — w179295
BWP 200.00 pp (2013)
68km or 3h15min SSW of Kaa North Gate (4WD)

Tel: +267 318 0774, Fax: +267 318 0775
dwnp@gov.bw
www.mewt.gov.bw

This camp is on the Polentswa 4x4 Trail in the Kgalagadi and offers a basic campsite with no facilities. Booking and prepayment required. A minimum of two vehicles and a maximum of five vehicles are allowed.

Facilities:
Activities:

Matopi Camp 1 & 2 — 4

Park Camp — w179349
BWP 30.00 pp (2013)
93km or 4h30min SW of Mabuasehube East Gate (4WD)

Tel: +267 318 0774, Fax: +267 318 0775
dwnp@gov.bw
www.mewt.gov.bw

The Matopi campsites are conveniently located between Nossob and Mabuasehube along the Boso Trail. As there are no facilities campers need to be fully self-sufficient. Booking and prepayment required.

Facilities:
Activities:

Mosomane Camp (KTMOS01) — 5

Wilderness Camp — w150457
BWP 200.00 pp (2013)
85km or 4h03min W of Mabuasehube East Gate (4WD)

Tel: +267 318 0774, Fax: +267 31 807 75
dwnp@gov.bw
www.mewt.gov.bw

The campsite at Mosomane Pan on the Mabu Trail is unfenced and has no facilities. Booking and prepayment required.

Facilities:
Activities:

Polentswa Camp 1 - 3 — 6

Park Camp — w195954
BWP 30.00 pp (2013)
62km or 1h35min from Nossob Camp (4WD)

Tel: +267 318 0774, Fax: +267 318 0775
dwnp@gov.bw
www.mewt.gov.bw

Three campsites each has a shower shelter, longdrop toile and a shade shelter. You need to bring your own water and be fully self-sufficient. Booking and prepayment required.

Facilities:
Activities:

...ooiputs Rest Camp   7

...WD Trail Camp   w151151
...WP 30.00 pp (2013)
...4km or 31min NNE of Twee Rivieren Gate (4WD)

...el: +267 318 0774, Fax: +267 318 0775
...wnp@gov.bw
...ww.mewt.gov.bw

...he camp is situated near Twee Rivieren and consists of
...x sites, each with own basic ablution facilities. Booking
...nd prepayment required.

Facilities: (icons)

Activities: (icon)

Sesatswe Camp (KTSES01)   8

Park Camp   w150504
BWP 200.00 pp (2013)
33km or 1h34min SE of Kaa North Gate (4WD)

Tel: +267 318 0774, Fax: +267 318 0775
dwnp@gov.bw
www.mewt.gov.bw

This camp is located on the edge of the dry Sesatswe Pan
where birdwatching and wildlife viewing can be enjoyed.
It is a basic campsite with no facilities on the Polen Trail.
Booking and prepayment required.

Facilities: (icons)

Activities: (icon)

...izatswe Camp (KTSIZ01)   9

...ark Camp   w189214
...WP 30.00 pp (2013)
...0.8km or 1h27min W of Kaa North Gate (4WD)

...el: +267 318 0774, Fax: +267 318 0775
...wnp@gov.bw
...ww.mewt.gov.bw

...his campsite is located next to Sizatswe Pan and has no
...cilities other than a braai pit. Booking and prepayment
...equired.

Facilities: (icons)

Activities: (icon)

Swartpan Camp   10

Camping   w242972
BWP 30.00 pp (2013)
79km or 03h41min W of Kaa (4WD)

Tel: +267 318 0774, Fax: +267 318 0775
dwnp@gov.bw
www.mewt.gov.bw

The Swartpan Camp is located in the Kaa Concession of
the Kgalagadi. It is situated at a waterhole and there are
two sites available. Facilities are very limited and you need
to be self-sufficient. Pre-booking is essential.

Facilities: (icons)

Activities: (icon)

...wartpan Camp 1 & 2   11

...ark Camp   w150676
...WP 30.00 pp (2013)
...7.1km or 03h41min NW of Kaa North Gate (4WD)

...el: +267 318 0774, Fax: +267 318 0775
...wnp@gov.bw
...ww.mewt.gov.bw

...wo sites are located on the Kaa Trail near the Swartpan
...aterhole. As the campsites have very limited resources
...ou need to be self-sufficient. There is a tap with drinkable
...ater. Booking and prepayment required.

Facilities: (icons)

Activities: (icon)

Thupapedi Camp (KTTH01)   12

Park Camp   w150599
BWP 30.00 pu (2013)
32.3km or 1h39min W of Kaa North Gate (4WD)

Tel: +267 318 0774, Fax: +267 318 0775
dwnp@gov.bw
www.mewt.gov.bw

The camp is next to the Thupapedi Pan in the northern
parts of the Kgalagadi. The campsite has no facilities, so
you need to be totally self-sufficient. Booking and prepayment required.

Facilities: (icons)

Activities: (icon)

GEMSBOK NP (Kgalagadi Transfrontier)

Two Rivers Camp 13

Park Camp w179189
BWP 30.00 pp (2013)
2km or 4min NE of Twee Rivieren Gate (4WD)

Tel: +267 31 807 74, Fax: +267 31 807 75
dwnp@gov.bw
www.mewt.gov.bw

The rest camp is situated opposite Twee Rivieren and offers comfortable, shaded campsites with clean ablution blocks. Booking and prepayment required.

Facilities:
Activities:

Photo: Karin Theron

MABUASEHUBE GR
(Kgalagadi Transfrontier)

Photo:Johann Groenewa

The Mabuasehube Game Reserve was also incorporated into th
Kgalagadi Transfrontier Park between Botswana and South Africa. Mabuasehub
means red earth and it is named after the red Kalahari sand. All campsites are ove
looking one of the few pans in this otherwise dry area. The pans fill with water durir
the rainy season and their hard surface layer ensures that the water remains in th
pans and is not immediately absorbed. These pans are of great importance to th
wildlife, which obtain valuable nutrients from the salts and the grasses of the pans

TRAVELLER DESCRIPTION:
There are a few campsites in this section of the Kgalagadi, all with basic ablu
tion facilities and shade shelters. Visitors have to be self-sufficient in terms of fuel
wood, food and water.

TRAVEL INFO:
You are not allowed to collect firewood.

188

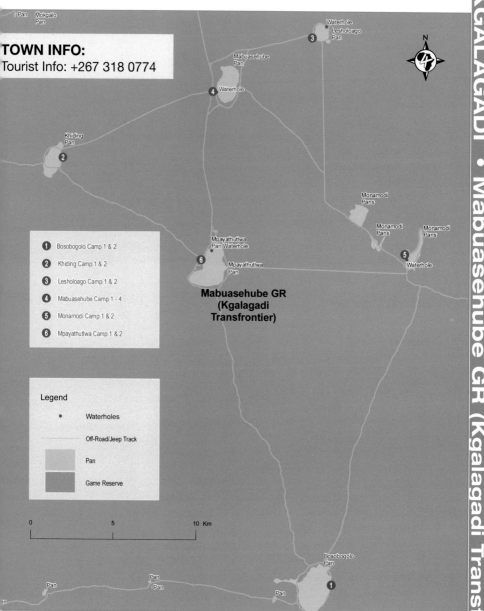

TOWN INFO:
Tourist Info: +267 318 0774

① Bosobogolo Camp 1 & 2

② Khiding Camp 1 & 2

③ Lesholoago Camp 1 & 2

④ Mabuasehube Camp 1 - 4

⑤ Monamodi Camp 1 & 2

⑥ Mpayathutlwa Camp 1 & 2

**Mabuasehube GR
(Kgalagadi
Transfrontier)**

Legend

•   Waterholes

    Off-Road/Jeep Track

    Pan

    Game Reserve

0   5   10 Km

TRAVEL TIP: Note that the numbers of the campsites do not correspond with the codes of the campsites. Make sure you are at the correct site.

MABUASEHUBE GR (Kgalagadi Transfrontier)

Bosobogolo Camp 1 & 2 — 1

Park Camp — w150902
BWP 30.00 pp (2013)
23.6km or 1h08min SSW of Mabuasehube East Gate (4WD)

Tel: +267 318 0774, Fax: +267 318 0775
dwnp@gov.bw
www.mewt.gov.bw

Two campsites are located at the Bosobogolo Pan. They have basic facilities like a shower shelter, longdrop toilet and a shade shelter each. No water available. Booking and prepayment required.

Facilities: [icons]
Activities: [icons]

Khiding Camp 1 & 2 — 2

Park Camp — w15074
BWP 30.00 pp (2013)
31km or 1h30min NW of Mabuasehube East Gate (4WD)

Tel: +267 318 0774, Fax: +267 318 0775
dwnp@gov.bw
www.mewt.gov.bw

Two campsites are close to each other and both have a stunning westerly view of Khiding Pan. The two campsites share ablution facilities. Booking and prepayment required.

Facilities: [icons]
Activities: [icons]

Lesholoago Camp 1 & 2 — 3

Park Camp — w150883
BWP 30.00 pp (2013)
22.5km or 1h04min NNW of Mabuasehube East Gate (4WD)

Tel: +267 318 0774, Fax: +267 318 0775
dwnp@gov.bw
www.mewt.gov.bw

Two campsites are located at Lesholoago Pan, which makes game viewing easy. The campsites have shade shelters, longdrop toilets and bucket showers. Booking and prepayment required.

Facilities: [icons]
Activities: [icons]

Mabuasehube Camp 1 - 4 — 4

Park Camp — w15075
BWP 30.00 pp (2013)
24.7km or 1h10min NNW of Mabuasehube East Gate (4WD)

Tel: +267 318 0774, Fax: +267 318 0775
dwnp@gov.bw
www.mewt.gov.bw

Four campsites are spread out around Mabuasehube Pan The facilities are basic and include rustic cold showers, longdrop toilets and A-frame shade shelters. Booking and prepayment required.

Facilities: [icons]
Activities: [icons]

Monamodi Camp 1 & 2 — 5

Park Camp — w150889
BWP 30.00 pp (2013)
7.2km or 21min NW of Mabuasehube East Gate (4WD)

Tel: +267 318 0774, Fax: +267 318 0775
dwnp@gov.bw
www.mewt.gov.bw

Two campsites are located next to the Monamodi Pans. Facilities are basic and include rustic showers, longdrop toilets and shade shelters. Booking and prepayment required.

Facilities: [icons]
Activities: [icons]

Mpayathutlwa Camp 1 & 2 — 6

Park Camp — w15075
BWP 30.00 pp (2013)
19.9km or 57min W of Mabuasehube East Gate (4WD)

Tel: +267 318 0774, Fax: +267 318 0775
dwnp@gov.bw
www.mewt.gov.bw

The campsites near Mpayathutlwa Pan each has a rustic shower, toilet and shade shelter. The water is too salty for drinking and cooking purposes. Booking and prepayment required.

Facilities: [icons]
Activities: [icons]

Photo:Johann Groenewald

MATA MATA
(Kgalagadi Transfrontier)

Photo:Deon Ko

Mata Mata is a border crossing between South Africa and Namibia as well as a rest camp in the Kgalagadi Transfrontier Park. Mata Mata lies within the Kalahari Gemsbok National Park in South Africa which forms part of the Kgalagadi Transfrontier Park. Coming from the South African side of the Park, it is possible to enter Namibia at Mata Mata.

TRAVELLER DESCRIPTION:
Mata Mata is a popular rest camp situated on the banks of the Auob River on the western boundary of the Park. It offers a range of accommodation types to suit a variety of tastes and budgets. A generator provides electricity for 18 hours per day. On the Namibian side of Mata Mata there also is a wide range of accommodation available.

TRAVEL INFO:
The shop at Mata Mata camp sells basic commodities. If you want to use the Mata Mata border post, you have to sleep two nights in the Kgalagadi Transfrontier Park and show proof of two days' accommodation reservation. Also, if you enter at Twee Rivieren you must spend two nights before exiting at Mata-Mata.

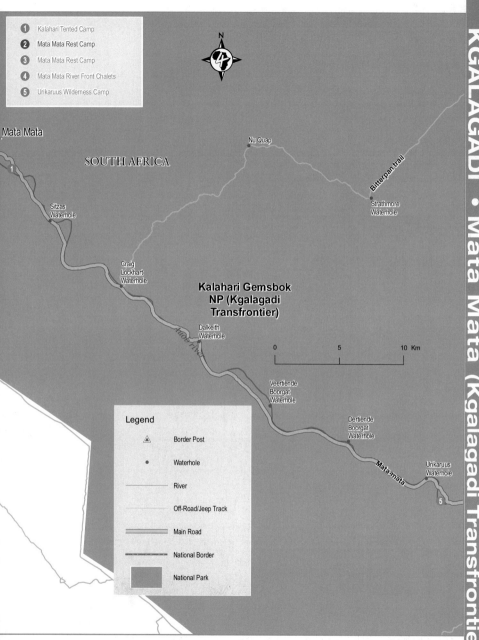

Legend

⚠	Border Post
•	Waterhole
—	River
—	Off-Road/Jeep Track
═	Main Road
══	National Border
▮	National Park

1. Kalahari Tented Camp
2. Mata Mata Rest Camp
3. Mata Mata Rest Camp
4. Mata Mata River Front Chalets
5. Urikaruus Wilderness Camp

Mata Mata

SOUTH AFRICA

Nu Quap

Sitzas Waterhole

Craig Lockhart Waterhole

Kalahari Gemsbok NP (Kgalagadi Transfrontier)

Dalkeith Waterhole

Strathmore Waterhole

Bitterpan trail

Veertiende Boorgat Waterhole

Dertiende Boorgat Waterhole

Urikaruus Waterhole

Mata-mata

0   5   10 Km

TRAVEL TIP: This camp is normally fully booked well in advance during the South African June school holidays.

MATA MATA (Kgalagadi Transfrontier Park)

Kalahari Tented Camp   1

Tented Camp   w151169
ZAR 1160.00 to 1315.00 pu (2013)
4km or 10min SE of Mata Mata (South Africa)

Tel: +27(0)54 561 2000, Fax: +27(0)54 561 2005
kgalagadi@sanparks.org
www.sanparks.org

Located close to Mata Mata Rest Camp. The camp offers family tents and honeymoon tents. Tents have a bathroom, ceiling fans and equipped kitchen. Water heated by gas.

Facilities:
Activities:

Mata Mata Rest Camp   2

Park Camp   w225478
ZAR 195.00 pu (2013)
In Mata Mata (South Africa)

Tel: +27(0)54 561 2000
kgalagadi@sanparks.org
www.sanparks.org

The Mata Mata Rest Camp is situated on the banks of the Auob River and offers camping. A generator provides electricity. Chalets are also available.

Facilities:
Activities:

Mata Mata Rest Camp   3

Self-catering   w179169
ZAR 665.00 to 1850.00 pu (2013)
In Mata Mata (South Africa)

Tel: +27(0)54 561 2000, Fax: +27(0)54 561 2005
kgalagadi@sanparks.org
www.sanparks.org

This camp has reopened after an extensive revamp in July 2010. It is situated on the banks of the Auob River. Chalets are available.

Languages: English

Facilities:
Activities:

Mata Mata River Front Chalets   4

Self-catering   w242974
ZAR 1210.00 to 1850.00 pu (2013)
In Mata Mata (South Africa)

Tel: +27(0)54 561 2000, Fax: +27(0)54 561 2005
kgalagadi@sanparks.org
www.sanparks.org

The 8 river chalets were revamped in July 2010 and are situated on the banks of the Auob River. They all overlook the dry river bed.

Languages: English

Facilities:
Activities:

Urikaruus Wilderness Camp   5

Self-catering   w151183
ZAR 1135.00 pu (2013)
50km or 1h16min SE of Mata Mata (South Africa)

Tel: +27(0)54 561 2000, Fax: +27(0)54 561 2005
kgalagadi@sanparks.org
www.sanparks.org

Overlooking the Auob River with old Camel thorn trees, there are self-catering cabins on stilts. Fully equipped kitchens with gas power. The camp is unfenced and guests must check in at Twee Rivieren.

Facilities: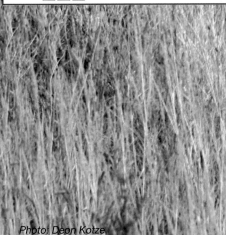
Activities:

Photo: Deon Kotze

NOSSOB
(Kgalagadi Transfrontier)

Photo: Willie Solomo

Nossob is one of the popular rest camps on the South African side of th Kgalagadi Transfrontier Park. An amalgamation of the Kalahari Gemsbok Nation Park in South Africa and the Gemsbok National Park in Botswana formed the Kga lagadi Transfrontier Park. Nossob lies in the dry riverbed of the Nossob River whic forms the border between South Africa and Botswana.

TRAVELLER DESCRIPTION:
Nossob rest camp is 3,5 hours' drive from Twee Rivieren. The camp offers camping facilities as well as accommodation in chalets, family cottages and guest houses The camp has a swimming pool and a generator supplies electricity for 18 hours pe day. Night drives and day walks can be organised.

TRAVEL INFO:
The shop at Nossob camp sells basic commodities. The nearest tow-in service i: based in Upington.

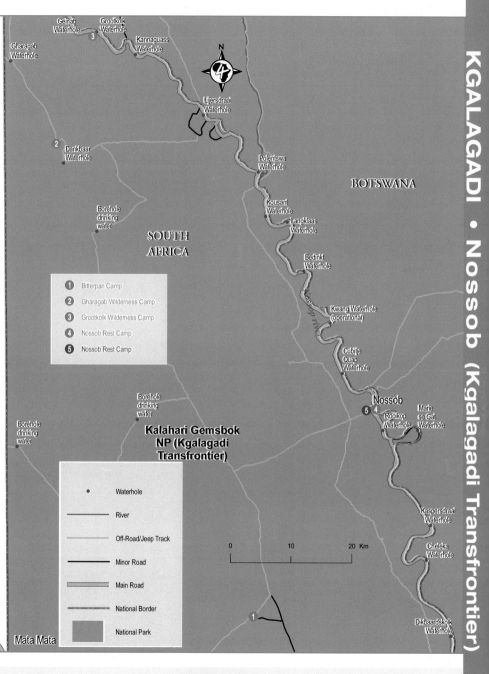

Gelnab Waterhole

Grootkolk Waterhole

Gharagab Waterhole

Kannaguass Waterhole

3

N

Lijersdraal Waterhole

2 Dankbaar Waterhole

Polentswa Waterhole

BOTSWANA

Kousant Waterhole

Langklaas Waterhole

Borehole drinking water

SOUTH AFRICA

Bedinkt Waterhole

1 Bitterpan Camp

2 Gharagab Wilderness Camp

3 Grootkolk Wilderness Camp

4 Nossob Rest Camp

5 Nossob Rest Camp

Nossop river

Kwang Waterhole (operational)

Cubitje Quap Waterhole

Borehole drinking water

Nossob

5 **4** Rooikop Waterhole

Marie se Gat Waterhole

Borehole drinking water

Kalahari Gemsbok NP (Kgalagadi Transfrontier)

Kaspersdraal Waterhole

	Waterhole
	River
	Off-Road/Jeep Track
	Minor Road
	Main Road
	National Border
	National Park

Chefeka Waterhole

0   10   20 Km

1

Dikbaardskolk Waterhole

Mata Mata

TOWN INFO:
Tow-in: +27(0)54 332 2641

197

NOSSOB (Kgalagadi Transfrontier Park)

Bitterpan Camp   1

Lodge   w151193
ZAR 1025.00 pu (2013)
107km or 02h31min SSW of Nossob (4WD)

Tel: +27(0)54 561 2000, Fax: +27(0)54 561 2005
kgalagadi@sanparks.org
www.sanparks.org

These elevated reed cabins, above the red sand dunes, have stunning desert surroundings. This is an unfenced camp and can only be accessed by 4x4 vehicles. Please bring own water and firewood.

Facilities:

Activities:

Gharagab Wilderness Camp   2

Lodge   w151201
ZAR 1045.00 pu (2013)
66km NW of Nossob (4WD)

Tel: +27(0)54 561 2000, Fax: +27(0)54 561 2005
kgalagadi@sanparks.org
www.sanparks.org

Situated in the far northern region of the park, the camp has log cabins. Cabins each has a fully equipped kitchen, a gas fridge, braai facilities on a lovely deck and hot and cold water.

Facilities:

Activities:

Grootkolk Wilderness Camp   3

Lodge   w151168
ZAR 1135.00 pu (2013)
R360, 106km or 2hrs35min NW of Nossob

Tel: +27(0)54 561 2000, Fax: +27(0)54 561 2005
kgalagadi@sanparks.org
www.sanparks.org

Accommodation is offered in cabins. Power is available but limited to a few hours. Guests are advised to bring their own drinking water. A lounge and fully equipped communal kitchen is available.

Facilities:

Activities:

Nossob Rest Camp   4

Lodge   w151113
ZAR 680.00 to 1380.00 pu (2013)
In Nossob

Tel: +27(0)54 561 2000, Fax: +27(0)54 561 2005
kgalagadi@sanparks.org
www.sanparks.org

This camp lies within the dry riverbed of the Nossob River, about 3,5 hrs drive north of Twee Rivieren Rest Camp. Accommodation is available in chalets, family cottages and guest houses.

Languages: English

Facilities:

Activities:

Nossob Rest Camp   5

Park Camp   w152155
ZAR 195.00 pu (2013)
In Nossob

Tel: +27(0)54 561 2000, Fax: +27(0)54 561 2005
kgalagadi@sanparks.org
www.sanparks.org

This camp lies within the dry riverbed of the Nossob River. There are 20 camping sites with electrical points. For alternative accommodation, there are also chalets.

Languages: English

Facilities:

Activities:

Photo: Willie Solomon

TWEERIVIEREN
(Kgalagadi Transfrontier)

Photo: Karin Theror

Twee Rivieren is the most southern camp of the Kgalagadi Transfrontie Park. The camp lies on the banks of the dry Nossop River which forms the borde between South Africa and Botswana. Two Rivers is the Botswana side of the borde post and shares the border post facilities with Tweerivieren. You will have to pas through the border control before you can enter the Transfrontier Park but if you sta on the SA side of the park you don't need to go through Botswana border control.

TRAVELLER DESCRIPTION:
Tweerivieren is the biggest camp in the park with the best facilities. It is the only camp with 24 hours' electricity and cell phone reception. The shop at the camp sells basic commodities and accepts credit cards. Hired cars can be collected here but only if an advance booking was made. The camp has its own tow-in service and ful mechanical workshop. Camp facilities include a swimming pool and very comfort-able campsites and cottages.

TRAVEL INFO:
The Tourist Info Office number is the number of the Kgalagadi Transfrontier Park office at Tweerivieren. The contact number for a tow-in service from Upington is +27(0)54 561 0903.

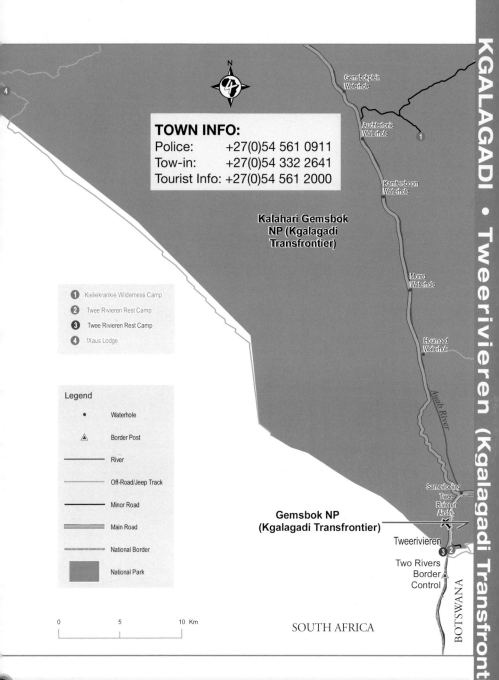

TOWN INFO:
Police: +27(0)54 561 0911
Tow-in: +27(0)54 332 2641
Tourist Info: +27(0)54 561 2000

Kalahari Gemsbok NP (Kgalagadi Transfrontier)

Gemsbokplein Waterhole
Auchterlonie Waterhole
Kamfersboom Waterhole
Monro Waterhole
Houmoed Waterhole
Auob River
Samevloeiing
Twee Rivieren Airstrip
Tweerivieren
Two Rivers Border Control

Gemsbok NP (Kgalagadi Transfrontier)

SOUTH AFRICA

BOTSWANA

1. Kieliekrankie Wilderness Camp
2. Twee Rivieren Rest Camp
3. Twee Rivieren Rest Camp
4. !Xaus Lodge

Legend

- • Waterhole
- ⚠ Border Post
- ── River
- ── Off-Road/Jeep Track
- ── Minor Road
- ── Main Road
- ⋯ National Border
- ▮ National Park

0   5   10 Km

TRAVEL TIP: If you enter at Twee Rivieren you must spend two nights before exiting at Mata-Mata. Both camps are normally fully booked well in advance during the South African June school holidays.

Kieliekrankie Wilderness Camp — 1

Self-catering — w152048
ZAR 1135.00 to 1220.00 pu (2013)
45km or 01h02min N of Twee Rivieren

Tel: +27(0)54 561 2000, Fax: +27(0)54 561 2005
kgalagadi@sanparks.org

This camp is unfenced. The dune cabins have solar electricity, ceiling fans, equipped kitchen and clean ablutions, with hot and cold water. No children under 12 years are allowed. Bring own drinking water and wood.

Languages: English

Facilities:

Activities:

Twee Rivieren Rest Camp — 2

Lodge — w179167
ZAR 890.00 to 1125.00 pu (2013)
Situated at Twee Rivieren

Tel: +27(0)54 561 2000, Fax: +27(0)54 561 2005
kgalagadi@sanparks.org
www.sanparks.org

This is the largest camp in the Kgalagadi Park and a very popular tourist destination. It is situated on the banks of the dry Nossob Riverbed. Fully equipped family cottages are available.

Facilities:

Activities:

Twee Rivieren Rest Camp — 3

Camping — w256094
ZAR 170.00 to 195.00 pu (2013)
Situated at Twee Rivieren

Tel: +27(0)54 561 2000, Fax: +27(0)54 561 2005
kgalagadi@sanparks.org
www.sanparks.org

This is the largest camp in the Kgalagadi Park and a very popular tourist destination. It is situated on the banks of the dry Nossob Riverbed.

Facilities:

Activities:

!Xaus Lodge — 4

Lodge — w13019C
ZAR 3100.00 pp (2013)
57km or 02h44min NW of Twee Rivieren

Tel: +27(0)21 701 7860, Fax: +27(0)21 701 7870
info@xauslodge.co.za
www.xauslodge.co.za

!Xaus means 'Heart'. There is a main building and 12 individual chalets. Enjoy a cosy lounge with a fireplace and a library of selected books for paging through before dinner. You would need at least a 2X4WD to reach this lodge.

Languages: English

Facilities:

Activities:

Photo: Karin Theron

HUKUNTSI

Photo: Johann Groenewald

Hukuntsi is 110 km from Kang, off the Gaborone-Ghanzi highway. The town lies between the Kgalagadi Transfrontier Park and the Central Kalahari Game Reserve and is surrounded by pans. It is one of the four major villages in the Kgalagadi region.

TRAVELLER DESCRIPTION:
Hukuntsi offers all the basic necessities overland travellers might need. You will be able to stock-up on fuel and food. The weather in Hukuntsi varies dramatically - very cold nights in the winter and very hot days in the summer. August winds are unpleasant.

TRAVEL INFO:
There are no private doctors in Hukuntsi; you can consult a doctor at the hospital.

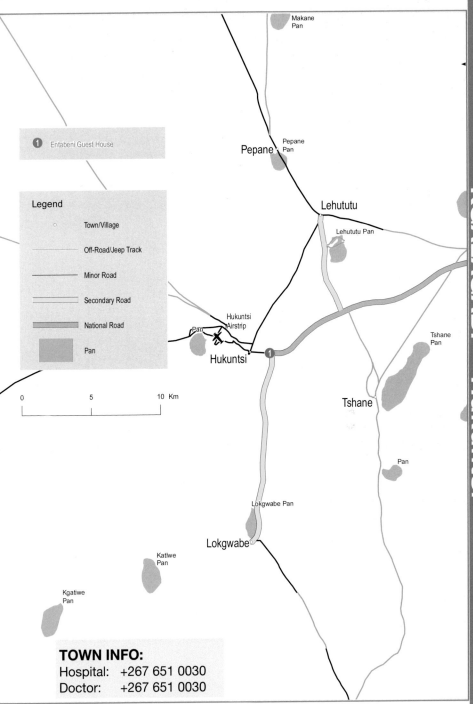

Entabeni Guest House

Legend

- ○ Town/Village
- Off-Road/Jeep Track
- Minor Road
- Secondary Road
- National Road
- Pan

0   5   10 Km

Makane Pan

Pepane Pan

Pepane

Lehututu

Lehututu Pan

Tshane Pan

Hukuntsi Airstrip

Pan

Hukuntsi

Tshane

Pan

Lokgwabe Pan

Lokgwabe

Katlwe Pan

Kgatiwe Pan

TOWN INFO:
Hospital: +267 651 0030
Doctor: +267 651 0030

HUKUNTSI

Entabeni Guest House	1

Guest House w151885
BWP 280.00 to 380.00 pu (2012)
Main Road, Hukuntsi

Tel: +267 651 0075

The guest house is located on the main road of Hukuntsi.
They offer accommodation in six comfortable rooms. No
credit cards accepted.

Facilities:

Photo:Karin Theron

McCARTHY'S REST

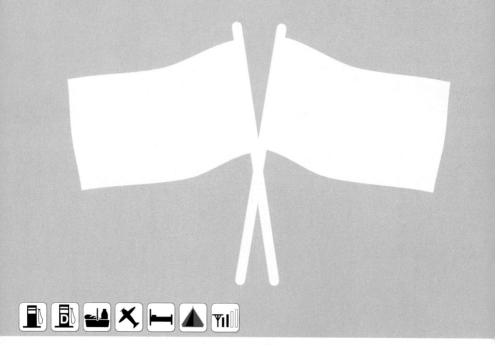

McCarthy's Rest is a border post on the Molopo River between Botswana and the Northern Cape of South Africa. It is mostly used by overlanders en-route to or from the Kgalagadi Transfrontier Park. The surrounding area is semi-arid desert.

TRAVELLER DESCRIPTION:
There are no facilities on the Botswana side of McCarthy's Rest. Camping and lodging are available on the South African side of the border. The fuel stop at McCarthy's Rest is often closed due to fuel shortages and is therefore not dependable. The next fuel stop on the South African side is about 180 km away. There is a shop at Springbokpan Guest Farm (on the SA side) that sells basic food supplies, water and ice.

TRAVEL INFO:
The border post is open 06:00 – 18:00. The contact number is +267 653 0056.

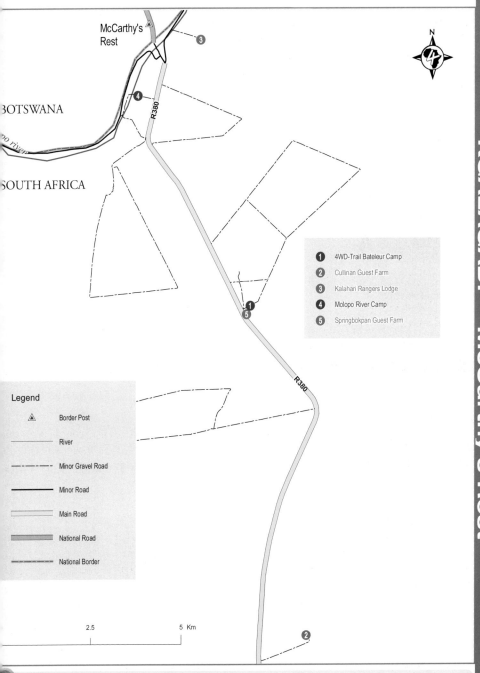

Legend

⚠   Border Post

――――   River

–·–·–·–   Minor Gravel Road

――――   Minor Road

――――   Main Road

――――   National Road

–··–··–··   National Border

McCarthy's Rest

BOTSWANA

SOUTH AFRICA

①   4WD-Trail Bateleur Camp
②   Cullinan Guest Farm
③   Kalahari Rangers Lodge
④   Molopo River Camp
⑤   Springbokpan Guest Farm

2.5   5 Km

TRAVEL TIP: Springbokpan Guest Farm (on the SA side) is a good place to stay.

McCARTHY'S REST

4WD-Trail Bateleur Camp   1

4WD Trail Camp   w131379
ZAR 80.00 pp (2013)
8km or 08min SSE of McCarthy's Rest

Fax: +27(0)86 648 7241, Cell: +27(0)82 224 5000
info@kalaharitours.co.za
www.4x4bateleurcamp.co.za

Situated in South Africa, close to the Botswana border, in McCarthy's Rest. Chalets and campsites are available. Self-drive safaris to Mabuasehube are offered here.

Languages: English, Afrikaans, Setswana

Facilities:

Activities:

Cullinan Guest Farm   2

Guest Farm   w130609
ZAR 250.00 to 680.00 pp (2012)
19km or 18min SSE of McCarthy's Rest

Fax: +27(0)86 511 0038, Cell: +27(0)82 826 1419
bnmarda@xsinet.co.za
www.cullinanplaas.co.za

Located about 19km from the McCarthy's Rest Border Control point. Accommodation available in one of 5 double rooms in the main guest house. Camping is also offered.

Languages: English, Afrikaans

Facilities:

Activities:

Kalahari Rangers Lodge   3

Lodge   w130102
ZAR 600.00 to 720.00 (2012)
2km or 02min NE of McCarthy's Rest

Fax: +27(0)86 624 0461, Cell: +27(0)79 580 4199
kalaharicc@mweb.co.za
www.kalahari-rangers.com

Situated in South Africa, near the Botswana border at McCarthy's Rest. Rooms are large and furnished with an African theme and each contains a dressing room, small lounge area, luxury bathroom and air-conditioning. Traditional cuisine and game is served.

Facilities:

Activities:

Molopo River Camp   4

Lodge Camp   w208462
ZAR 80.00 pp (2013)
2km or 02min SW of McCarthy's Rest

Cell: +27(0)82 224 5000
info@kalaharitours.co.za

Located in South Africa, near the Botswana border, in McCarthy's Rest. The camp offers very basic facilities with no electricity, but there is water.

Languages: English, Afrikaans

Facilities:

Springbokpan Guest Farm   5

Guest Farm   w208511
ZAR 300.00 to 500.00 pp (2013)
8km or 08min SSE of McCarthy's Rest

Fax: +27(0)86 765 6475, Cell: +27(0)82 224 5000
info@springbokpan.co.za
www.springbokpan.co.za

Situated in South Africa, close to McCarthy's Rest Border Control point. The main farm house provides luxury en-suite rooms, or there are also thatched chalets set amongst Camel thorn trees.

Languages: English, Afrikaans

Facilities:

Activities:

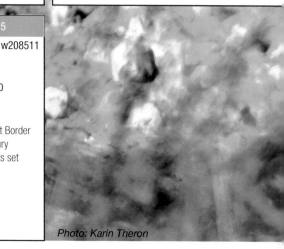
Photo: Karin Theron

KGALAGADI • McCarthy's Rest

TSABONG

Photo: Johann Groenewal

Tsabong is the administrative centre of the Kgalagadi region and its primar
hospital serves a huge outlying area. It has several refuges where tuberculosi
patients and their families can stay while undergoing lengthy outpatient treatmen
Near Tsabong is one of the largest kimberlite fields in the world. Kimberlite is a typ
of volcanic rock sometimes containing diamonds and is named after South Africa'
famous diamond town, Kimberley.

TRAVELLER DESCRIPTION:
Only 27 km from the McCarthy's Rest border post between Botswana and South
Africa, this town offers the overlander all the services and supplies you might need
for your trip into Botswana.   Don't count on getting fuel in Tsabong because they
quite often run dry. An interesting sight around the area is the police patrolling on
camels.

TRAVEL INFO:
The ATM at the Barclays Bank accepts Visa and Master Card. Contact AB Spares
(tel: +267 654 0885) for batteries, tyres, shocks, gaskets and bearings.

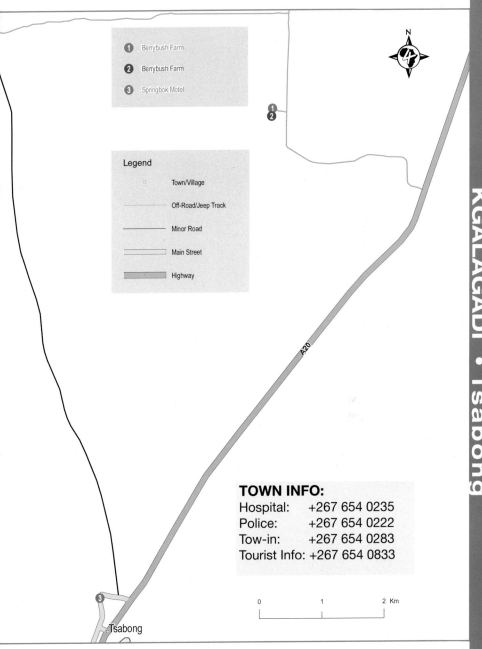

1 Berrybush Farm

2 Berrybush Farm

3 Springbok Motel

Legend

○ Town/Village

Off-Road/Jeep Track

Minor Road

Main Street

Highway

A20

Tsabong

TOWN INFO:
Hospital: +267 654 0235
Police: +267 654 0222
Tow-in: +267 654 0283
Tourist Info: +267 654 0833

0   1   2 Km

TRAVEL TIP: Allow yourself enough time to get to Mabuasehube from Tsabong as the road has deep sand that slows you down a lot.

TSABONG

Berrybush Farm 1

Lodge w149904
BWP 50.00 to 225.00 pp (2013)
12km or 15min NNE of Tsabong

Tel: +267 654 0584, Fax: +267 65 407 79,
Cell: +267 72 195 269
kalahariberrybush@gmail.com

Berrybush is a self-sufficient farm, producing their own organic dairy and meat products. They offer rustic en-suite accommodation and meals and drinks on request. Game drives can be organised at the nearby game farms.

Facilities:

Activities:

Berrybush Farm 2

Farm Camp w211017
BWP 40.00 pp (2013)
12km or 15min NNE of Tsabong

Tel: +267 654 0584, Fax: +267 654 0779,
Cell: +267 72 195 269
kalahariberrybush@gmail.com

Berrybush is a self-sufficient farm, producing their own organic dairy and meat products. They offer secure camping and ablutions. Meals and drinks available on request. Fresh water and wood are supplied.

Facilities:

Activities:

Springbok Motel 3

Motel w245022
BWP 458.00 to 570.00 pu (2013)
In Tsabong

Tel: +267 654 0747, Fax: +267 654 0473,
Cell: +267 7240 9277
joy@springbokmotel.com, www.springbokmotel.com

The Springbok Motel is situated in town close to the bank and shops. They offer accommodation in standard, double and executive rooms.

Facilities:

Photo: Johann Groenewald

T4A AUTOMOTIVE NAVIGATION

KGALAGADI • Tsabong

iGO primo

Automotive Navigation
iGO Navigation Software

TRACKS4AFRICA

MAKGADIKGADI

Sunrise at Lekhubu Island. (Hannes Thirion)

This region features some of the largest salt pans in the world, collectively known as the Makgadikgadi Pans.

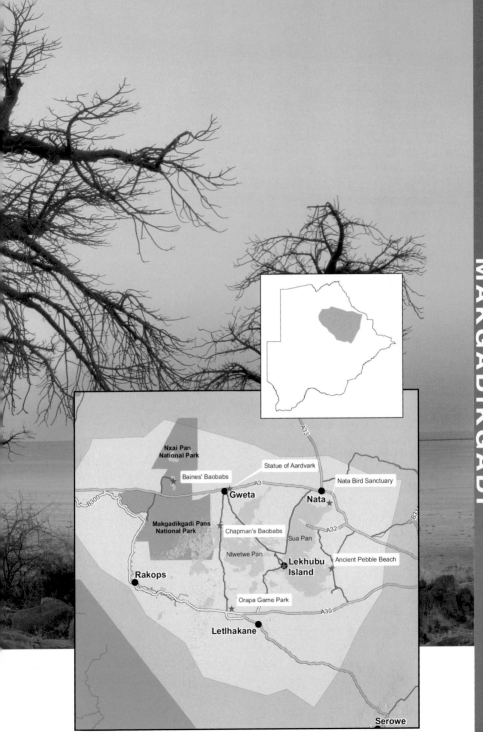

Nxai Pan
National Park

Baines' Baobabs

Statue of Aardvark

Nata Bird Sanctuary

A3

Gweta

Nata

Makgadikgadi Pans
National Park

Chapman's Baobabs

Sua Pan

A32

Ntwetwe Pan

**Lekhubu
Island**

Ancient Pebble Beach

Rakops

Orapa Game Park

A30

Letlhakane

Serowe

A33

B300

It is difficult to believe that millions of years ago these pans were a sea filled with life, but today an ancient pebble beach bears testimony to that era.

The contrast between the dry and the wet seasons in these pans is quite spectacular. In the dry season you won't see many animals, but as soon as the rain arrives the landscape is filled with thousands of animals. Unfortunately the roads are quite treacherous during this season and overlanding becomes very challenging.

During the rainy summer season these pans provide breeding ground for flamingos, pelicans and waders, while the surrounding grasslands are home to antelope and are visited seasonally by migrating wildebeest, zebra and a range of predators.

The pans may seem to be in the middle of nowhere, but people have been visiting them for millennia to enjoy their isolation and stark beauty. Some of these pans fall within the Nxai Pan National Park and the Makgadikgadi Pans National Park, but the biggest part of it lies outside the parks.

Sua Pan is probably the most famous of these pans and both Lukhubu Island (also known as Kubu Island) and Kukonje Island are situated within this pan. They are rock islands with numerous Baobab trees within this vast expanse of nothingness. Lekhubu Island is described as one of those must-see places and offers amazing photographic opportunities. At sunrise and sunset the Baobabs create a ghostly feeling of wandering spirits, which is also reflected in the lore of the locals who go there to honour the spirits on a regular basis.

The nearby Nata Bird Sanctuary offers a refuge to the wildlife, pelicans, flamingos and other water birds of Sua Pan. This is a community camp.

Other well-known Baobabs in the Makgadikgadi region are Green's, Baines' and Chapman's Baobabs. These giants are sometimes referred to as 'the upside down' trees because, when they shed their leaves during the dry season, they look like they were planted with their roots in the air.

The Orapa Game Park near Letlhakane was developed in 1985 from a badly degraded cattle-grazing and recreational area surrounding the mine. Today the park includes wildlife like springbok, blue wildebeest, eland, zebra, waterbuck and giraffe.

The Boteti River is generally dry and lies on the western side of the Makgadikgadi Pans National Park. There are a few places down the western side of the river that are quite popular among overlanders.

When you pass the small village of Gweta, stop and have a look at the statue of an aardvark.

A rain storm over Sua Pan. (Lindy Lourens)

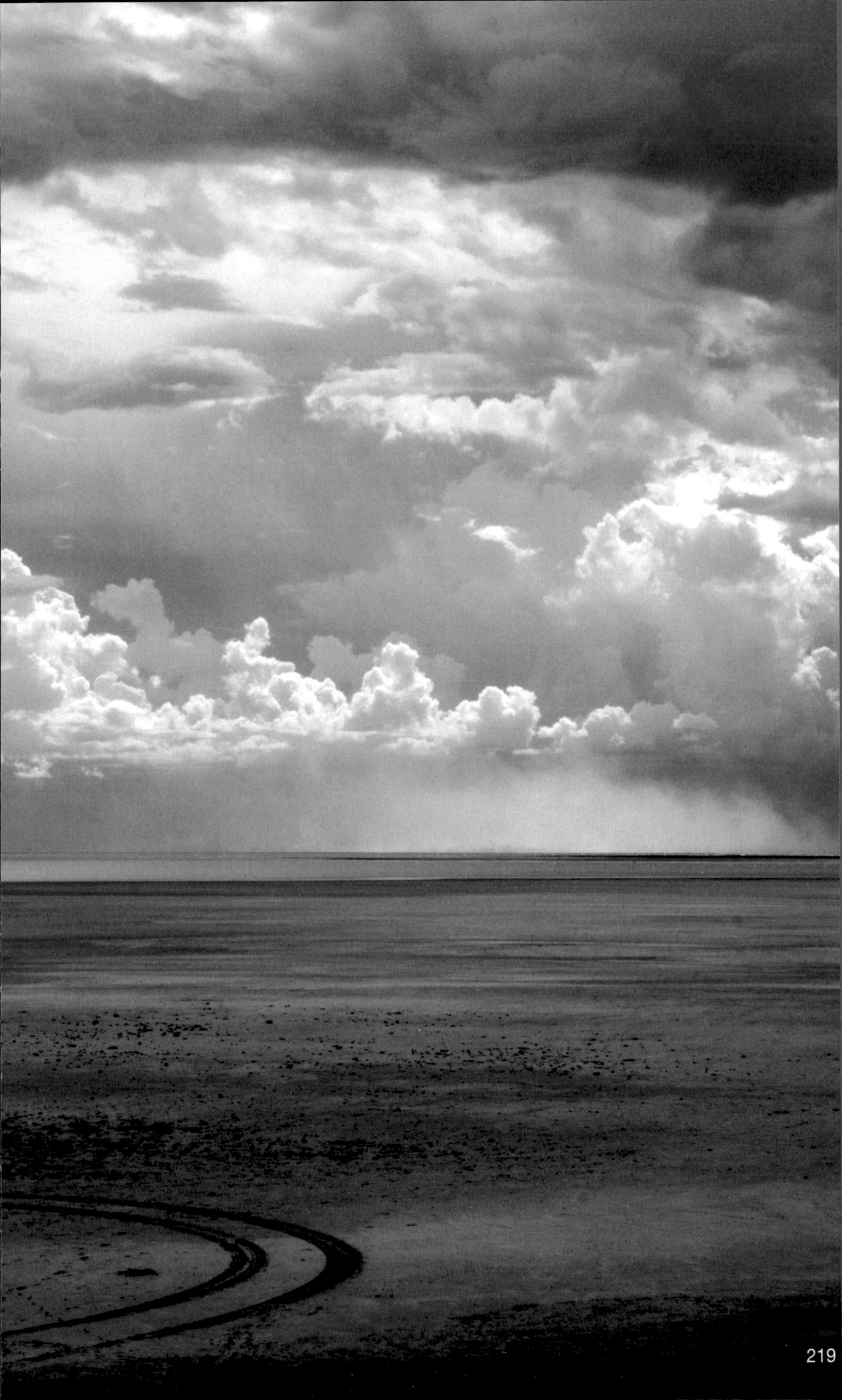

MAKGADIKGADI

GWETA

Gweta is a small village on the edge of the Makgadikgadi Pans. It lies on the A3, about 205 km east of Maun and 100 km west of Nata. The village has a hospital with a pharmacy. At the local supermarket and butchery you'll be able to replenish food supplies. There is a good choice of lodge and camping accommodation available in the area.

TRAVELLER DESCRIPTION:
Gweta is the gateway to the Makgadikgadi Pans and Nxai Pan National Parks and a convenient town to replenish food supplies before entering the parks.

TRAVEL INFO:
Although there is no private doctor in town, you can consult one at the hospital. The pharmacy is at the hospital.

 TRAVEL TIP: Due to a vet fence you're not allowed to take raw meat from cloven hooved animals, cheese and unpasteurised milk from Maun east to Nxai Pan or Makgadigadi Pans National Parks. Gweta is the nearest town where you can buy food supplies.

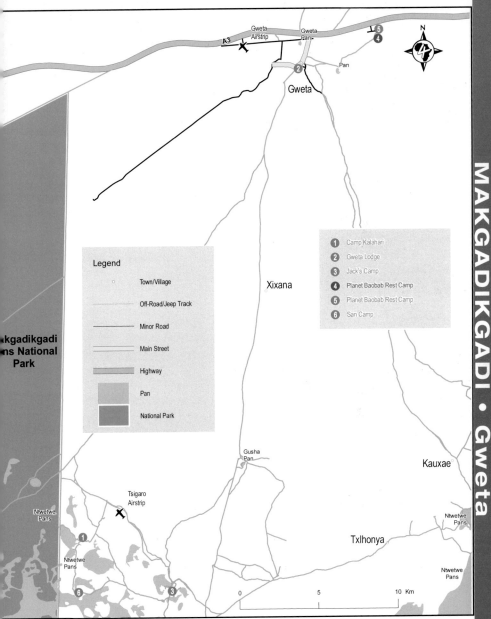

Legend

○	Town/Village
	Off-Road/Jeep Track
	Minor Road
	Main Street
	Highway
	Pan
	National Park

1 Camp Kalahari
2 Gweta Lodge
3 Jack's Camp
4 Planet Baobab Rest Camp
5 Planet Baobab Rest Camp
6 San Camp

Gweta Airstrip
Gweta Pan
A3
Pan
Gweta
Xixana
Kauxae
Makgadikgadi Pans National Park
kgadikgadi ns National Park
Gusha Pan
Tsigaro Airstrip
Ntwetwe Pans
Ntwetwe Pans
Ntwetwe Pans
Ntwetwe Pans
Txlhonya
0   5   10 Km

TOWN INFO:
Hospital: +267 621 2333
Police: +267 621 2204

GWETA

Camp Kalahari — 1

Tented Camp — w189277
USD 430.00 to 590.00 pp (2013)
36km or 01h34min SSW of Gweta (4WD)

Tel: +27(0)11 447 1605, Fax: +27(0)11 447 6905
res1@unchartedafrica.com
www.unchartedafrica.com

The former Makgadikgadi Camp, now Camp Kalahari, is located adjacent to the Makgadikgadi National Park. Accommodation is offered in twin, double or family size Meru-style tents with outdoor en-suite bathrooms.

Facilities:
Activities:

Gweta Lodge — 2

Lodge — w17933
BWP 400.00 to 835.00 pu (2013)
Centre of Gweta Village

Tel: +267 62 122 20, Fax: +267 62 12 458,
Cell: +267 74 315 307
gwetalodge@botsnet.bw, www.gwetalodge.com

The lodge offers accommodation in luxury rooms, family rooms, en-suite double rooms or rondavels. Off-site activities and safaris can be organized by the lodge. There is a restaurant, outdoor kitchen and a fire pit if you want to braai.

Facilities:
Activities:

Jack's Camp — 3

Tented Camp — w150138
USD 1400.00 to 14375.00 pp (2013)
No self-drive access

Tel: +27(0)11 447 1605, Fax: +27(0)86 677 5387,
Cell: +27(0)82 575 5076
res1@unchartedafrica.com, www.unchartedafrica.com

Jack's Camp is an authentic safari camp with 10 twin or double stylish and roomy canvas tents with en-suite bathrooms and outdoor showers. Charter planes from Maun available. Pre-booking required.

Facilities:
Activities:

Planet Baobab Rest Camp — 4

Park Camp — w150414
BWP 45.00 to 68.00 pp (2012)
7km or 7min ENE of Gweta

Tel: +27(0)11 447 1605, Fax: +27(0)86 677 5496,
Cell: +27(0)82 575 5076
res2@unchartedafrica.com, www.unchartedafrica.com

The camp is situated on the edge of the Makgadikgadi Pans and is surrounded by large Baobab trees. Six campsites share ablutions. Campers can relax at the funky bar or enjoy traditional food at their restaurant.

Facilities:
Activities:

Planet Baobab Rest Camp — 5

Lodge — w151703
BWP 215.00 to 795.00 pp (2012)
7km or 7min ENE of Gweta

Tel: +27(0)11 447 1605, Fax: +27(0)11 447 6905,
Cell: +267 72 338 344
res2@unchartedafrica.com, www.unchartedafrica.com

The camp is surrounded by Baobab trees and accommodation is offered in traditional huts with en-suite bathrooms. You can cook your own food on the communal fire or enjoy traditional food at their restaurant.

Facilities:
Activities:

San Camp — 6

Tented Camp — w195984
USD 1100.00 to 1425.00 pp (2013)
39km or 01h40min SSW of Gweta (4WD)

Tel: +27(0)11 447 1605, Fax: +27(0)86 677 5387
res1@unchartedafrica.com
www.unchartedafrica.com

San Camp offers accommodation in luxury Meru-style tents spread out facing the Makgadikgadi Pans. The camp is only open during the dry season.

Facilities:
Activities:

Photo: Willie Solomon

LETLHAKANE

Letlhakane has developed into a buzzing town, thanks to the three diamond mines close-by. Letlhakane mine, Orapa mine and Damtshaa mine are all within 15–20 km of Letlhakane and are operated by Debswana.

TRAVELLER DESCRIPTION:

If you want to enter the Makgadikgadi Pans National Park at Khumaga gate, coming from Palapye on the A14, this is a good place to stock-up. You will find all the services that you need in Letlhakane, from medical to mechanical.

TRAVEL INFO:

The telephone number for the doctor is the same as for the hospital. Hospital reception will put you through to the doctor. TDS Tyre Services also provides tow-in services. You can contact them on +267 297 6502 or +267 71 480 727. Good quality meat is available at the Spar.

TOWN INFO:

Hospital:	+267 297 8242
Police:	+267 297 8222
Doctor:	+267 297 8242
Tow-in:	+267 297 6914
Tourist Info:	+267 297 8585

① Mikelele Motel

Legend

∘	Town
——	River
– – –	Off-Road/Jeep Track
——	City Street
═══	Main Street
═══	Secondary Road
▬▬	Highway

A30

A14

Letlhakane

0   2   4 Km

TRAVEL TIP: Although there are two service stations, fuel may not always be available.

LETLHAKANE

Mikelele Motel 1

Motel   w150905
BWP 460.00 pp (2012)
Lot 95 Tawana Ward Letlhakane Link Road

Tel: +267 297 6639, Fax: +267 297 6268
ratsietape@gmail.com

Mikelele Motel offers accommodation in en-suite rooms
which are air-conditioned and have satellite television.

Facilities:

Activities:

Photo: Hannes Thirion

MAKGADIKGADI PANS

Photo: Lindy Lourens

The Makgadikgadi Pans area is quite remarkable and boasts some
of the largest salt pans in the world. The pans may seem in the middle of nowhere, but people have been visiting them for millennia. The contrast between the dry and the wet seasons around these pans is quite spectacular. In the dry season you won't see many animals, but as soon as the rain arrives, the landscape is filled with thousands of animals. During the rainy summer season these pans provide breeding ground for flamingos, pelicans and waders while the surrounding grasslands are home to antelope and are visited seasonally by migrating wildebeest, zebra, and a range of predators. Lekhubu Island and Kukonje Island are popular destinations in one of the biggest pans of the region, Sua Pan. Most of the rock islands in this area are remnants of ancient sand dunes. Lekhubu is the most famous and is different from the other islands. Many of Lekhubu's granite rocks are stained white with fossilized bird droppings. This ancient guano bears testimony to a large bird population that used to live on the island. This island of rocks and majestic Baobab trees in the middle of a sea of salt offers stunning photographic opportunities. The island is littered with artefacts from different ages: Stone-age cutting tools, shards of pottery at least 2 000 years old, and the remains of a low, circular wall.

ai Pan National Park adjoins the northern border of the Makgadikgadi Pans
tional Park. Wildlife migrates freely between these parks. The landscapes of the
rks are dotted with clusters of Acacia trees and Mopane woodland and smaller
ns and they host a big variety of wildlife.

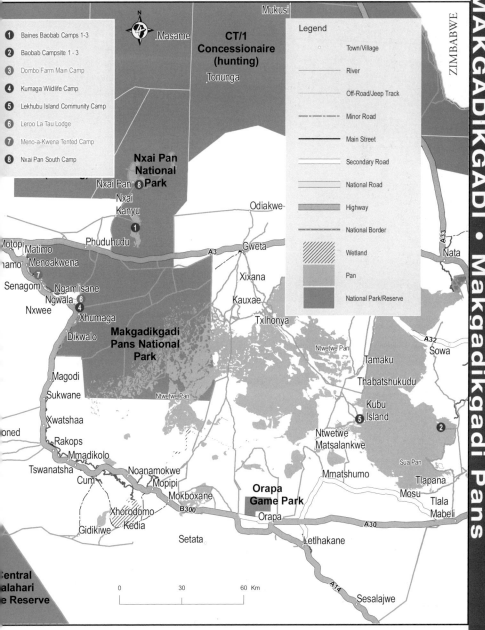

- ❶ Baines Baobab Camps 1-3
- ❷ Baobab Campsite 1 - 3
- ❸ Dombo Farm Main Camp
- ❹ Kumaga Wildlife Camp
- ❺ Lekhubu Island Community Camp
- ❻ Leroo La Tau Lodge
- ❼ Meno-a-Kwena Tented Camp
- ❽ Nxai Pan South Camp

Legend

○	Town/Village
	River
	Off-Road/Jeep Track
	Minor Road
	Main Street
	Secondary Road
	National Road
	Highway
	National Border
	Wetland
	Pan
	National Park/Reserve

MAKGADIKGADI PANS

Photo: Lindy Loure

TRAVELLER DESCRIPTION:
It is best to travel this area in your own 4x4 and camp, but bear in mind that the roads are quite treacherous during the rainy season and overlanding becomes very challenging. Visitors are advised to phone before travelling to the area during the wet season to check water levels and accessibility. Kukonje Island is a remote area with just a campsite under a large tree. There is a community campsite on the outskirts of Lekhubu Island. Campers must please remove all their litter from the islands. You need a 4WD and have to be self-sufficient if you want to visit the Makgadikgadi Pans and Nxai Pan National Parks. Campsites are unfenced. Bookings have to be made and paid in advance, but park en vehicle entry fees can be paid at the gates.

TRAVEL INFO:
Park entry fees are payable to the Department of Wildlife and National Parks (DWNP). You can contact them at +267 318 0774 or pay the entry fees at the gate.

TOWN INFO: Tourist Info: +267 661 265

TRAVEL TIP: Due to a vet fence you're not allowed to take raw meat from cloven hooved animals, cheese and unpasteurised milk from Maun east to Nxai Pan or Makgadigadi Pans National Parks. The nearest food supply is in Gweta.

230

aines Baobab Camps 1-3   1

ilderness Camp   w150837
VP 80.00 to 350.00 pp (2013)
5.8km or 1h17min NE of Nxai Pan Nat Park Gate on A3
WD)

l: +267 686 2221, Fax: +267 686 2262,
ell: +267 73 867 221
maesites@botsnet.bw, www.xomaesites.com

e camp, situated on the border of Kudiakam Pan, was
ded when the boundaries of the Nxai Pan National Park
ere extended. The camp is unfenced and undeveloped.
e-booking and prepayment are essential.

cilities:

tivities:

Baobab Campsite 1 - 3   2

Wilderness Camp   w152320

171km or 03h03min W of Francistown

(We were unable to confirm the information for this listing.
Please use at your own discretion). Three campsites are
situated under large Baobab trees on Kukonje Island. A
longdrop toilet is the only facility. Camping is free for now.

---

ombo Farm Main Camp   3

odge   w239742
URO 95.00 to 119.00 pp (2013)
2km or 01h36min E of Maun (4WD)

ell: +267 74 121 332
fo@dombofarm.com
ww.dombofarm.com

tuated outside the Makgadikgadi Pans National Park, this
hall lodge only has 4 beds available. They offer German
spitality and individual service. Booking is essential. No
lf-drive allowed around the farm.

nguages: English, German

cilities:

tivities:

Kumaga Wildlife Camp   4

Park Camp   w179304
USD 50.00 pp (2013)
2km or 5 min N of Khumaga Gate (4WD)

Tel: +267 686 5365, Fax: +267 686 5367
sklcamps@botsnet.bw
www.sklcamps.com

The camp is situated on the banks of the Boteti River in
the Makgadikgadi Pans National Park. Ten campsites share
an ablution block that has flush toilets. The water is drinkable. Booking and prepayment required.

Facilities:

Activities:

---

ekhubu Island Community Camp   5

ommunity Camp   w151867
VP 60.00 to 100.00 pp (2013)
km or 02h36min NNE of Letlhakane (4WD)

l: +267 297 9612, Fax: +267 297 9612,
ell: +267 75 49 4669
bu.island@botsnet.bw, www.kubuisland.com

ampsites are scattered around Lekhubu Island and facili-
s include long drop toilets and braai pits. Reception is
en Monday to Friday during normal working hours. Fire
ood is for sale at reception. Pre-booking required.

cilities:

tivities:

Photo: Lindy Lourens

MAKGADIKGADI PANS

Leroo La Tau Lodge	6

Tented Camp w179368
USD 476.00 to 586.00 pp (2013)
141km or 01h38min ESE of Maun (4WD)

Tel: +267 686 1559, Fax: +267 686 0037
info@desertdelta.com
www.desertdelta.com

The lodge on the bank of the Boteti River overlooks the Makgadikgadi Pans National Park. Accommodation is offered in en-suite Meru-style tents on wooden decks. No children under the age of six allowed. Booking is essential.

Languages: English

Facilities:

Activities:

Meno-a-Kwena Tented Camp	7

Tented Camp w17921*
USD 250.00 to 600.00 pp (2013)
118km or 01h24min ESE of Maun (4WD)

Tel: +267 686 0981, Fax: +267 68 60 493,
Cell: +267 71 326 085
kkreservations@ngami.net, www.menoakwena.com

The camp on the edge of the Makgadikgadi Pans National Park offers accommodation in eight tents that can each take up to 16 people. Getting directions from their office is essential.

Languages: English

Facilities:

Activities:

Nxai Pan South Camp	8

Park Camp w179296
BWP 80.00 to 350.00 pp (2013)
38.9km or 1h12min NNE of Nxai Pan Nat Park Gate (4WD)

Tel: +267 686 2221, Fax: +267 686 2262,
Cell: +267 73 86 2221
xomaesites@botsnet.bw, www.xomaesites.com

The camp is situated close to the entrance gate of Nxai Pan NP. There are ten campsites in a well-wooded area. Each site has its own braai pit but share ablutions. Pre-booking and prepayment are essential.

Facilities:

Activities:

Photo:Hannes Thirion

NATA

RITE CENTRE
SUPERMARKET

Nata is a small town on the edge of the Makgadikgadi Pans National Park. It lie at the junction of the A3 from Maun in the west and Francistown in the south with th A33 that runs along the Botswana/Zimbabwe border to Kasane. Nata is located 20 km northwest of Francistown, 300 km east of Maun and 300 km south of Kasane Aids is having a devastating effect on the village, but thanks to active communit work it is seen as a 'Village of hope'.

TRAVELLER DESCRIPTION:
You can buy all the basic necessities from local shops and have your vehicle repaired by a backyard mechanic in town. From Nata you can visit the nearby Nata Bird Sanctuary and Sua Pan.

TRAVEL INFO:
The contact number for the Nata Clinic is +267 621 1244. There is only one private doctor in the village. In case of emergency you can contact Dr Joseph Kaseba or his cell phone +267 71 771 765. Only Master and Visa cards work at the ATM, provided by Barclays Bank.

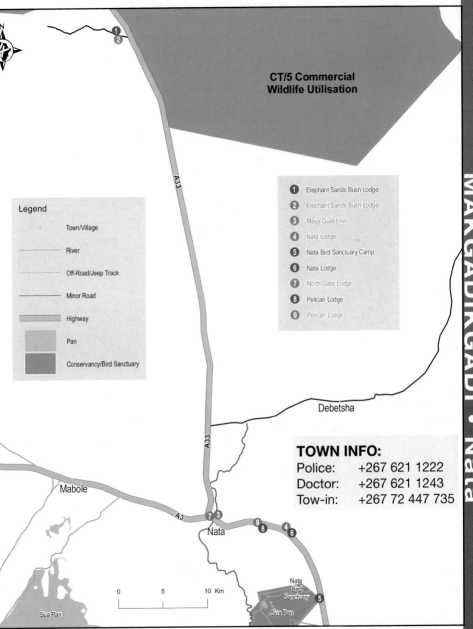

Legend

○	Town/Village
——	River
——	Off-Road/Jeep Track
——	Minor Road
▬	Highway
▬	Pan
▬	Conservancy/Bird Sanctuary

CT/5 Commercial Wildlife Utilisation

1. Elephant Sands Bush Lodge
2. Elephant Sands Bush Lodge
3. Maya Guest Inn
4. Nata Lodge
5. Nata Bird Sanctuary Camp
6. Nata Lodge
7. North Gate Lodge
8. Pelican Lodge
9. Pelican Lodge

Debetsha

Mabole

Nata

TOWN INFO:
Police:	+267 621 1222
Doctor:	+267 621 1243
Tow-in:	+267 72 447 735

Nata Bird Sanctuary

Sua Pan

Sua Pan

0   5   10 Km

TRAVEL TIP: The local butcheries are not for the faint hearted. Due to a vet fence you're not allowed to take raw meat from cloven hooved animals, cheese and unpasteurised milk from Maun east to Nata.

NATA

Elephant Sands Bush Lodge 1

Wilderness Camp   w179143
BWP 70.00 pu (2013)
54km or 44min NNW of Nata

Cell: +267 73 445 162
bookings@elephantsandsbotswana.com
www.elephantsands.com

Elephant Sands is a conservancy on privately owned land.
They offer unfenced campsites. Sites are not allocated; you
can pick your own site. Ablutions and a bar are available.

Languages: English, Dutch, Afrikaans, Setswana

Facilities:
Activities:

Elephant Sands Bush Lodge 2

Self-catering   w249819
BWP 350.00 to 690.00 pu (2013)
54km or 44min NNW of Nata

Cell: +267 73 445 162
bookings@elephantsandsbotswana.com
www.elephantsands.com

Elephant Sands is a conservancy on privately owned land.
They offer twin and family size en-suite chalets and a bar.
To be safe, inform the lodge of your expected arrival time
in winter.

Facilities:
Activities:

Maya Guest Inn 3

Inn   w219948
BWP 310.00 pu (2012)
A3 main road, Nata, Makgadikgadi

Tel: +267 621 1295, Fax: +267 62 112 96,
Cell: +267 74 771 118
www.mayaguestinn.com

Maya Guest Inn offers accommodation in chalets and in
rooms set in a garden filled with palm trees. All rooms and
chalets are air-conditioned and have coffee/tea making
facilities.

Facilities:
Activities:

Nata Lodge 4

Lodge   w179292
BWP 700.00 to 880.00 pu (2013)
10km or 7min E of Nata

Tel: +267 62 000 70, Fax: +267 62 000 71,
Cell: +267 74 533 417
reservations@natalodge.com, www.natalodge.com

Nata Lodge offers accommodation in wooden chalets and
safari tents. The air-conditioned wooden chalets are on
stilts and have outdoor showers and indoor baths. The
safari tents have en-suite bathrooms and outdoor showers.

Languages: English, Afrikaans, Setswana

Facilities:
Activities:

Nata Bird Sanctuary Camp 5

Community Camp   w151681
BWP 35.00 pp (2012)
18km or 13min ESE of Nata (4WD)

Cell: +267 71 54 4342

The campsite is near the entrance gate to Nata Bird
Sanctuary. The camp is dominated by an old fallen Baobab
tree growing horizontally. Sites have braai areas and clean
ablutions. Please support this community based project.

Facilities:
Activities:

Photo: Lindy Lourens

Nata Lodge	6

Lodge Camp   w179300
BWP 80.00 pp (2013)
10km or 8min E of Nata

Tel: +267 620 0070, Fax: +267 62 000 71,
Cell: +267 74 53 3417
reservations@natalodge.com, www.natalodge.com

Nata Lodge looks like an oasis, set amongst Mokolwane
palms. The lodge also has a campsite with ablutions.

Languages: English, Afrikaans, Setswana

Facilities:

Activities:

North Gate Lodge	7

Lodge   w192588
BWP 555.00 to 945.00 pu (2013)
Kasane/Maun Junction, Nata

Tel: +267 62 111 56, Fax: +267 621 1154,
Cell: +267 74 273 722
northgatelodge@yahoo.com, www.northgate.co.bw

North Gate Lodge offers accommodation in chalets as well
as executive and family rooms. All chalets and rooms are
en-suite and air-conditioned and have a television, coffee/
tea making facility, mosquito nets and ceiling fans.

Facilities:

Activities:

Pelican Lodge	8

Lodge Camp   w258285
BWP 70.00 pp (2012)
6km or 05min E of Nata

Tel: +27(0)13 751 2220, Cell: +267 71 314 603
pelicanlodge1@madbookings.com
www.pelicanlodgebotswana.com

The campsite at Nata Pelican Lodge has private ablution
facilities. Each site has its own electricity point and a braai
area.

Languages: English

Facilities:

Activities:

Pelican Lodge	9

Lodge   w258281
BWP 680.00 pu (2012)
6km or 05min E of Nata

Tel: +27(0)13 751 2220, Cell: +267 71 314 603
pelicanlodge1@madbookings.com
www.pelicanlodgebotswana.com

The lodge offers accommodation in single thatched bungalows and double chalets. All rooms are en-suite, have
air conditioning, TV, a fridge, internet access and coffee/
tea making facilities. The presidential rooms each has a
Jacuzzi.

Facilities:

Activities:

MAKGADIKGADI • Nata

Photo: Peter Levey

RAKOPS

Photo:Peter Levey

Rakops is a small town on the Boteti River in the Central District of Botswana. The town has most of the necessities and travellers are able to restock here with the basics. It is a useful stop to fill up with fuel before entering the Makgadikgadi Pans National Park.

TRAVELLER DESCRIPTION:
In the recent past Rakops still had old mechanical fuel pumps that had to be operated by hand, but these have now been replaced with modern electric pumps. Although there are no gas refill facilities in town, refilled cylinder bottles are for sale. Xere Motel has a restaurant that is open to the public.

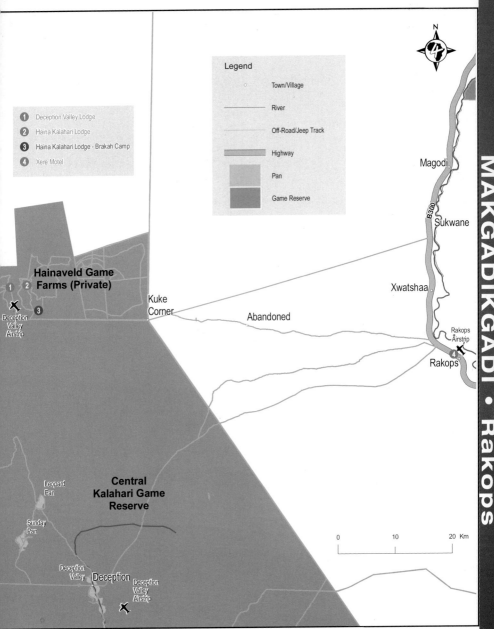

Legend

- Town/Village
- River
- Off-Road/Jeep Track
- Highway
- Pan
- Game Reserve

1 Deception Valley Lodge
2 Haina Kalahari Lodge
3 Haina Kalahari Lodge - Brakah Camp
4 Xere Motel

Magodi

B300

Sukwane

Hainaveld Game Farms (Private)

Xwatshaa

Kuke Corner

Abandoned

Rakops Airstrip

Rakops

Deception Valley Airstrip

Leopard Pan

Central Kalahari Game Reserve

Sunday Pan

Deception Valley · Deception · Deception Valley Airstrip

0   10   20 Km

TOWN INFO:
Police: +267 297 5115

RAKOPS

Deception Valley Lodge — 1

Game/Safari Lodge w189270
USD 440.00 to 1576.00 pp (2013)
106km or 03h08min W of Rakops

Tel: +27(0)11 781 1661, Fax: +27(0)86 766 9369,
Cell: +27(0)76 940 7650
res2@africananthology.co.za, www.dvl.co.za

The main lodge can accommodate up to 16 people and
there are also eight en-suite chalets available with outside
shower each. Guests can be transferred by light aircraft
from Maun Airport to the lodge.

Languages: English, German, Afrikaans

Facilities:

Activities:

Haina Kalahari Lodge — 2

Tented Camp w152313
USD 315.00 to 513.00 pp (2013)
102km or 02h55min W of Rakops (4WD)

Tel: +267 683 0239, Fax: +267 683 0239,
Cell: +267 72 991 580,
reservations@hainakalaharilodge.com
www.hainakalaharilodge.com

The superior luxury tents have private decks and full
en-suite bathrooms. The family tent is built around trees.
Guests can relax in the lounge, at the bar or on the
sundeck.

Facilities:

Activities:

Haina Kalahari Lodge - Brakah Camp — 3

Lodge Camp w196005
USD 22.00 pp (2012)
98km or 02h45min W of Rakops (4WD)

Tel: +267 683 0239, Fax: +267 683 0238
reservations@hainakalaharilodge.com
www.hainakalaharilodge.com

Five campsites are set under big thorn trees. Facilities
include a flush toilet and a sink for washing dishes. Drinkable water is available at the main lodge which is 3 km
from the camp.

Facilities:

Activities:

Xere Motel — 4

Motel w230015
BWP 500.00 pu (2012)
4km or 5min SSW of Rakops (4WD)

Cell: +267 71 723 907

The Xere Motel is situated along the Rakops-Maun road.
Rooms are en-suite, with satellite television and air conditioning. Pre-booking required.

Languages: English

Facilities:

Activities:

MAKGADIKGADI • Rakops

Photo: Peter Levey

OKAVANGO / MOREMI

A bird's-eye view of the Okavango Delta.
(Lindy Lourens)

The Okavango/Moremi region

has a lot to offer in terms of Botswana's natural beauty and wildlife, and it is a popular tourist destination. Maun is the tourist capital of Botswana and a transportation and service hub to camps, lodges and overlanding safaris.

There are many upmarket private concessions with tented camps and lodges in this area. The Nhabe Museum in Maun has a few displays

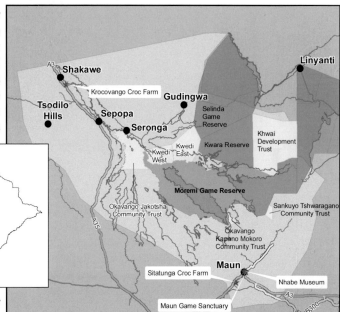

about the history of the Ngamiland district and some temporary exhibitions of photography, basket-weaving and art.

The Okavango is without a doubt one of the highlights of any trip to Botswana. The Okavango is a mysterious network of ever-expanding and increasingly smaller channels, hemmed by reeds, islands and palm forests - a unique oasis of life right in the centre of the Kalahari Desert. The best way to explore the Okavango Delta is by mokoro.

The delta has a thriving crocodile population and there are two crocodile farms where these prehistoric animals can be viewed from close-up, one near Maun and the other near Shakawe.

Located on the eastern side of the Okavango Delta, the relatively small **Moremi Game Reserve** combines Mopane woodland and Acacia forests, floodplains and lagoons. The reserve boasts a variety of wildlife that moves freely (even through campsites) and is a real paradise for bird lovers, as it is home to nearly 500 species of birds. You need a 4WD to tour Moremi, as you have to negotiate deep sand in summer and mud in winter. Note that the following activities are not allowed in the reserve: off-road driving, night drives, walking safaris and fishing.

Moremi's main entrance, North Gate or Khwai Gate as the locals call it, is situated on the Khwai River. A large number of San (Bushmen) live in the Khwai Village after they relocated from the reserve area. The Khwai Development Trust just to the north of Moremi Game Reserve offers the ideal stop-over en-route between Moremi and Savuti in the Chobe National Park.

There are a number of Community Trusts in this region, like the Khwai Development Trust. These conservation areas are run by the local communities who also support eco-tourism. As the proceeds go to the local communities and it creates job opportunities, we urge you to support them.

Apart from Moremi and the Community Trust conservation areas, Botswana's wildlife can also be enjoyed at the private concession areas like the Kwara Reserve and Selinda Game Reserve. **Selinda Game Reserve** straddles both the Okavango Delta in the west and the Linyanti waterways and savannah in the east. The Selinda Reserve follows the course of the Selinda Spillway as it connects the Okavango to the Linyanti/Kwando River systems. The Selinda Spillway is like no other. It is a river that can flow in two directions, depending on where the water levels are the highest, the Linyanti waterways or the Okavango Delta.

Also worth visiting in this region is Tsodilo Hills. With one of the highest concentrations of rock art in the world, Tsodilo has been called the 'Louvre of the Desert'. Over 4 500 paintings are preserved in an area of only 10km² of the Kalahari Desert and Tsodilo Hills,

Houses in the Khwai Village. (Hannelie Bester)

An elephant walking through Magotho Camp in the Khwai Development Trust. (Hannelie Bester)

which have been declared a World Heritage Site.

Most of these paintings were done by the San people of the Kalahari (the Bushmen). They believe the hills are a resting place for the spirits of the deceased as well as the site of first Creation. The exact age of the paintings is not known although some are thought to be more than 20 000 years old. The archaeological record of the area gives a chronological account of human activities and environmental changes over at least 100 000 years.

GUDIGWA

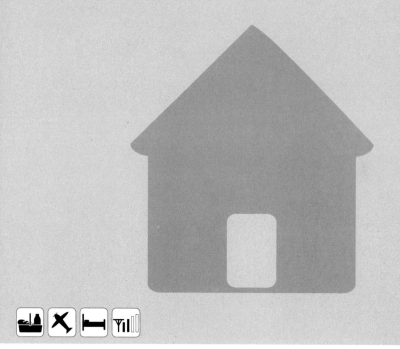

Gudigwa is a small rural village at the eastern tip of the Okavango Delta. The village has nothing but a school and a typical spaza type shop with basic essentials on sale and possibly something to drink.

TRAVELLER DESCRIPTION:
There are about seven small villages in this area where the Bayei and San people continue with their way of life much as they have done for hundreds of years. At Gudigwa Lodge, 5 km from Gudingwa village, you can learn from the San about the medicinal uses of plants, how to track animals on foot, how to find underground water, make fire by rubbing two sticks together, find out what plants are edible (and what not) and how to survive off nature's resources.

TRAVEL INFO:
The nearest hospital is at Maun and doctor at the Seronga clinic.

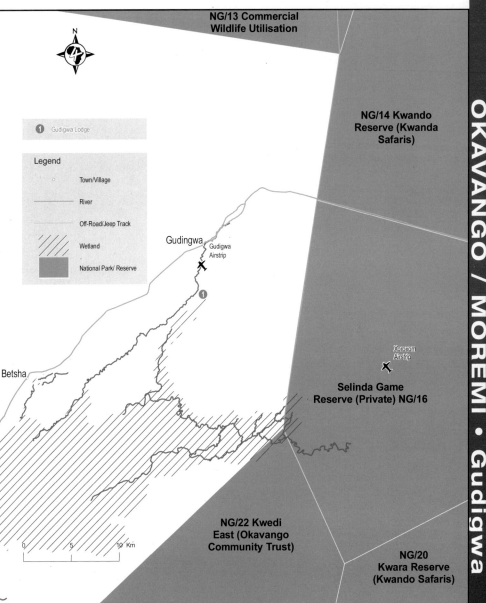

TRAVEL TIP: Sometimes fuel is sold in cans along the road. Be aware of the quality.

GUDIGWA

Gudigwa Lodge 1

Lodge w195866
USD 300.00 to 450.00 pp (2013)
8km or 5min S of Gudigwa (4WD)

Fax: +267 39 27770, Cell: +267 71 843 657
gudigwaculturallodge@gmail.com
www.gudigwa.com

Gudigwa Lodge offers accommodation in comfortable
thatched huts with private open air bathrooms. They serve
traditional meals and guests can learn about the San
(Bushmen) culture and medicinal plants. Pre-booking is
essential.

Facilities:

Activities:

Photo: Hannelie Bester

MAUN

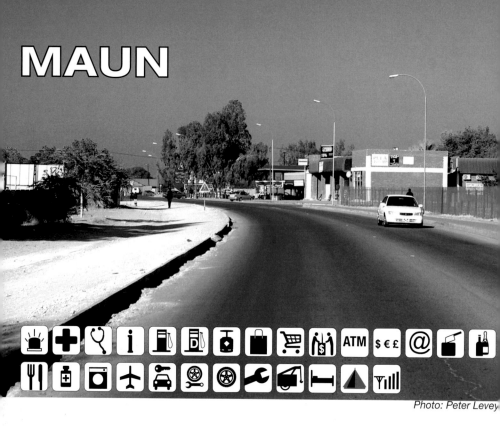

Photo: Peter Levey

Maun is one of the largest towns in Botswana and is situated along the banks of the Thamalakane River. It is considered the gateway to the Okavango Delta and acts as a transport and service hub to camps and lodges in the Delta as well as an important rendezvous point for most overlanding trips into the natural wonders of the Okavango. Maun boasts its own international airport to cater for foreign visitors wanting to explore the Delta.

TRAVELLER DESCRIPTION:
Maun is the tourist capital of Botswana and offers a wide variety of shopping possibilites, services and outdoor activities. The town really has a lively adventure vibe to it. Although it has all the necessary modern facilities, the atmosphere remains rural because of the donkeys, cattle and goats that can be seen grazing around town.

TRAVEL INFO:
Riley's Garage also offers tow-in services. You can contact them on +267 686 0203. There is a Shoprite in Maun.

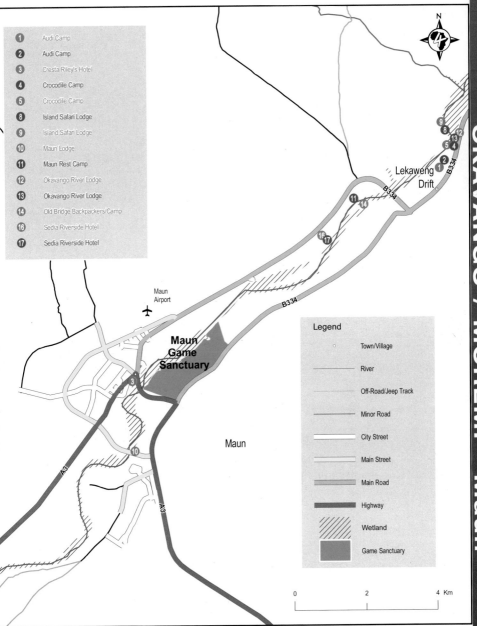

1	Audi Camp
2	Audi Camp
3	Cresta Riley's Hotel
4	Crocodile Camp
5	Crocodile Camp
8	Island Safari Lodge
9	Island Safari Lodge
10	Maun Lodge
11	Maun Rest Camp
12	Okavango River Lodge
13	Okavango River Lodge
14	Old Bridge Backpackers/Camp
16	Sedia Riverside Hotel
17	Sedia Riverside Hotel

Lekaweng Drift

Maun Airport

Maun Game Sanctuary

Maun

Legend

○	Town/Village
	River
	Off-Road/Jeep Track
	Minor Road
	City Street
	Main Street
	Main Road
	Highway
▨	Wetland
▨	Game Sanctuary

0   2   4 Km

TRAVEL TIP: You can order meat from The Beef Boys butchery. Phone them on +267 686 4771. Remember that you are allowed to take raw meat west but not east from Maun past the vet fences.

MAUN

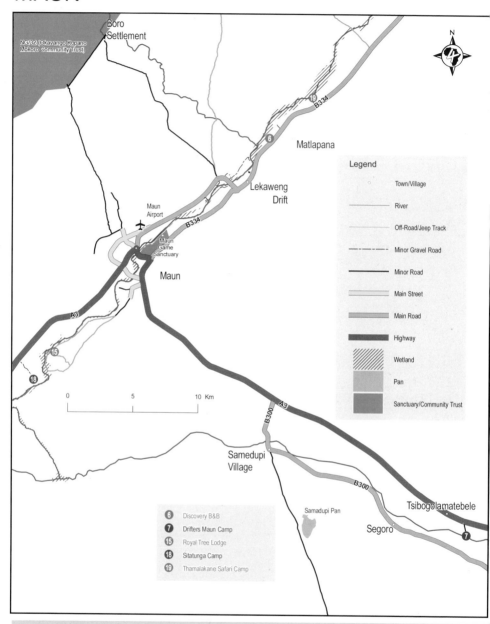

Boro Settlement

NG/32 (Okavango Kopano Mokoro Community Trust)

B334

Matlapana

Lekaweng Drift

Maun Airport

B334

Maun Game Sanctuary

Maun

A3

15

18

0   5   10 Km

A3

B300

Samedupi Village

B300

Tsibogolamatebele

Samadupi Pan

Segoro

Legend

	Town/Village
	River
	Off-Road/Jeep Track
	Minor Gravel Road
	Minor Road
	Main Street
	Main Road
	Highway
	Wetland
	Pan
	Sanctuary/Community Trust

6	Discovery B&B
7	Drifters Maun Camp
15	Royal Tree Lodge
18	Sitatunga Camp
19	Thamalakane Safari Camp

TOWN INFO:

Hospital: +267 687 9000
Doctor: +267 686 1411
Tourist Info: +267 686 1056

Police: +267 686 0223
Tow-in: +267 71 303 788

udi Camp   1

ented Camp   w204785
NP 140.00 to 1815.00 pu (2012)
2km or 15min ENE of Maun

el: +267 686 0599, Fax: +267 686 5388
fo@okavangocamp.com
ww.okavangocamp.com

udi Camp, situated on the banks of the Thamalakane
ver, offers accommodation in luxurious tents raised on
ooden decks. There is also a house with 4 rooms avail-
le on a full board or self-catering basis.

acilities:

ctivities:

Audi Camp   2

Tour Operator Camp   w204786
BWP 60.00 to 70.00 pp (2012)
13km or 15min ENE of Maun

Tel: +267 686 0599, Fax: +267 686 0581
info@okavangocamp.com
www.okavangocamp.com

Some of the campsites at Audi Camp have electricity
points, but not all. Campers are welcome to use all facilities and enjoy activities like cultural village tours, horse
riding and bird watching.

Facilities:

Activities:

resta Riley's Hotel   3

otel   w179130
NP 1039.00 to 1334.00 pu (2012)
verside, in Maun

el: +267 686 0204, Fax: +267 686 0580
esrileys@cresta.co.bw
ww.crestahotels.com

ccommodation is offered in spacious en-suite rooms with
r conditioning, satellite television and coffee/tee making
cilities. The hotel has a beautiful garden, hair salon and a
ecure parking area. Pre-booking required.

anguages: English

acilities:

ctivities:

Crocodile Camp   4

Holiday Resort Camp   w179216
USD 10.00 pp (2013)
13km or 14min ENE of Maun

Fax: +267 680 1257, Cell: +267 75 60 6864
sales@crocodilecamp.com
www.crocodilecamp.com

The camp is situated on the banks of the Thamalakane
River. Camp grounds are beautifully maintained and popular for its shady trees and security. Each site has its own
water and electricity point and braai area.

Facilities:

Activities:

rocodile Camp   5

elf-catering   w256085
SD 100.00 to 125.00 pp (2013)
2km or 14min NE of Maun

ax: +267 680 1257, Cell: +267 75 60 6864
ales@crocodilecamp.com
ww.crocodilecamp.com

rocodile Camp is situated on the banks of the Thamala-
ane River. Standard, Family and Deluxe Chalets are avail-
ble. All chalets are en-suite, with private verandas and
nosquito nets and are serviced. 24 Hour security.

acilities:

ctivities:

Discovery B&B   6

Bed and Breakfast   w179285
BWP 325.00 to 750.00 pu (2013)
15km or 18min NE of Maun

Cell: +267 72 448 298
discoverybnb@info.bw
www.discoverybedandbreakfast.com

Accommodation is offered in en-suite chalets. There is
also a communal shower under the stars. Pre-booking
is preferred. The last 300 m to the entrance can be a bit
sandy.

Languages: English, Dutch

Facilities:

Activities:

MAUN

Drifters Maun Camp — 7

Tour Operator Camp　w151015
ZAR 100.00 pp (2013)
Gravel road off A3, 36km or 27min SE of Maun

Tel: +27(0)11 888 1160, Fax: +27(0)11 888 1020,
Cell: +267 72 304 472
drifters@drifters.co.za, www.drifters.co.za

The camp is built on the banks of the Boteti River. Campsites are set out on a lawn under thorn trees. Electricity is supplied by generator and water comes from a borehole. You can enjoy cold drinks at the bar.

Languages: English, Afrikaans

Facilities:
Activities:

Island Safari Lodge — 8

Lodge Camp　w17919
BWP 50.00 to 75.00 pp (2012)
12km or 13min NE of Maun

Tel: +267 686 0300, Fax: +267 686 2932,
Cell: +267 71 38 6170
enquire@africansecrets.net, www.islandsafarilodge.com

Shady trees divide the camp on the banks of the Thamalakane River into spacious individual campsites. There is a central braai area and clean ablutions. Campers are welcome to use the facilities at the lodge.

Facilities:
Activities:

Island Safari Lodge — 9

Lodge　w179365
BWP 195.00 to 830.00 pp (2012)
12km or 12min NE of Maun

Tel: +267 686 0300, Fax: +267 686 2932,
Cell: +267 71 386 170
enquire@africansecrets.net, www.islandsafarilodge.com

The lodge offers comfortable accommodation set amongst the trees on the banks of the Thamalakane River. En-suite chalets are air-conditioned and have television. Budget rooms are also available.

Facilities:
Activities: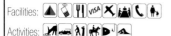

Maun Lodge — 10

Hotel　w17936
BWP 790.00 to 960.00 pu (2012)
Plot No 459, Boseja, Maun

Tel: +267 686 3939, Fax: +267 68 63 969
maun.lodge@info.bw
www.maunlodge.com

Accommodation is available in en-suite twin, double or family rooms as well as riverfront suites and chalets. All rooms, suites and chalets are air-conditioned; have coffee, tea making facilities and satellite television.

Facilities:
Activities:

Maun Rest Camp — 11

Tour Operator Camp　w179148
BWP 70.00 pp (2013)
9km or 9min NE of Maun

Tel: +267 686 2623, Fax: +267 686 3472
simonjoyce@info.bw

You can either erect your own tent or stay in one of the large pre-erected tents. These tents are fully carpeted and have two single beds each. Ablutions are clean and have separate laundry tubs and sinks for washing dishes.

Facilities:
Activities:

Okavango River Lodge — 12

Backpackers Hostel　w17923
BWP 100.00 to 500.00 pu (2013)
13km or 15min from Maun

Tel: +267 686 3707, Fax: +267 686 3707,
Cell: +267 72 249 272
info@okavango-river-lodge.com
www.okavango-river-lodge.com

The lodge, situated on the banks of the Thamalakane River, offers budget backpackers' accommodation in a dormitory en-suite thatched chalets, family rooms and double chalets. Campers are also welcome. Languages: English

Facilities:
Activities:

Kavango River Lodge | 13

Lodge Camp   w256091

WP 70.00 to 80.00 pp (2013)
3km or 15min from Maun

Tel: +267 686 3707, Fax: +267 686 3707,
Cell: +267 72 249 272
info@okavango-river-lodge.com, www.okavango-river-
lodge.com

Kavango River Lodge has a large shady campsite with a
central boma, electricity points and braai areas with lights.

Languages: English

Facilities:

Activities:

Royal Tree Lodge | 15

Lodge   w179194

USD 210.00 to 305.00 pp (2013)
14km or 29min SW of Maun

Tel: +267 680 0757, Fax: +267 680 0757
treelodge@botsnet.bw
www.royaltreelodge.com

The lodge is situated on a wildlife estate along the
Thalamakane River. Accommodation is offered in luxury
tents and chalets. Booking is essential and transfers from
Maun can be organised.

Languages: English

Facilities:

Activities:

Sedia Riverside Hotel | 17

Lodge Camp   w223050

WP 50.00 to 300.00 pp (2012)
334, 7km or 7min ENE of Maun

Tel: +267 686 0177, Fax: +267 686 2574
sedia@info.bw
www.sediahotel.com

The campsite on the hotel grounds leads down to the
banks of the Thamalakane River. The camp is beautiful
with plenty of trees and a lawn. They also have pre-erected
tents with twin beds and electricity.

Facilities:

Activities:

Old Bridge Backpackers/Camp | 14

Tented Camp   w189403

BWP 155.00 to 425.00 pp (2013)
11km or 12min NE of Maun

Tel: +267 686 2406
info@maun-backpackers.com
www.maun-backpackers.com

Some of the tents are en-suite with own verandas and
others share ablutions with hot water. There is also a dorm
with 8 beds right on the edge of the river. A fully equipped
kitchen is available for self-catering purposes.

Facilities:

Activities:

Sedia Riverside Hotel | 16

Hotel   w179288
BWP 860.00 to 1380.00 pp (2012)
7km or 6min NE of Maun

Tel: +267 686 0177, Fax: +267 686 2574
sedia@info.bw
www.sediahotel.com

The hotel offers accommodation in rooms with private
verandas and in chalets. Afro Trek Safaris is situated on
the hotel premises and offers a range of safari activities
like mokoro trips. This is a bird paradise.

Facilities:

Activities:

Sitatunga Camp | 18

Tour Operator Camp   w150525
BWP 45.00 pp (2012)
15km or 21min SW of Maun

Tel: +267 680 0380, Fax: +267 680 0381
info@deltarain.com

Sitatunga offers large, well shaded campsites with individual braai areas and electricity points. They have full time
security guards. Facilities include a bar.

Facilities:

Activities:

MAUN

Thamalakane Safari Camp   19

Lodge   w195799
BWP 1286.00 to 1746.00 pu (2012)
20km or 24min NE of Maun

Tel: +267 68 002 17, Fax: +267 686 4313,
Cell: +267 72 506 184
reservations@thamalakane.com, www.thamalakane.com

Located on the riverbank, the lodge offers accommodation
in thatched chalets with en-suite bathrooms, coffee/tea
making facilities, ceiling fans, mosquito nets and private
viewing decks. Facilities include a spa and library.

Facilities:

Activities:

OKAVANGO / MOREMI • Maun

MOREMI GAME RESERVE

Photo:Sonia Joube

Located on the eastern side of the Okavango Delta in Botswana, the rela tively small Moremi Game Reserve is lush and varied. It is a patchwork of lagoons shallow flooded pans, plains and forests. The reserve has a huge variety and high density of wildlife and is a real paradise for bird lovers, as it is home to nearly 500 species of birds. Moremi extends east and northwards to join Chobe National Park ensuring a continuous area of protected land all the way to Kasane. Because neither Moremi nor Chobe is fenced, animals can follow their own migration routes without interference. In Moremi you will really experience African wildlife as not even the camps are fenced. A number of camps are run by either National Parks or private safari operators. There is a small tuck shop in the Moremi Game Reserve where you can buy necessities.

TRAVELLER DESCRIPTION:
The Moremi Game Reserve offers a real African wildlife experience and is a bird lover's paradise. A number of camps are run by either DWNP or private safari oper ators. Booking and prepayment are essential. Park and vehicle entry fees can be paid at the main gates (South or North Gate) but not at Third Bridge Gate. North Gate is also the main entrance gate and current headquarters of the reserve.

TRAVEL INFO:
There is a small shop in Khwai Village in the north of the reserve where you can buy necessities.

Betsha

Xoroxom
Airstrip

NG/15 (Linyanti
Sable Safaris (Linyanti
Investment

Selinda
Game Rese
(Private) NG

1	3rd Bridge Rest Camp
2	Camp Moremi
3	Camp Okuti
4	Chiefs Camp
5	Gcudikwa Camp
6	Khwai - North Gate Camp
7	Little Mombo Camp
8	Mboma Island Camp
9	South Gate Camp
10	Xakanaxa Campsites
11	Xakanaxa Lodge
12	Xigera Camp

N

NG/18 (Khwai
Development
Trust)

Vumbura   Lechomos

umbura
Airstrip

NG/22 Kwedi East
(Okavango
Omdop Airstrip   Community Trust)
(Duba Plains)

NG/20 Kwara Reserve
(Kwando Safaris)

Xugane
Airstrip

NG/21 Kwando
WMA

Shindi
Lodge
Airstrip

Mombo
Airstrip

Camp
Okavango
Airstrip

11 Xakanaxa
3
2   10
Xakanaxa
Airstrip

Kings
Airstrip

Khwai

7

8

5

1   Moremi

6

4

Piajio Airstrip
(Chiefs Camp)

Moremi Game Reserve (NG/28)

Txichira
Airstrip

12

Chitabe
Airstrip

9

Nxabega
Airstrip

Delta Camp
Airstrip

Ntswi Airstrip
(Gunn's Camp)

Santantadibi
Airstrip

NG/31 Commercial
Photographic
WMA

Legend

Xaxaba
Airstrip

NG/27A
(Matsebe)

G/26
ephant
Safaris)

Kuruneraga
Airstrip

NG/27B Commercial
Photographic
WMA

Town/Village

Pompom
Airstrip

Kiri Camp
Airstrip

Stanley's
Airstrip

River

Riverboat Trail

Xudum
Airstrip

NG/32 (Okavango Kopano
Mokoro Community Trust)

Minor Road

Off-Road/Jeep Track

NG/30
(Hunting):
Rann Safaris

Wetland

Major River

NG/29
(Hunting):
Safari South

Boro
Settlement

Game Reserve

15   30 Km

Matlapana

TRAVEL TIP: Fishing is not allowed in the game reserve.

MOREMI GAME RESERVE

3rd Bridge Rest Camp — 1

Park Camp   w150947
BWP 80.00 to 350.00 pp (2013)
50.1km or 2h23min NW of Moremi South Gate (4WD)

Tel: +267 686 2221, Fax: +267 686 2262,
Cell: +267 73 867 221
xomaesites@botsnet.bw, www.xomaesites.com

The camp is located at the third bridge from the south gate and has seven sites with braai pits. There is a newly built ablution facility. Baboons can sometimes be a problem in the camp. Transfers available.

Facilities:
Activities:

Camp Moremi — 2

Tented Camp   w195856
USD 476.00 to 856.00 pp (2013)
135km or 04h17min N of Maun (4WD)

Tel: +267 686 1559, Fax: +267 686 0037
info@desertdelta.com
www.desertdelta.com

The camp can accommodate a maximum of 22 people. Luxury tents are raised on wooden decks. No children under the age of six allowed. Pre-booking is essential.

Languages: English

Facilities:
Activities:

Camp Okuti — 3

Tented Camp   w179354
USD 495.00 to 820.00 (2013)
135km or 04h18min N of Maun (4WD)

Tel: +267 686 1226, Fax: +267 686 1282
info@kerdowney.bw
www.kerdowneybotswana.com

Camp Okuti offers accommodation in en-suite tents raised on decks. Guests can relax at the camp or enjoy activities like motorboat safaris, 4WD trips and bird watching.

Languages: English

Facilities: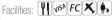
Activities:

Chief's Camp — 4

Lodge   w195822
USD 995.00 to 2035.00 pp (2013)
No self-drive access

Tel: +27(0)11 438 4650, Fax: +27(0)86 218 1482
southernafrica@sanctuaryretreats.com

The camp on Chief's Island offers accommodation in luxury en-suite tents with private viewing decks. Facilities include a boma, curio shop, bar and spa. Activities include mokoro excursions. Pre-booking required.

Languages: English

Facilities:
Activities:

Gcudikwa Camp — 5

Wilderness Camp   w152116
BWP 400.00 to 635.00 pp (2013)
No self-drive access. Access by boat only

Tel: +267 686 2221, Fax: +267 686 2262,
Cell: +267 73 86 2221
xomaesites@botsnet.bw, xomaesites.com

Facilities at Gcudikwa are limited and visitors should be self-sufficient. The camp is situated close to the Gcudikwa Lagoon and is only accessible via boat transfer from Third Bridge Boat Station. Pre-booking is essential.

Facilities:
Activities:

Khwai - North Gate Camp — 6

Park Camp   w150410
ZAR 50.00 pp (2013)
At Moremi North Gate (4WD)

Tel: +267 686 5366, Fax: +267 686 5367
reservations@sklcamps.co.bw
www.sklcamps.com

This camp is known for its wide variety of animals and the San Bushmen, who have a growing community nearby. New ablution blocks with solar lights were built in 2010. Booking and prepayment are essential.

Facilities:
Activities:

Little Mombo Camp   7

Tented Camp   w195832
USD 1715.00 to 2431.00 pp (2013)
No self-drive access

Tel: +27(0)21 702 7500, Fax: +27(0)21 701 0765
enquiry@wilderness.co.za

The camp offers accommodation in tents raised from the
ground; with verandas, en-suite bathrooms and outdoor
showers. No children under 6 years. Pre-booking required.

Languages: English

Facilities: ▲ 🍴 VISA ✕ 👥

Activities: 🚶 🚗 ⛰

Mboma Island Camp   8

Tented Camp   w179353
BWP 540.00 to 4445.00 pp (2013)
No self-drive access

Tel: +267 686 5788, Fax: +267 68 65 757
mankwe@info.bw
www.mankwe.com

Guests will be transferred from the Mboma boat station
to the island by boat or mokoro. Guests have the choice
of full board or self-catering accommodation at the lodge.
Booking is essential.

Facilities: ▲ 🧴 VISA FC 👥

Activities: 🚶

South Gate Camp   9

Park Camp   w179127
BWP 100.00 to 260.00 pp (2012)
At Moremi South Gate (4WD)

Tel: +267 686 1448, Fax: +267 686 1448,
Cell: +267 71 308 283
kwalatesafari@gmail.com

This shady camp with clean ablutions is situated at the
southern entrance to the Moremi Game Reserve. Solar
panels are used for hot water and lights. Park and vehicle
entry fees are payable at the gate.

Facilities: 🚽 VISA 🔥 👥

Activities: 🚶

Xakanaxa Campsites   10

Park Camp   w151541
BWP 100.00 to 260.00 pp (2012)
45km or 02h09min W of Khwai (4WD)

Tel: +267 686 1448, Fax: +267 686 1448,
Cell: +267 71 308 283
kwalatesafari@gmail.com

Most of the eight campsites are under trees. They share
ablution facilities but have individual braai areas. Solar
panels are used for hot water and lights. Park and vehicle
entry fees are payable at the gate.

Facilities: 🚽 🔥 ✕

Activities: 🚶 ⛰

Xakanaxa Lodge   11

Tented Camp   w179224
USD 531.00 to 893.00 pp (2012)
45km or 02h09min W of Khwai (4WD)

Tel: +27(0)11 463 3999, Fax: +27(0)11 463 3564
info@moremi-safaris.com
www.xakanaxa-camp.com

Xakanaxa Lodge is located in the Moremi GR and offers
accommodation in Meru-style tents on a wooden platform.
Electricity is provided from 05h30 to 19h00 by generator.
Boat trips are available.

Facilities: ▲ 🍴 @ ✕ 👥

Activities: 🚶 🚗 ⛰

Xigera Camp   12

Tented Camp   w195823
USD 708.00 to 1218.00 pp (2013)
No self-drive access

Tel: +27(0)21 702 7500, Fax: +27(0)21 701 0765
enquiry@wilderness.co.za

Xigera Camp offers accommodation in en-suite tents on
wooden decks. Outside showers are available. Dinners
are served in a boma under the beautiful African skies. No
children under 6 years. Pre-booking required.

Languages: English

Facilities: ▲ 🍴 VISA ✕ 👥

Activities: 🚶 🚗 🎣 📷 ⛰

OKAVANGO / MOREMI • Moremi GR

MOREMI GAME RESERVE AREA

The area surrounding the Moremi Game Reserve is a conservation area which is either run under concession by tour operators or by Community Trusts. The camps and lodges that are run by tour operators cater mainly for upmarket fly-in tourists and most of them do not have self-drive access. The community campsites are worth supporting. The Khwai Development Trust support employment opportunities and eco-tourism. A large number of San (Bushmen) live in the Khwai Village after relocating from the reserve area. They participate actively in the conservation of the environment.

TRAVELLER DESCRIPTION:
The Khwai Development Trust borders Moremi Game Reserve on the north and Chobe National Park on the west and is the ideal place to sleep over en-route between these two popular conservation areas. Although crafts and basic food and drinks are for sale in the village there are no modern communications, electricity, schools or a health centre.

TRAVEL INFO:
Basics can be bought from street vendors in Khwai village, but there is no fresh fruit.

20   40 Km

N

Gudingwa

Betsha

diro

onga Gunitsuga

Kabamukuni
Village

Vumbura Lechomos

NG/14 Kwando
Reserve (Kwanda
Safaris)

Selinda
Game Reserve
(Private) NG/16

NG/22 Kwedi
East (Okavango
Community Trust)

NG/20 Kwara
Reserve (Kwando
Safaris)

NG/23 Kwedi West
(Okavango Community
Trust)   16

6

(Okavango
ha
unity Trust)

31   NG/21
        Kwando WMA

3   27   14

NG/25 (Ngamiland
Adventure Safaris)

15

8

9
10

26
1

22

NG/26
(Elephant
Back Safaris)

NG/27A
(Matsebe)

23   11

NG/27B
Commercial
Photographic
WMA

7   5 8 21

Moremi Game
Reserve
(NG/28)

Xakanaxa

Moremi

Khwai

2   17   18
       25 12

NG/34 (Sankuyo
Tshwaragano
Community Trust)

19
20

Rakuku

NG/31
Commercial
Photographic
WMA

24

4

13

Shukumukwa

Shorobe

NG/32
(Okavango
Kopano Mokoro
Community
Trust)

Boro
Settlement

Lekaweng
Drift

Maun

30

29

NG/29 (Hunting)- Safari South

1	Abu's Camp
2	Banoka Bush Camp
3	Camp Okavango
4	Chitabe Camp
5	Delta Camp
6	Duba Plains Camp
7	Eagle Island Camp
8	Gunn's Main Camp
9	Jacana Camp
10	Jao Camp
11	Kanana Camp

12	Khwai River Lodge
13	Kaziikini Community camp
14	Kwara Camp
15	Kwetsani Camp
16	Little Vumbura Camp
17	Machaba Camp
18	Magotho Camp
19	Mankwe Bush Lodge
20	Mankwe Mopani Campsites
21	Moremi Crossing
22	Nxabega Safari Camp
23	Pompom Camp

24	Sandibe Safari Lodge
25	Sango Safari Camp
26	Seba Camp
27	Shinde Lodge
28	Tubu Tree Camp
29	Xaranna Camp
30	Xudum Lodge
31	Xugana Island Lodge

Town/Village

River

Off-Road/Jeep Track

Minor Road

Main Street

Main Road

Highway

Wetland

Major River

TOWN INFO:
Tourist Info: +267 680 1211

MOREMI GAME RESERVE AREA

Abu's Camp   1

Tented Camp   w195837
USD 1715.00 to 2431.00 pp (2013)
No self-drive access

Tel: +27(0)21 702 7500, Fax: +267 686 1005
enquiry@wilderness-safaris.com
www.abucamp.com

Abu's Camp offers accommodation in luxury tents with
en-suite bathrooms. Activities offered include night drives
and elephant back safaris. Pre-booking required.

Languages: English

Facilities:

Activities:

Banoka Bush Camp   2

Lodge   w230010
USD 558.00 to 691.00 pp (2013)
135km or 05h19min NNE of Maun (4WD)

Tel: +27(0)21 702 7500, Fax: +27(0)21 701 0765
enquiry@wilderness.co.za

Banoka is situated on the banks of the Khwai River. The
en-suite tented rooms have private verandas. The whole
camp is raised on stilts resulting in beautiful views of the
lagoon. Pre-booking is essential.

Facilities:

Activities:

Camp Okavango   3

Tented Camp   w152118
USD 476.00 to 856.00 pp (2013)
Fly-in access only

Tel: +267 686 1559, Fax: +267 686 0037
info@desertdelta.com
www.desertdelta.com

Camp Okavango is situated on Nxaragha Island and offers
accommodation in en-suite safari tents raised on wooden
decks, and a thatched honeymoon suite. No children under
the age of six allowed. Pre-booking is essential.

Languages: English

Facilities:

Activities:

Chitabe Camp   4

Tented Camp   w189266
USD 868.00 to 1333.00 pp (2013)
No self-drive access

Tel: +27(0)21 702 7500, Fax: +27(0)21 701 0765
enquiry@wilderness.co.za
www.wilderness-safaris.com

Chitabe Camp offers accommodation in meru-style tents
built on wooden platforms. Air transfers to the camp are
available on request. Pre-booking required.

Facilities:

Activities:

Delta Camp   5

Lodge   w195819
USD 450.00 to 785.00 pp (2013)
No self-drive access

Tel: +27(0)17 631 5133, Cell: +27(0)82 355 6910
res3@footsteps-in-africa.com
www.footsteps-in-africa.com

The camp is situated on Chief's Island and is surrounded
by water. Mokoro is the way of transport. Accommodation
is provided in luxury en-suite chalets that are raised and
built from reed and wood. Pre-booking required.

Languages: English

Facilities:

Activities:

Duba Plains Camp   6

Tented Camp   w195826
USD 868.00 to 1209.00 pp (2012)
No self-drive access

Tel: +27(0)21 702 7500, Fax: +27(0)21 701 0765
enquiry@wilderness.co.za

This remote camp offers accommodation in en-suite tents
with private verandas which allow spectacular views of the
surrounding floodplains. Activities include elephant back
safaris and night drives. Pre-booking is essential.

Facilities:

Activities:

Eagle Island Camp 7

Tented Camp   w195842
USD 680.00 to 1430.00 pp (2013)
No self-drive access

Tel: +27(0)21 483 1600, Fax: +27(0)21 422 5045
safaris@orient-express.com
www.eagleislandcamp.com

The camp is situated on the remote Xaxaba Island and
offers accommodation in luxury tents raised on wooden
decks. Tents are air-conditioned and en-suite. Scenic
helicopter flights are available. Pre-booking required.

Facilities: ⊞ 🅥 @ ✗ 🏕 🛗

Activities: 🚶 🎣 ▶ 🏊

Gunn's Main Camp 8

Lodge   w195818
USD 371.00 to 591.00 pp (2013)
No self-drive access

Tel: +267 686 4436, Fax: +267 686 0040
reservations@gunns-camp.com
www.gunns-camp.com

Gunn's Camp is located on Ntswi Island. Rooms are
en-suite and a honeymoon suite is also available. Activities include Mokoro excursions and island camping. No
children under 12 years. Pre-booking required.

Facilities: ▲ ⊞ FC @ ✗ 🏕

Activities: 🚶 🎣 🏊

Jacana Camp 9

Tented Camp   w195974
USD 708.00 to 1164.00 pp (2013)
No self-drive access

Tel: +27(0)21 702 7500, Fax: +27(0)21 701 0765
enquiry@wilderness.co.za
www.wilderness-safaris.com

The camp is found north east of Jao camp, and offers accommodation in 5 meru-style tents raised on decks, with
verandas and great views. All tents are en-suite.

Facilities: ⊞ 🅥 @ ✗ 🛗

Activities: 🚶 🚗 ▶ 🏊

Jao Camp 10

Tented Camp   w195839
USD 1194.00 to 1986.00 pp (2013)
No self-drive access

Tel: +27(0)21 702 7500, Fax: +27(0)21 701 0765
enquiry@wilderness.co.za
www.wilderness-safaris.com

Jao Camp is located in a private game reserve. The en-
suite Meru-style tents are raised on wooden decks and
surrounded by Mahogany trees. No children under 6 years
are allowed and pre-booking is required.

Facilities: ⊞ 🅥 FC ✗ 🛗

Activities: 🚶 🚗 🎣 ▶ 🏊

Kanana Camp 11

Tented Camp   w195846
USD 495.00 to 820.00 (2013)
No self-drive access

Tel: +267 686 1226, Fax: +267 686 1282
info@kerdowney.bw
www.kerdowneybotswana.com

Kanana Camp offers accommodation in Meru-style tents
with en-suite bathrooms. Activities include boat excursions,
star gazing and Mokoro trips to the local heronry. Pre-
booking is essential.

Languages: English

Facilities: ⊞ 🅥 FC ✗ 🛗

Activities: 🚶 🚗 🎣 ▶ 🏊

Khwai River Lodge 12

Tented Camp   w179234
USD 680.00 to 1430.00 pp (2013)
128km or 04h02min NNE of Maun (4WD)

Tel: +27(0)21 483 1600, Fax: +27(0)21 422 5045
safaris@orient-express.com
www.orient-express-safaris.co.za

Khwai River Lodge is situated on the edge of a forest
and offers accommodation in tents on raised wooden
platforms. The en-suite tents are air-conditioned and have
private viewing decks. Facilities include a gym and spa.

Facilities: ⊞ 🅥 FC @ ✗ 🛗

Activities: 🚶 🚗 🎣 🏊

MOREMI GAME RESERVE AREA

Kaziikini Community camp 13

Community Camp w150422
USD 24.00 pp (April 2013)
62km or 01h13min NE of Maun

Tel: +267 680 0664, Fax: +267 680 0665,
Cell: +267 7566 2865
santawanistmt@botsnet.bw, www.kaziikinicampsite.com

The camp is run by the Sankuyo Community. Ablution blocks are clean and each campsite has running water and braai facilities. There also are twin bedded huts available. Pre-booking required.

Facilities:

Activities:

Photo: PieterTheron

Kwara Camp 14

Tented Camp w152117
USD 515.00 to 918.00 pp (2013)
No self-drive access

Tel: +267 686 1449, Fax: +267 686 1457
reservations@kwando.co.bw
www.kwando.co.bw

Kwara Camp offers accommodation in safari-style tents with spectacular views over the lagoon and surrounding plains. Guests can enjoy activities like boat trips and bird watching. Pre-booking required.

Facilities:
Activities:

Kwetsani Camp 15

Tented Camp w195975
USD 708.00 to 1218.00 pp (2013)
No self-drive access

Tel: +27(0)21 702 7500, Fax: +27(0)21 701 0765
enquiry@wilderness.co.za
www.wilderness-safaris.com

Kwetsani Camp offers accommodation in luxury en-suite tents with thatched roofs under shady palm trees. Activities include night drives. No children under 6 years. Pre-booking required.

Facilities:
Activities:

Little Vumbura Camp 16

Tented Camp w195828
USD 1194.00 to 1986.00 pp (2013)
No self-drive access

Tel: +27(0)21 702 7500, Fax: +27(0)21 701 0765
enquiry@wilderness.co.za

Little Vumbura Camp offers accommodation in en-suite tents with beautiful views and outside showers. Activities include bird watching, night drives and Mokoro trips. Pre-booking required.

Facilities:
Activities:

Machaba Camp 17

Tented Camp w150771
USD 249.00 to 765.00 pp (2013)
No self-drive access

Fax: +27(0)86 662 9002, Cell: +27(0)82 579 5249
enquiries@machabacamp.com
www.machabacamp.com

The camp is built in a classic 1950's style, with 10 safari tents, en-suite bathrooms and outdoor shower and living areas. The camp is on the Khwai River with great views of the Moremi Game Reserve.

Facilities:
Activities:

Magotho Camp

Community Camp   w179145
BWP 290.00 pp (2013)
50km or 2h25min NNE of Moremi South Gate

Tel: +267 680 1211, Fax: +267 680 1210
khwai@botsnet.bw

Magotho is the only one of the three camps run by the Kwai Development Trust that is open to the public. This is a large camp with no facilities. Pre-booking is essential. Please support this community camp.

Languages: English

Facilities:

Activities:

Photo: Mietsie Visser

Mankwe Bush Lodge   19

Tented Camp   w179175
BWP 600.00 to 2950.00 pp (2013)
92km or 02h23min NE of Maun

Tel: +267 68 657 88, Fax: +267 686 5787
mankwe@info.bw
www.mankwe.com

Accommodation is available in Meru-style tents on a full board or self-catering basis. Campers are welcome. Ablutions are available but campers need to bring their own drinking water and firewood. Pre-booking is essential.

Facilities:

Activities:

Mankwe Mopani Campsites   20

Lodge Camp   w151542
BWP 125.00 to 250.00 pp (2013)
91km or 02h22min NE of Maun

Tel: +267 68 657 88, Fax: +267 68 657 88
mankwe@info.bw
www.mankwe.com

Mankwe Mopani has six campsites under Mopani and Camel thorn trees. There is a clean ablution block with flush toilets and bucket showers. Campers have to bring their own firewood and drinking water. Pre-booking is required.

Facilities:

Activities:

Moremi Crossing   21

Tented Camp   w195815
USD 331.00 to 481.00 pp (2012)
No self-drive access

Tel: +267 686 4436, Fax: +267 68 60040
reservations@moremicrossing.com
www.moremicrossing.com

Moremi Crossing is located on a secluded island. Accommodation is available in 16 en-suite tents on raised decks, with their own verandas. There is also a family tent and a honeymoon tent available. Pre-booking required.

Facilities:

Activities:

Nxabega Safari Camp   22

Tented Camp   w195844
USD 570.00 to 1145.00 pp (2013)
No self-drive access

Tel: +27(0)11 809 4300, Fax: +27(0)11 809 4400,
Cell: +27(0)83 960 3391
safaris@andBeyond.com, www.andbeyondafrica.com

The camp, located on the edge of the Okavango Delta, features en-suite safari tents raised on wooden decks. Activities include bush picnics, cocktails on a river island and boat excursions. Pre-booking is essential.

Facilities:

Activities:

MOREMI GAME RESERVE AREA

Pompom Camp — 23

Tented Camp — w195810
USD 456.00 to 796.00 pp (2013)
No self-drive access

Tel: +267 686 4436, Fax: +267 686 0040
reservations@pompomcamp.com
www.pompomcamp.com

The camp offers a real bush experience with en-suite traditional safari tents and open-air ablution blocks. Activities include Mokoro trips. Guests can relax at the bar and enjoy the company at the boma. Pre-booking required.

Facilities:
Activities:

Sandibe Safari Lodge — 24

Lodge — w195809
USD 570.00 to 1145.00 pp (2013)
No self-drive access

Tel: +27(0)11 809 4300, Fax: +27(0)11 809 4400
safaris@andBeyond.com
www.sandibe.com

Sandibe Safari Lodge is located on the southern tip of Chief's Island. Guests stay in en-suite cottages and enjoy breakfast and dinner in a boma. Mokoro excursions and river cruises are available. Pre-booking required.

Facilities:
Activities:

Sango Safari Camp — 25

Lodge — w227132
USD 235.00 to 540.00 pp (2013)
123km or 03h47min NNE of Maun (4WD)

Tel: +267 686 3763, Fax: +267 680 0937
reservations@sangosafaricamp.com
sangosafaricamp.com

Sango Safari Camp is situated under large trees on the banks of the Khwai River. En-suite Meru tents with open-air bucket showers and hand crafted furnishings ensure a true safari feeling. Pre-booking is essential.

Languages: English

Facilities:
Activities:

Seba Camp — 26

Tented Camp — w195976
USD 708.00 to 1164.00 pp (2013)
No self-drive access

Tel: +27(0)21 702 7500, Fax: +27(0)21 701 0765
enquiry@wilderness.co.za
www.wilderness-safaris.com

Seba Camp has en-suite tents with private decks. Mokoro excursions, boat trips, and sundowners around a traditional African campfire can be enjoyed. Pre-booking is essential and is done through the central Cape Town office.

Languages: English

Facilities:
Activities:

Shinde Lodge — 27

Tented Camp — w152108
USD 495.00 to 950.00 (2013)
No self-drive access

Tel: +267 686 1226, Fax: +267 686 1282
info@kerdowney.bw
www.kerdowneybotswana.com

Shinde Lodge offers accommodation in en-suite safari-style tents with twin beds. Delicious meals are served in a boma. Guest can enjoy night drives, mokoro trips and bird watching. Pre-booking required.

Languages: English

Facilities:
Activities:

Tubu Tree Camp — 28

Tented Camp — w189439
USD 868.00 to 1333.00 pp (2013)
No self-drive access

Tel: +27(0)21 702 7500, Fax: +27(0)21 701 0765
enquiry@wilderness.co.za
www.wilderness-safaris.com

Tubu Tree Camp offers accommodation in en-suite tents with private viewing decks. Guests can also enjoy outside showers. Reservations are done through the Cape Town office. Pre-booking is essential.

Facilities:
Activities:

Xaranna Camp 29

Tented Camp   w195979
USD 650.00 to 1550.00 pp (2013)
No self-drive access

Tel: +27(0)11 809 4300, Fax: +27(0)11 809 4400
safaris@andBeyond.com
www.andbeyondafrica.com

The remote Xaranna Camp is located in the southern,
seasonal part of the Delta. During the high water season,
it can only be reached by boat. It is an intimate camp with
only nine tented suites. Pre-booking required.

Languages: English

Facilities:

Activities:

Xudum Lodge 30

Lodge   w195977
USD 650.00 to 1550.00 pp (2013)
No self-drive access

Tel: +27(0)11 809 4300, Fax: +27(0)11 809 4400
safaris@andBeyond.com
www.andbeyondafrica.com

Xudum Lodge is located in the seasonal part of the Delta.
Unique rooftop hideouts are furnished as private safari
suites that overlook the lagoon. The intricate water channels can be explored by Mokoro. Pre-booking required.

Facilities:

Activities:

Xugana Island Lodge 31

Lodge   w179306
USD 476.00 to 856.00 pp (2013)
Fly-in access only

Tel: +267 686 1559, Fax: +267 68 60 037
info@desertdelta.com
www.desertdelta.com

Xugana Island Lodge is located in the heart of the permanent Okavango Delta. Xugana offers accommodation in
luxury safari chalets with en-suite bathrooms and private
decks. No children under 6 years. Booking is essential.

Languages: English

Facilities:

Activities:

Photo: Billy Boshoff

SEPOPA

Photo: Peter Levey

Sepopa is one of the gateways into the pan handle of the Okavango Delta. Sepopa has a beautiful rest camp where you can rent a houseboat. You can also take a ferry from Sepopa to Seronga.

TRAVELLER DESCRIPTION:
Sepopa is not really a touristy town, even though it is one of the gateways into the pan handle of the Okavango Delta.

TRAVEL INFO:
There is a clinic in Sepopa. Liquor is only available at the bar.

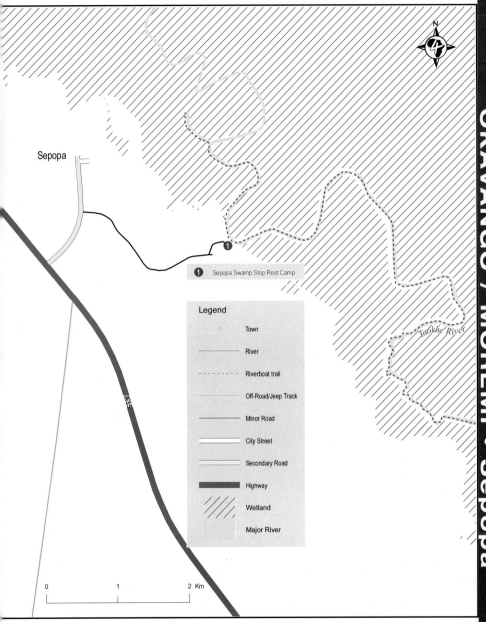

Sepopa

1 Sepopa Swamp Stop Rest Camp

Taokhe River

Legend

○	Town
——	River
- - -	Riverboat trail
——	Off-Road/Jeep Track
——	Minor Road
══	City Street
══	Secondary Road
██	Highway
/////	Wetland
	Major River

0   1   2 Km

TOWN INFO:
Police: +267 687 7027

SEPOPA

Sepopa Swamp Stop Rest Camp   1

Transit Camp   w151105
BWP 100.00 pp (2012)
3km or 9min ESE of Sepupa

Fax: +267 686 2932, Cell: +267 75 670 252
carl@ngami.net
www.swampstop.com

The camp is abounding in trees and has clean ablutions.
Pre-erected tents, a few air-conditioned chalets and a
houseboat are available.

Facilities:

Activities:

Photo: Peter Levey

SERONGA

Photos: Christo Spykerma

Seronga is the largest village on the eastern side of the Okavango Delta panhandle and an important regional centre for a number of small settlements further east. It is at the base of the panhandle and therefore ideal for exploring the Delta.

TRAVELLER DESCRIPTION:
Water taxis run from Sepopa to Seronga. Mokoro trips are available to explore the Delta.

TRAVEL INFO:
You can consult a doctor at the local clinic.

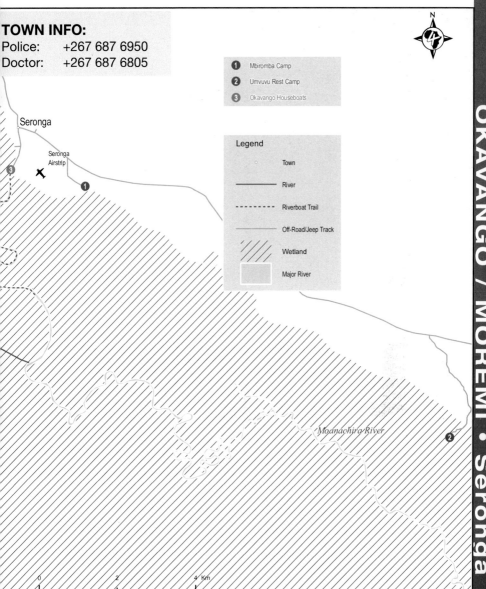

TOWN INFO:
Police: +267 687 6950
Doctor: +267 687 6805

❶ Mbiromba Camp
❷ Umvuvu Rest Camp
❸ Okavango Houseboats

Seronga

Seronga
Airstrip

Legend

○   Town

———   River

- - - - -   Riverboat Trail

———   Off-Road/Jeep Track

////   Wetland

▭   Major River

Moanachira River

0   2   4   Km

TRAVEL TIP: Only limited amounts of fuel in containers are available, mainly for the boats.

SERONGA

Mbiromba Camp   1

Tour Operator Camp   w150366
BWP 78.00 pp (2013)
2km or 6min SE of Seronga

Tel: +267 687 6861, Fax: +267 687 6939
okavangodelta@botsnet.bw
www.okavangodelta.co.bw

Gas is used for heating water for the bucket showers in the ablutions. Tents, sleeping bags and mattresses are to rent. Self-drivers have to cross the Okavango River by public ferry at Mohembo to reach the camp.

Facilities:
Activities:

Umvuvu Rest Camp   2

Wilderness Camp   w152241
BWP 100.00 to 168.00 pp (2012)
No self-drive access

Cell: +267 72 57 4643
umvuvubots@gmail.com

Guests leave their vehicles in a secure parking area and are transported by boat to Gau Island. You can camp or stay in one of their tents with beds and bedding provided. To book it is best to email or send a text message.

Languages: English, Setswana

Facilities:
Activities:

Okavango Houseboats   3

Houseboat   w151536
BWP 6000.00 to 6360.00 pu (2013)
1km SSW of Seronga

Tel: +267 686 0802, Fax: +267 686 0812
krause@info.bw
www.okavangohouseboats.com

Three houseboats are operated from Seronga, namely the Inkwazi, the Inyankuni and the Madikubu houseboats. The crew includes a boatman and chef. The area of operation is between Seronga and Sepupa in the Okavango mainstream. Rates are per houseboat.

Facilities:
Activities:

Photo: Okavango Houseboats

Photo: Francois Malan

SHAKAWE

Photo: Peter Levey

Shakawe is no longer a sleepy little outpost deep in the Okavango Delta. It has become a hub for overlanders traversing Botswana, Namibia and Angola. It is in very close proximity of Mohembo Border Post which gives access to the Caprivi Strip of Namibia. Due to the Shakawe Airport, the town has become the gateway to the northern part of the Okavango Delta.

TRAVELLER DESCRIPTION:
Shakawe is a friendly town on the banks of the Okavango River in which you will get just about anything you need. The fuel stations are usually quite reliable. Various types of accommodation are available around Shakawe, of which the most famous is Drotsky's Cabins - a family owned business offering camping and chalets on the Okavango River. Shakawe is the ideal place for those keen on fishing and birding.

TRAVEL INFO:
There is a clinic in Shakawe. Their contact number is +267 687 5016. There are bush mechanics and backyard workshops if you're in dire need of mechanical repairs, but you have to ask around in town.

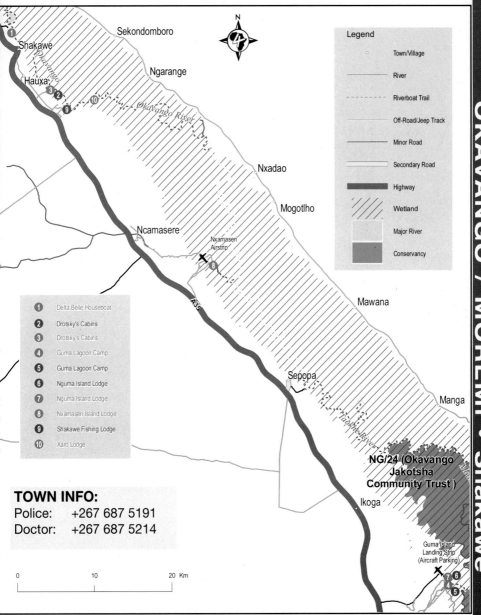

Legend

Town/Village
River
Riverboat Trail
Off-Road/Jeep Track
Minor Road
Secondary Road
Highway
Wetland
Major River
Conservancy

1. Delta Belle Houseboat
2. Drotsky's Cabins
3. Drotsky's Cabins
4. Guma Lagoon Camp
5. Guma Lagoon Camp
6. Nguma Island Lodge
7. Nguma Island Lodge
8. Nxamaseri Island Lodge
9. Shakawe Fishing Lodge
10. Xaro Lodge

TOWN INFO:
Police: +267 687 5191
Doctor: +267 687 5214

0   10   20 Km

TRAVEL TIP: Shakawe is a convenient base for a visit to the Tsodilo Hills a mere 40 km away, as well as for a fishing trip into the Okavango Panhandle.

SHAKAWE

Delta Belle Houseboat   1

Houseboat   w249812
BWP 7500.00 pu (2012)
3km or 4min NNW of Shakawe

Cell: +267 75 323 990
deltabelle.bw@gmail.com
www.deltabelle.com

The Delta Belle is moored at Shakawe and during excursions the houseboat moves to a different location each night. It has four en-suite cabins and accommodates 8 - 10 people. It can also be used as a stationery B&B.

Languages: English, Afrikaans

Facilities: FC @

Activities:

Drotsky's Cabins   2

Lodge Camp   w179126
BWP 125.00 pp (2013)
10km or 13min SE of Shakawe

Tel: +267 687 5035, Fax: +267 683 0227,
Cell: +267 72 12 2971
drotsky@botsnet.bw

Campsites are set amongst the trees close to the river. Sites have braai stands and firewood is provided. Boats are available for hiring. The bar is a popular meeting place. Pre-booking required.

Languages: English

Facilities: VISA FC

Activities:

Drotsky's Cabins   3

Lodge   w179321
BWP 1250.00 pu (2013)
10km or 13min SE of Shakawe

Tel: +267 687 5035, Fax: +267 683 0227,
Cell: +267 72 12 2971
drotsky@botsnet.bw

This is a family-owned resort situated on the banks of the Okavango River. Drotsky's has A-frame chalets and is famous for its bar with restaurant. Boats for fishing can be hired with a driver. Pre-booking required.

Languages: English

Facilities: VISA FC

Activities:

Guma Lagoon Camp   4

Tented Camp   w179190
BWP 941.00 pu (2012)
102km or 01h25min SE of Shakawe (4WD)

Tel: +267 687 4626, Fax: +267 687 4626
info@guma-lagoon.com
www.guma-lagoon.com

The camp is situated at one of the biggest lagoons in the Okavango panhandle. Tented cabins as well as campsites are available. All guests can use the communal kitchen. Transfers from Etsha 13 village. Full board available.

Facilities: VISA FC

Activities:

Guma Lagoon Camp   5

Lodge Camp   w256086
BWP 124.00 pp (2013)
102km or 01h25min SE of Shakawe (4WD)

Tel: +267 687 4626, Fax: +267 687 4626
info@guma-lagoon.com
www.guma-lagoon.com

Guma Lagoon Camp has seven campsites available. Campers are welcome to enjoy the lodge facilities. Guma offers mokoro excursions. Packed lunches can be ordered.

Facilities: VISA FC

Activities:

Nguma Island Lodge   6

Lodge Camp   w179199
BWP 117.00 to 140.00 pp (2012)
98km or 01h11min SE of Shakawe (4WD)

Tel: +267 68 301 59, Fax: +267 683 0158,
Cell: +267 73 560 120
nguma@dynabyte.bw, www.ngumalodge.com

Campers can erect their own tents on the green lawns or stay in the pre-erected cottage tents. These tents have beds and fully equipped kitchens. Although these units are self-catering they are fully serviced daily.

Facilities: VISA FC

Activities:

Nguma Island Lodge — 7

Tented Camp — w179367
BWP 1373.00 to 2822.00 pp (2012)
98km or 01h11min SE of Shakawe (4WD)

Tel: +267 68 30 159, Fax: +267 683 0158,
Cell: +267 73 560 120
nguma@dynabyte.bw, www.ngumalodge.com

En-suite Meru-style tents are raised on a wooden platform
overlooking the lagoon. The last 12km is only suitable for
4WD but sedan vehicles can be left in a secure parking
area from where guests are transferred to the lodge.

Facilities:

Activities:

Nxamaseri Island Lodge — 8

Lodge — w179344
USD 415.00 to 525.00 pp (2013)
No self-drive access

Tel: +267 72 113 764, Fax: +267 68 78 016,
Cell: +267 73 361 026
info@nxamaseri.com, www.nxamaseri.com

The lodge offers accommodation in en-suite chalets with
private decks. Access to the lodge is by prior arranged
transfer only. Vehicles are left in a car park from where
guests are transferred by boat to the lodge.

Facilities: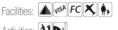

Activities:

Shakawe Fishing Lodge — 9

Lodge Camp — w204762
BWP 90.00 to 110.00 pp
14km or 15min SE of Shakawe

Fax: +267 660 493

(We were unable to confirm the information for this listing.
Please use at your own discretion). The campsites near the
Lodge is situated on a grassy place near the river bank,
under shady trees. The campsite has clean ablution blocks.

Facilities:

Activities:

Xaro Lodge — 10

Tented Camp — w179195
BWP 1050.00 pp (2013)
No self-drive access

Fax: +267 683 0227, Cell: +267 72 610 064
xarolodge@info.bw

Eight Meru-style tents are en-suite and have sliding doors
opening onto wooden decks. Tents are river facing and
sleep two people. Pre-booking is essential as guests are
transferred by boat from Drotsky's Cabins.

Languages: English

Facilities:

Activities:

OKAVANGO / MOREMI • Shakawe

Photo: Peter Levey

TSODILO HILLS

Tsodilo Hills is a cultural site in the Kalahari Desert and means 'The mountain of the gods'. As the only World Heritage Site in Botswana, it offers 400 sites with 4 500 rock paintings, most of which date between 850 AD and 1 100 AD. On one of these, the map of Africa is engraved - a subject of much discussion. The Tsodilo Hills consist of four hills - male, female, child and grandchild. The male is the highest point above sea level. Legend has it that the cliffs were a family and when the mother and father divorced, the mother moved away with the children and cursed them all to turn into rocks.

TRAVELLER DESCRIPTION:
There is a San village, museum and curio shop. Tsodilo Hills Museum displays, amongst other archaeological finds, three excavated rock shelters, namely the White Painting, Depression Rock and the Rhino Cave. Pottery, metal spearheads, stone tools, glass beads and fish bones are some of the discoveries that have helped archaeologists form a picture of ancient life here. Apparently there are plans to set up a community camp in the area which will offer traditional culture events sometime in the future.

TRAVEL INFO:
No food is sold at the site. The contact number for the office at reception is +267 687 8025.

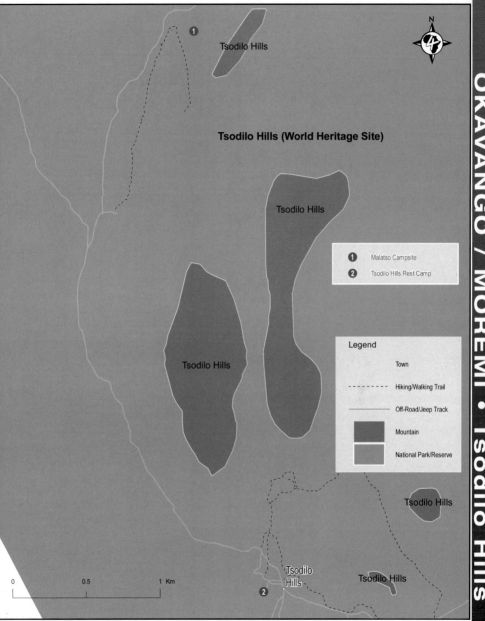

Tsodilo Hills

Tsodilo Hills (World Heritage Site)

Tsodilo Hills

1	Malatso Campsite
2	Tsodilo Hills Rest Camp

Legend

○	Town
- - - -	Hiking/Walking Trail
——	Off-Road/Jeep Track
■	Mountain
■	National Park/Reserve

Tsodilo Hills

Tsodilo Hills

Tsodilo Hills

Tsodilo
Hills

Tsodilo Hills

0   0.5   1 Km

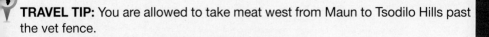

TRAVEL TIP: You are allowed to take meat west from Maun to Tsodilo Hills past the vet fence.

TSODILO HILLS

Malatso Campsite	1
Wilderness Camp	w151533

(Free 2012)
75km or 1h18min SSW of Shakawe (4WD)

Tel: +267 687 8025, Fax: +267 687 8731

This bush camp has no facilities, but there are facilities available at the main camp nearby. Camping is free but guests have to sign in and pay a small park fee.

Activities:

Tsodilo Hills Rest Camp	2
Park Camp	w179131

(Free 2012)
71km or 01h11min SSW of Shakawe (4WD)

Tel: +267 687 8025

(We were unable to confirm the information for this listing. Please use at your own discretion). There are no facilities at the campsite. Camping is free.

Facilities:

Activities:

Photo: Lindy Lourens

SOUTHERN BOTSWANA

Tourism in Southern Botswana is mainly confined to trave
lers passing through to destinations, such as the Central Kalahari Game Reserve, c
following the Trans Kalahari Highway to Namibia.

Although this region doesn't have major conservation areas it does offer the passer
by opportunities to see wildlife without having to visit the remote conservation area
that are mostly only accessible by 4WD. The St Claire Lion Park, Cheetah Conserva
tion Research Camp and Cheetah Enclosure are worth a visit.

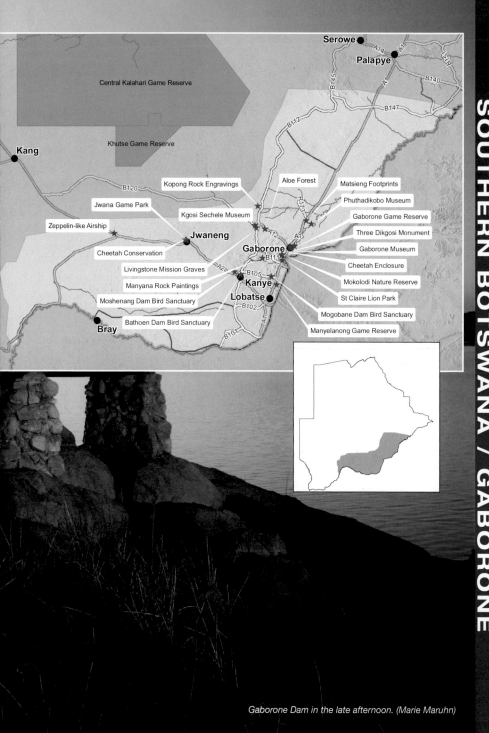

Central Kalahari Game Reserve

Khutse Game Reserve

Serowe

Palapye

Kang

Kopong Rock Engravings

Aloe Forest

Matsieng Footprints

Jwana Game Park

Phuthadikobo Museum

Kgosi Sechele Museum

Gaborone Game Reserve

Zeppelin-like Airship

Three Dikgosi Monument

Jwaneng

Gaborone

Gaborone Museum

Cheetah Conservation

Cheetah Enclosure

Livingstone Mission Graves

Mokolodi Nature Reserve

Manyana Rock Paintings

Kanye

St Claire Lion Park

Moshenang Dam Bird Sanctuary

Lobatse

Mogobane Dam Bird Sanctuary

Bathoen Dam Bird Sanctuary

Manyelanong Game Reserve

Bray

B120

B112

B147

B145

B140

A14

A1

B171

RA173

A72

A1

B111

B105

B102

A2

A1

B101

Gaborone Dam in the late afternoon. (Marie Maruhn)

The area that was to become **Jwana Game Park** was initially a fenced mine lease area surrounding the Jwaneng mine. Today the park has a wide variety of antelope, giraffe, zebra, warthog, baboon, cheetah, ostrich, leopard, caracal and numerous smaller animal species.

The Gaborone Game Park has a prolific bird life and offers a wide variety of game. Although it is much smaller than most reserves in Botswana it is now the country's third busiest reserve. The park has a good network of roads and also features a visitors' education centre, a number of picnic sites, a game hide as well as a remotely situated bird hide which overlooks a well-vegetated wetland.

Manyelanong Game Reserve was founded in 1965 after Cape Vultures had nested in the hills of Manyelanong for hundreds of years. Otse Hill, which stands with its summit at a height of almost one and a half kilometers, is the highest point in Botswana. The cliff and its lower wooded slope were fenced off to serve as a sanctuary for nesting Cape Griffon Vultures and for many years the area was known as Otse Vulture Colony. The name Manyelanong is said to mean, 'where vultures defecate' in Setswana, and refers to the guano covered cliffs where the vultures live. The reserve currently boasts one of Botswana's largest vulture colonies.

Mokolodi Nature Reserve has played a pivotal role in educating people about cheetah and predators in general since it was founded in 1994. The Mokolodi Rhino Fund was established in 2012, following the substan-

tial increase in rhino poaching. With this fund they hope to contribute to the management and conservation of their own white rhino population as well as this endangered species in general.

Bird lovers can enjoy the prolific bird life at the bird sanctuaries at Bathoen Dam, Mogobane Dam and Moshenang Dam.

This region is host to the capital of Botswana, Gaborone. Gaborone, named after Kgosi (Chief) Gaborone, is a vibrant African city and offers everything a self-drive tourist could ever need before setting off to explore the wilderness to the north.

There is a lot to see in and around Gaborone like an Aloe Forest, the Livingstone Mission Graves, Three Dikgosi Monument, Gaborone Museum, Kgosi Sechele I Museum, Phuthadikobo Museum, Kopong rock engravings, Manyana rock paintings and Matsieng engraved footprints.

The Jwaneng Diamond Mine is the richest diamond mine in the world. Not far from Jwaneng a Zeppelin-like airship can be viewed. It was shipped to South Africa in November 2005 for the De Beers mining company who was going to use it for the exploration of new diamond reserves in Southern Africa.

However, this Zeppelin, one of only three such airships in the world, was damaged beyond repair when heavy winds detached the 7 m ship from its moorings near the Jwaneng mine in September 2007.

Kgale Hills outside Gaborone. (Marie Maruhn)

BRAY

Bray is a relatively quiet border post between Botswana and South Africa. Bray is a no-nonsense border post to pass through and is popular for people travelling between Mabuasehube and Vryburg in the North-West province of South Africa. Coming from the south, one can reach the Trans-Kalahari route through this border post.

TRAVELLER DESCRIPTION:
Other than a fuel stop, there are no facilities on the Botswana side of the border. On the South African side Bray has limited facilities and only two un-tarred streets. It will serve as a stop to fill up with fuel and basic goods and refreshments. It also offers accommodation if you want to stay close to the border. There is a police station on the South African side.

TRAVEL INFO:
The Bray border post is open 08:00 – 16:00.
The telephone number is +267 653 0068.

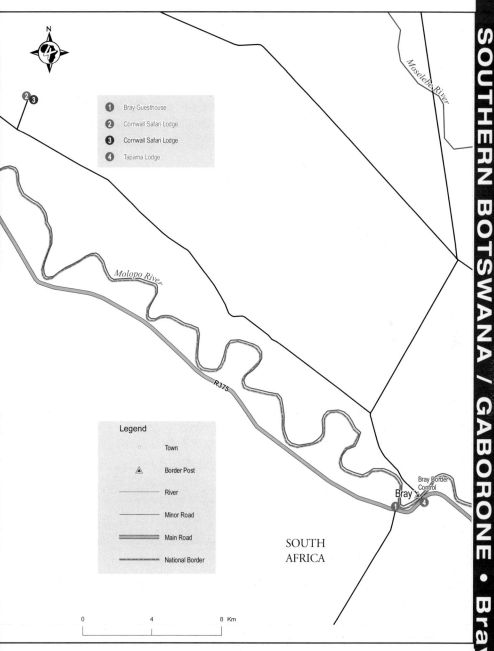

Legend

○	Town
⚠	Border Post
—	River
—	Minor Road
▬	Main Road
▬▬	National Border

1 Bray Guesthouse
2 Cornwall Safari Lodge
3 Cornwall Safari Lodge
4 Tapama Lodge

Moselebe River

Molopo River

R375

Bray Border Control

Bray

SOUTH AFRICA

0   4   8 Km

TOWN INFO:
Police: +27 (0) 53 937 0006

BRAY

Bray Guesthouse   1

Guest House   w231205
ZAR 300.00 to 585.00 pu (2013)
3 Main street, Bray, South Africa

Fax: +27(0)53 937 0013, Cell: +27(0)82 896 0949
caroll@cornergate.com

The Bray Guesthouse is located near the Bray Border
Control between South Africa and Botswana. They offer 4
rooms. Hunting is offered as well.

Languages: English, Afrikaans

Facilities:
Activities:

Cornwall Safari Lodge   2

Lodge   w230020
BWP 175.00 to 375.00 pp (March 2013)
25km or 40min E of Werda

Tel: +267 73 520 433, Cell: +27(0)72 798 5051
info@cornwallsafaris.co.za
www.cornwallsafaris.co.za

Cornwall Safari Lodge is situated on a private farm from
where hunting excursions and safaris are run into the
concession areas around the Kgalagadi Transfrontier Park.
The accommodation is also open to non-hunters.

Facilities:
Activities:

Cornwall Safari Lodge   3

Lodge Camp   w249811
BWP 110.00 pp (March 2013)
25km or 40min E of Werda

Tel: +267 73 520 433, Cell: +27(0)72 798 5051
info@cornwallsafaris.co.za
www.cornwallsafaris.co.za

Cornwall Safari Lodge is situated on a private farm. There
is a campsite with electricity at the lodge as well as a
campsite with no electricity in their Esjanti Bush Camp.

Facilities:
Activities:

Tapama Lodge   4

Lodge   w247103
ZAR 430.00 to 560.00 pu (2012)
Off the R375, at the Bray Border Control

Tel: +27(0)53 937 0020, Fax: +27(0)53 937 0053,
Cell: +27(0)82 821 3780
tapama@lantic.net

They offer en-suite rooms, 4 of which have showers and
the rest have bathtubs only. There is satellite television,
ceiling fans and tea/coffee making facilities. Room services
are also available.

Languages: Afrikaans

Facilities:
Activities:

Photo:Wouter Brand

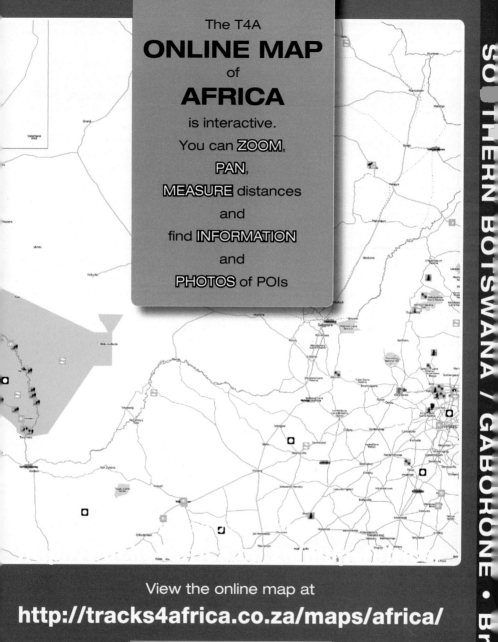

The T4A
ONLINE MAP
of
AFRICA
is interactive.
You can ZOOM,
PAN,
MEASURE distances
and
find INFORMATION
and
PHOTOS of POIs

View the online map at
http://tracks4africa.co.za/maps/africa/

Travel Africa Informed

GABORONE

Gaborone, the capital of Botswana, is a well-organised city, easy to explore and well worth a stop-over. Gaborone, named after Kgosi (Chief) Gaborone, is a vibrant African city. Although small in international terms, Gaborone offers all the modern services one would expect of a capital city and has something on offer for everyone's taste. Most travellers will not spend too much time in Gaborone as the real gems of Botswana are further north. Driving around Gaborone is easy as the traffic is relatively orderly and roads are generally well-maintained. However, potholes could be a problem in the rainy season.

TRAVELLER DESCRIPTION:
Gaborone is a vibrant African city that offers everything a self-drive tourist could ever need before setting off to explore the African wilderness lying to the north. For overlanders Gaborone offers a wide range of services like good accommodation, well-stocked shopping centres, vehicle repair services and many things to see and do. If you need to sleep over, there is a wide range of accommodation available, from camping to the most luxurious lodges and hotels.

TRAVEL INFO:
Tow-in services are also offered by Weststar Towing: Tel: +267 318 7571. An alternative number for the police is: +267 315 9022.

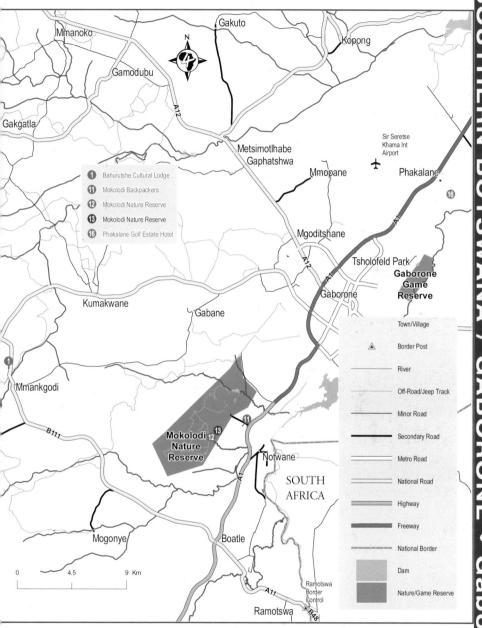

Mmanoko

Gakuto

Kopong

Gamodubu

A12

Gakgatla

N

Sir Seretse
Khama Int
Airport

Metsimotlhabe
Gaphatshwa

Mmopane

Phakalane

1	Bahurutshe Cultural Lodge
11	Mokolodi Backpackers
12	Mokolodi Nature Reserve
13	Mokolodi Nature Reserve
16	Phakalane Golf Estate Hotel

16

Mgoditshane

A12

A1

Tsholofeld Park

Gaborone
Game
Reserve

Kumakwane

Gabane

Gaborone

1

Mmankgodi

B111

Mokolodi
Nature
Reserve

12 13

11

Notwane

A1

SOUTH
AFRICA

	Town/Village
⚠	Border Post
	River
	Off-Road/Jeep Track
	Minor Road
	Secondary Road
	Metro Road
	National Road
	Highway
	Freeway
	National Border
	Dam
	Nature/Game Reserve

0   4.5   9 Km

Mogonye

Boatle

Ramotswa
Border
Control

A11

Ramotswa

B48

TRAVEL TIP: If you fancy camping, the Mokolodi Game Reserve just outside
Gaborone on the Lobatse road is very popular.

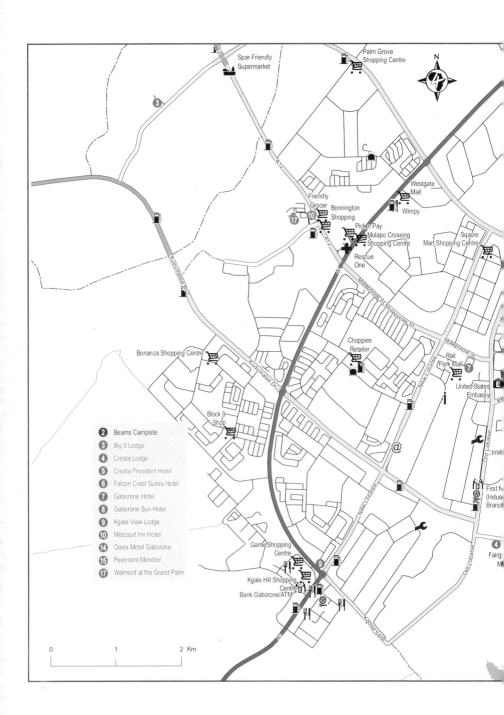

Spar-Friendly Supermarket

Palm Grove Shopping Centre

3

Friendly Grocer
Bonnington Shopping

17
10

Westgate Mall

Wimpy

Pick'n Pay
Molapo Crossing Shopping Centre

Sqaure Mart Shopping Centre

Rescue One

Molepolole St
Molepolole St

Choppies Retailer

Rail Park Mall

7

United States Embassy

Bonanza Shopping Centre

Block 9 Shop

Kudumatse Dr.

First N (Indus Branch

2 Beams Campsite
3 Big 5 Lodge
4 Cresta Lodge
5 Cresta President Hotel
6 Falcon Crest Suites Hotel
7 Gaborone Hotel
8 Gaborone Sun Hotel
9 Kgale View Lodge
10 Metcourt Inn Hotel
14 Oasis Motel Gaborone
15 Peermont Mondior
17 Walmont at the Grand Palm

@

Fairg M

Game Shopping Centre

9

Kgale Hill Shopping Centre
Bank Gaborone/ATM

Kgola Sere

New Lobatse

Old Lobatse

0   1   2 Km

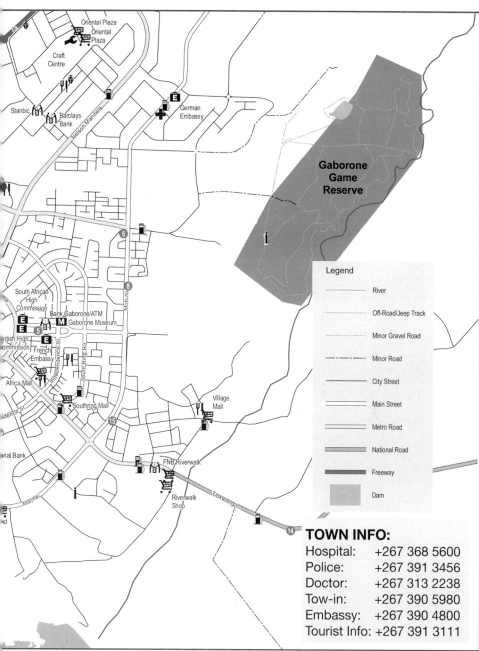

Gaborone Game Reserve

Oriental Plaza
Oriental Plaza

Craft Centre

Stanbic
Barclays Bank

German Embassy

Nelson Mandela

South African High Commission

Bank Gaborone/ATM
Gaborone Museum

British High Commission

French Embassy

Africa Mall

Southring Mall

Village Mall

FNB Riverwalk

Riverwalk Shop

Tlokweng Rd

Machel

Mobuto

Independence St

South Ring Rd

Legend

	River
	Off-Road/Jeep Track
	Minor Gravel Road
	Minor Road
	City Street
	Main Street
	Metro Road
	National Road
	Freeway
	Dam

TOWN INFO:

Hospital:	+267 368 5600
Police:	+267 391 3456
Doctor:	+267 313 2238
Tow-in:	+267 390 5980
Embassy:	+267 390 4800
Tourist Info:	+267 391 3111

GABORONE

Bahurutshe Cultural Lodge   1

Lodge   w151099
BWP 300.00 pp (2012)
37km or 36min W of Gaborone

Fax: +267 316 3324, Cell: +267 72 41 9170
culturallodge@gmail.com
www.bahurutshelodge.com

Accommodation is available in thatched en-suite chalets built from hand moulded bricks. During visits to the local village, you can learn how to brew beer, mill flour and decorate floors using cow dung. Pre-booking required.

Facilities: ⬛
Activities: ⬛

Beams Campsite   2

Lodge Camp   w179177
BWP 90.00 pp (2013)
Off Legolo Road, Madibeng, Gaborone

Tel: +267 391 1912, Fax: +267 391 1912,
Cell: +267 724 12105
info@beamscampsite.co.bw, www.beamscampsite.co.bw

Beams Campsite is situated right in the city centre of Gaborone. They offer comfortable, rustic and affordable camping facilities.

Languages: English

Facilities: ⬛
Activities: ⬛

Big 5 Lodge   3

Lodge   w179186
BWP 660.00 pu (2012)
8km or 11min WNW of Gaborone

Tel: +267 35 005 00, Fax: +267 350 0555
bigfivelodge@gmail.com

Big 5 Lodge offers comfortable accommodation in chalets with satellite television, air conditioning and en-suite bathrooms. Chalets are available in single, double and family size. They have a secure parking area.

Languages: English

Facilities: ⬛
Activities: ⬛

Cresta Lodge   4

Lodge   w179222
BWP 1238.00 to 1408.00 pu (2012)
Samora Machel Drive, Gaborone

Tel: +267 39 753 75, Fax: +267 39 00 635,
Cell: +267 71 375 375
reslodge@cresta.co.bw, www.crestahotels.com

Cresta Lodge offers accommodation in comfortable rooms with en-suite bathrooms, air conditioning and satellite television. Facilities include a cocktail bar. Pre-booking is essential.

Languages: English

Facilities: ⬛
Activities: ⬛

Cresta President Hotel   5

Hotel   w195997
BWP 1238.00 to 3596.00 pu (2012)
Botswana Road, Main Mall, Gaborone

Tel: +267 39 53 631, Fax: +267 35 1840
respresident@cresta.co.bw
www.crestahotels.com

All rooms of the Cresta President Hotel are en-suite and have air conditioning, satellite television, a mini bar and coffee/tea making facilities. Safe and secure on-site parking is available. Pre-booking required.

Languages: English

Facilities: ⬛
Activities: ⬛

Falcon Crest Suites Hotel   6

Hotel   w245002
BWP 985.00 to 1150.00 pu (2012)
Plot 2571, Nyerere Drive, Gaborone

Tel: +267 393 5373, Fax: +267 3935374,
Cell: +267 7147 9484
falconcrest@falconcrest.co.bw, www.falconcrest.co.bw

The hotel is centrally located and conveniently close to shopping malls. There are only eight rooms, all en-suite with verandas overlooking a beautiful garden. Wi-fi is available in the rooms. Airport transfer available.

Languages: English

Facilities: ⬛
Activities: ⬛

Gaborone Hotel　　　　7

Hotel　　　　w179198
BWP 425.00 to 480.00 pu (2012)
Central Bus Rank, Gaborone

Tel: +267 39 22 777, Fax: +267 392 2727
gh@info.bw
www.gaboronehotel.com

Gaborone Hotel offers comfortable en-suite rooms which
are air-conditioned and have satellite television. Facilities
include squash and tennis courts as well as a bar and
casino for entertainment.

Facilities:

Activities: ▨

Gaborone Sun Hotel　　　　8

Hotel　　　　w179322
BWP 1566.00 to 1855.00 pu (2012)
Chuma Drive Gaborone, Gaborone

Tel: +27(0)11 780 7810, Fax: +267 39 02 555
mb_bw_Reservations@za.suninternational.com
www.suninternational.com

Rooms are en-suite and have air conditioning, satellite television, mini bar and 24 hour room service. The hotel also
has a golf course, tennis and squash courts, gymnasium
and casino. Pre-booking required.

Facilities: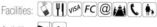

Activities: ▨▨▨

Kgale View Lodge　　　　9

Lodge　　　　w179162
BWP 570.00 to 680.00 pp (2012)
Phase 4, Plot 22258, Gaborone

Tel: +267 312 1755, Fax: +267 312 1755,
Cell: +267 72 111 011
kgaleviewlodge@brobemail.co.bw
www.kgaleviewlodge.com

The lodge with beautiful garden is conveniently situated
close to the Kgale View Mall and business district. Eight
rooms are en-suite and have satellite television. Breakfast
included.

Facilities: ▨▨▨

Activities: ▨

Metcourt Inn Hotel　　　　10

Hotel　　　　w189305
BWP 720.00 to 825.00 pu (2012)
Bonnington Farm, Molepolole Road, Gaborone

Tel: +267 36 377 77, Fax: +267 391 0402,
Cell: +267 72 696 942
metres@grandpalm.bw, www.metcourt.com

Rooms are luxurious with double beds, en-suite bathrooms, air conditioning, television and coffee/ tea making
facilities. Amenities include a hair salon, health club, bar
and casino. Airport shuttle service provided.

Languages: English, Setswana

Facilities: ▨▨▨▨

Activities: ▨

Mokolodi Backpackers　　　　11

Backpackers Hostel　　　　w219964
BWP 185.00 to 580.00 pp (2013)
14km or 15min SW of Gaborone

Cell: +267 74 111 165
admin@backpackers.co.bw
www.backpackers.co.bw

Two 2-bed chalets and four 4-bed chalets share a communal kitchen and bathroom. There are three braai areas
as well as an entertainment area. Pre-booking is advised
as large groups sometimes book out the whole camp.

Languages: English, Afrikaans

Facilities: ▨▨▨▨

Activities: ▨▨▨

Mokolodi Nature Reserve　　　　12

Self-catering　　　　w179334
BWP 680.00 to 1240.00 pu (2012)
19km or 21min SW of Gaborone (4WD)

Tel: +267 31 61 955, Fax: +267 31 65 488,
Cell: +267 71 321 021
bookings@mokolodi.com, www.mokolodi.com

Mokolodi Nature Reserve offers accommodation in fully
equipped, comfortable chalets. Rates do not include
entrance fees to the reserve.

Facilities:

Activities: ▨▨▨▨▨▨

GABORONE

Mokolodi Nature Reserve — 13

Park Camp w179346
BWP 120.00 pp (2012)
18km or 20min SW of Gaborone (4WD)

Tel: +267 31 619 55, Fax: +267 316 5488,
Cell: +267 71 321 021
bookings@mokolodi.com, www.mokolodi.com

Campsites are surrounded by historical stonewalls dating back to 1901. Traditional dances and game tracking can be enjoyed. Rates do not include entrance to the nature reserve..

Facilities:
Activities:

Oasis Motel Gaborone — 14

Motel w179174
BWP 660.00 to 1300.00 pu (2012)
6km or 8min ESE of Gaborone

Tel: +267 392 8396, Fax: +267 32 8568
reservations@oasis-motel.com
www.oasis-motel.com

The motel has single, double and family size rooms with satellite television. They also offer accommodation in chalets with double rooms, separate lounges and kitchenettes. Pre-booking required. Airport transfers available.

Facilities:
Activities:

Peermont Mondior — 15

Hotel w179146
BWP 1390.00 to 2550.00 pu (2012)
Plt 21117, Cnr Mobuto/Maratadiba Roads, Gaborone

Tel: +267 319 0600, Fax: +267 319 0660
ndulamo@mondiorsummit.co.bw
www.mondior.com

The hotel offers comfortable accommodation in en-suite air-conditioned rooms equipped with satellite television and small kitchenettes. Airport transfers available. Pre-booking required. This was previously the Syringa Hotel.

Languages: English, Setswana

Facilities:
Activities:

Phakalane Golf Estate Hotel — 16

Hotel w179338
BWP 1210.00 to 1576.00 pu (2012)
In Phakalane, near Gaborone

Tel: +267 360 4000, Fax: +267 315 9663
reservations@phakalane.co.bw
www.phakalane.com

The hotel offers accommodation in luxurious en-suite rooms with air conditioning. There is also the choice of comfortable and fully equipped self-catering chalets or villas. Guests can play golf on an 18 hole golf course.

Facilities:
Activities:

Walmont at the Grand Palm — 17

Hotel w179303
BWP 1745.00 pu (2012)
Molepolole Road, Gaborone

Tel: +267 36 377 77, Fax: +267 363 2989
metres@grandpalm.bw
www.grandpalm.bw

This five storey hotel with casino offers comfortable en-suite rooms with air conditioning, satellite television and coffee/tea making facilities. Secure parking and airport transfers are available. Pre-booking required.

Languages: English

Facilities:
Activities:

Photo: Peter Levey

Travel
Africa
Informed

Photo: Mokolodi Nature Reserve

JWANENG

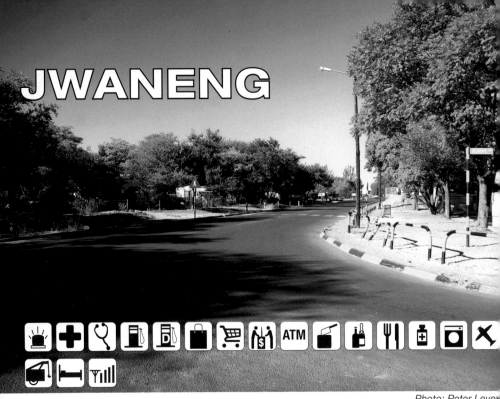

Photo: Peter Levey

The town was formed around the Jwaneng diamond mine, considered the richest in the world in terms of its content of gem-quality diamonds. At its inception it was a 'closed town', meaning that in order to live there permission was needed from the owners of the mine, Debswana.

TRAVELLER DESCRIPTION:
The mine is surrounded by the Jwana Game Park which also hosts a Cheetah Conservation Research Centre. Jwaneng is a good stop-over for replenishing fresh food supplies if you're on your way to Mabuasehube.

TRAVEL INFO:
The number listed is for the mine hospital. The clinic number is +267 588 0360.

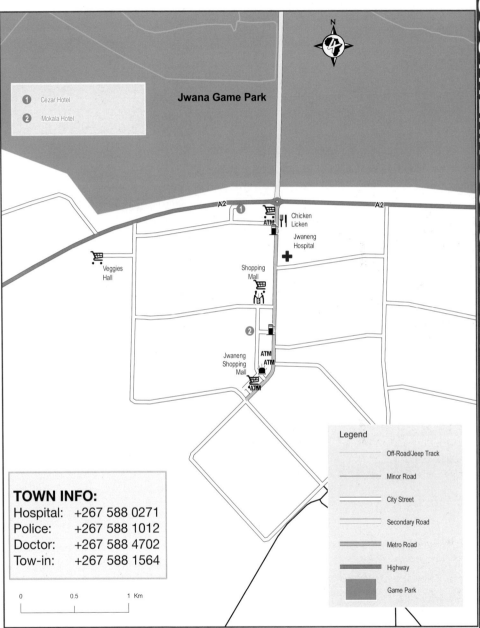

Jwana Game Park

1 Cezar Hotel

2 Mokala Hotel

A2

ATM

Chicken Licken

Jwaneng Hospital

Veggies Hall

Shopping Mall

2

A2

ATM
ATM

Jwaneng Shopping Mall

ATM

Legend

	Off-Road/Jeep Track
	Minor Road
	City Street
	Secondary Road
	Metro Road
	Highway
	Game Park

TOWN INFO:
Hospital: +267 588 0271
Police: +267 588 1012
Doctor: +267 588 4702
Tow-in: +267 588 1564

0   0.5   1 Km

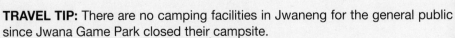

TRAVEL TIP: There are no camping facilities in Jwaneng for the general public since Jwana Game Park closed their campsite.

JWANENG

Cezar Hotel   1

Hotel   w179187
BWP 550.00 to 800.00 pu (2012)
Mathethe Road, Unit 4, Plot No 5483, Jwaneng

Tel: +267 588 1090, Fax: +267 588 1052
cezarhotel@ymail.com
www.cezarhotel.com

The comfortable en-suite rooms are air-conditioned and have ceiling fans, satellite television and coffee/tea making facilities. Standard and deluxe rooms are available to cater for different budgets. Pre-booking required.

Facilities:

Activities: ⛰

Mokala Hotel   2

Hotel   w151797
BWP 600.00 to 750.00 pp (2012)
In Jwaneng

Tel: +267 588 0835, Fax: +267 588 0839
mokala@botsnet.bw

Mokala Hotel offers comfortable accommodation in air-conditioned en-suite rooms with satellite television. Hotel facilities include a bar and casino. Pre-booking is essential.

Facilities:

Activities:

Photo: Peter Levey

FIND  AFRICA *ON YOUR* PHONE

or tablet with the
T4A Overland Navigator for Android.

- Offline navigation (you do not require internet to use the maps)
- Turn-by-turn navigation with voice guidance
- Plan and save routes on the app
- Tour guide information included on POI
- Coverage includes Southern and Eastern Africa
- For more information visit our website or scan the QR code

www.tracks4africa.co.za

TRACKS4AFRICA

KANYE

Kanye is the administrative centre of the Southern District and is as such one of the major towns of Botswana. It is the capital of the Bangwaketse tribe, one of the biggest tribes in Botswana. Kanye was founded in 1853 and today it is a fully fledged town that offers everything one might need.

TRAVELLER DESCRIPTION:
Kanye nestles in the mountainous area between Lobatse and Jwaneng on the Trans Kalahari Highway. It is a large town that spreads out over the surrounding area and travellers need to adhere to the speed limits that are in place. Bird lovers can visit the bird sanctuaries at Bathoen Dam and Moshenang Dam just outside Kanye.

TRAVEL INFO:
The contact number for the private clinic is +267 544 1555. Afri-Car Body is the local tow-in service.

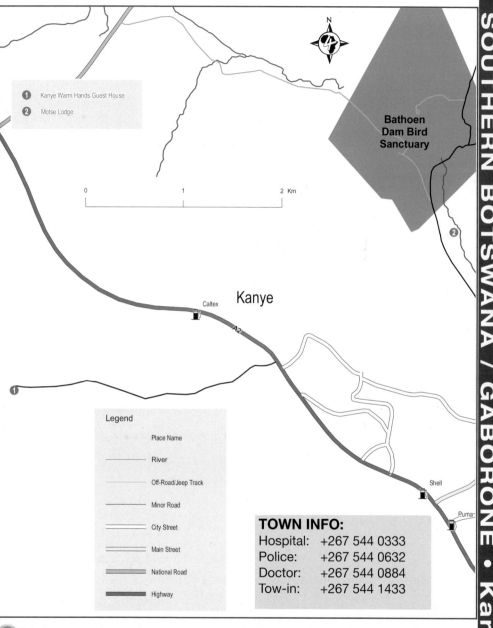

Kanye

1 Kanye Warm Hands Guest House

2 Motse Lodge

Bathoen
Dam Bird
Sanctuary

0   1   2 Km

Caltex

A2

Shell

Puma

Legend

Place Name

River

Off-Road/Jeep Track

Minor Road

City Street

Main Street

National Road

Highway

TOWN INFO:
Hospital: +267 544 0333
Police: +267 544 0632
Doctor: +267 544 0884
Tow-in: +267 544 1433

TRAVEL TIP: You will find everything that you need in Kanye and you can pay by credit card in most places.

KANYE

Kanye Warm Hands Guest House   1

Guest House   w256071
BWP 390.00 pu (2013)
In Kanye

Tel: +267 544 3862, Fax: +267 544 3865,
Cell: +267 713 07967
medline30@botsnet.bw, warmhandsbots.com

Accommodation is offered in tastefully decorated rooms,
all with double beds. Pre-booking required.

Facilities:

Motse Lodge   2

Lodge   w179369
BWP 200.00 to 570.00 pu (2012)
4km or 5min NNE of Kanye

Tel: +267 5480 363, Fax: +267 548 0370,
Cell: +267 71 659 964
motselodge@botsnet.bw, www.motselodge.com

Motse Lodge offers comfortable air-conditioned single,
double and family rooms with satellite television and en-
suite bathrooms. Self-catering chalets and campsites are
also available.

Facilities:
Activities:

Photo: Peter Levey

SOUTHERN BOTSWANA / GABORONE • Kanye

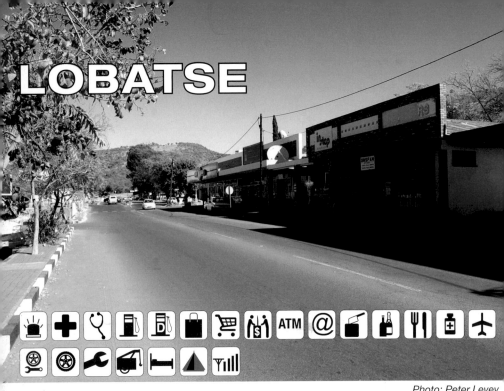

LOBATSE

Photo: Peter Levey

Lobatse is home to the High Court of Botswana, the headquarters of the Department of Geological Surveys as well as the Lobatse Mental Hospital, the only mental institution in Botswana. It is an industrial town.

TRAVELLER DESCRIPTION:
Lobatse lies 70 km south of Gaborone and is the first major town after you have entered Botswana from South Africa. Lobatse offers good accommodation and all services that a traveller might need.

TRAVEL INFO:
Lobatsy Body Works (landline: +267 533 2737) offers a 24 hours tow-in service. For emergency only medical services you can contact Dr Mezher on his cell number +267 74 165 761.

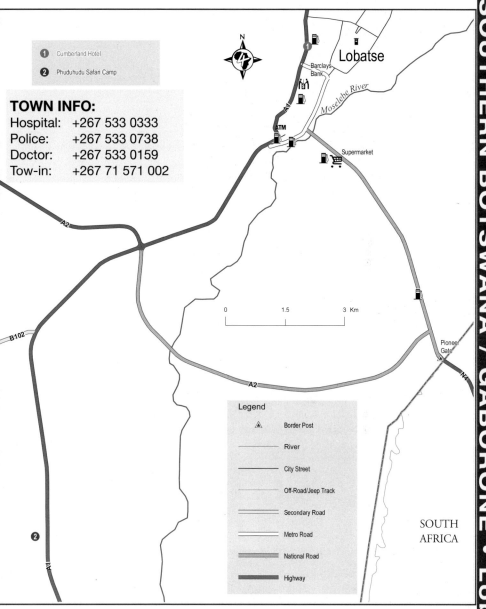

1 Cumberland Hotel

2 Phuduhudu Safari Camp

Lobatse

Barclays Bank

Moselebe River

TOWN INFO:
Hospital: +267 533 0333
Police: +267 533 0738
Doctor: +267 533 0159
Tow-in: +267 71 571 002

Supermarket

0   1.5   3 Km

Pioneer Gate

Legend

⚠ Border Post

River

City Street

Off-Road/Jeep Track

Secondary Road

Metro Road

National Road

Highway

SOUTH AFRICA

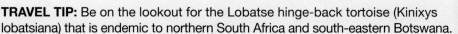

TRAVEL TIP: Be on the lookout for the Lobatse hinge-back tortoise (Kinixys lobatsiana) that is endemic to northern South Africa and south-eastern Botswana.

LOBATSE

Cumberland Hotel — 1

Hotel   w150814
BWP 395.00 to 850.00 pu (2012)
Plot 474, Khama Avenue, Lobatse

Tel: +267 533 0281, Fax: +267 5 332 106
cumberland@botsnet.bw
www.cumberlandhotel.co.bw

All rooms are en-suite and air-conditioned, have satellite television and coffee/tea making facilities. Baby sitting and 24 hour room services are available. Guests can relax in the beautiful garden. Safe parking available.

Languages: English

Facilities:

Activities:

Phuduhudu Safari Camp — 2

Farm Camp   w256001
ZAR 100.00 pp (2013)
15km or 16min SW of Lobatse

Fax: +267 530 0999, Cell: +267 71 304 897
sharondoepie@gmail.com

The camp is situated on a game farm and overlooks a dam where game often wonders around. The camp is spacious and has ample shower facilities. Pre-booking required.

Languages: English, Afrikaans, Setswana

Facilities:

Activities:

Photo: Peter Levey

T4A GPS Maps cover almost 724 000 km of navigable roads in Africa and feature over 124 000 POIs.

Simply plug die SD Card into your Garmin map capable GPS and navigate from Cape Town to Cairo.

The SD Card includes:

- The T4A Africa Guide.
- Installation files for PC and Mac for trip planning.

T4A GPS Maps are also available as individual downloads per region from www.tracks4africa.co.za.

Travel Africa Informed

Lake Ngami is seasonally filled and is an important habitat for birds and wildlife, especially in flood years. (Lindy Lourens)

WESTERN BOTSWANA

Western Botswana is mainly cattle farming area. However, Ghanzi is the ideal stop-over for self-drive tourists to replenish their stock and freshen up. Ghanzi is in reach of Moremi and Shakawe (the gateway to the Okavango Delta) to the north, the Central Kalahari National Park to the east and the Kgalagadi Transfrontier Park to the south. It is also less than a day's drive from Windhoek in Namibia, all on an excellent tarred highway.

For those interested in caving the **Gcwihaba caverns** are well worth a visit. Gcwihaba is a fascinating underground labyrinth of caverns, pits, linked passages, fantastica stalagmite and stalactite formations and beautifully coloured flowstones that seem like waterfalls of rock. The main cavern is called Drotsky's cavern, named after the Ghanzi farmer Martinus Drotsky, who was the first European to be shown the caves by the !Kung San in 1934. The caves also hold important clues to the way prehistoric peoples related to their environment. Gcwihaba is a designated National Monument and a proposed UNESCO World Heritage Site.

Straddling the Botswana/Namibia

attractive simply because they're so remote, and you can camp wherever you like once you asked permission from the chief of the nearest village. Clambering around is not much fun because the Aha Hills are made of endless jagged little blocks. You need good walking shoes with strong soles to climb these hills.

Within the Aha Hills there are two dolomite sinkholes known by the local people as Waxhu, which means 'house of god'. These can only be climbed down to by using specialist climbing/caving equipment.

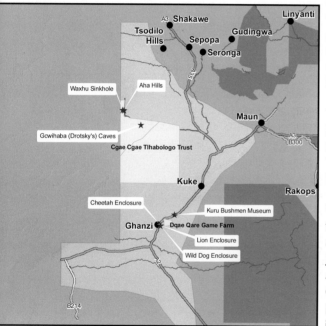

The caves and sinkholes fall into an area run by the Cgae Cgae Tlhabolongo Trust, which is a community trust.

While in Ghanzi, pop in to visit the cheetah, lion and wild dog enclosures just outside of town. About 24 km north of Ghanzi the **Dqae Qare Private Game Farm** is a community based tourism project of the

border, the **Aha Hills** lie about 50 km northwest of Gcwihaba, and are visible from it. This is one of the most remote and little-visited destinations in Botswana. The range covers about 245 km², most of which is in Botswana, and very little of which has been properly mapped or documented. In some ways the hills are

San (Bushmen) people from D'Kar Village.

Here you can experience the Bushmen culture and through your support help to preserve it.

GHANZI

Photo:Loureen Bester

Ghanzi is seen as the gateway to the Kalahari and is a convenient stop-over for Gaborone, Maun and Namibia. Ghanzi is primarily a farming community that supplies the Botswana Meat Commission with most of the required beef produce. Thirty-five kilometres north of Ghanzi is the small village of D'Kar, home to various extended family groups of Bushmen people. Do take the time to stop here, as one of the best co-operative galleries displaying and selling Bushman art and crafts is situated here. Every year during August, D'Kar also hosts the Kuru Traditional Dance and Music Festival. With all aspects of traditional Bushmen culture on display, this event is well worth visiting.

TRAVEL TIP: Good quality meat can be bought here at good prices but be aware of veterinary line restrictions on the movement of meat.

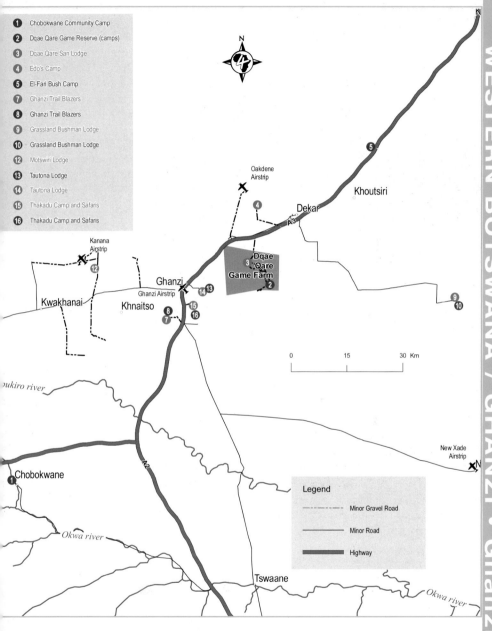

1 Chobokwane Community Camp
2 Dqae Qare Game Reserve (camps)
3 Dqae Qare San Lodge
4 Edo's Camp
5 El-Fari Bush Camp
7 Ghanzi Trail Blazers
8 Ghanzi Trail Blazers
9 Grassland Bushman Lodge
10 Grassland Bushman Lodge
12 Motswiri Lodge
13 Tautona Lodge
14 Tautona Lodge
15 Thakadu Camp and Safaris
16 Thakadu Camp and Safaris

Oakdene
Airstrip

Khoutsiri

Dekar

A3

Kanana
Airstrip

Dqae
Qare
Game Farm

Ghanzi

Ghanzi Airstrip

Kwakhanai

Khnaitso

9
10

oukiro river

0   15   30 Km

New Xade
Airstrip

Chobokwane

A2

Okwa river

Legend

Minor Gravel Road

Minor Road

Highway

Tswaane

Okwa river

WESTERN BOTSWANA / GHANZI • Ghanzi

TRAVELLER DESCRIPTION:

Ghanzi is the unofficial capital of the Kalahari and is situated in the middle of nowhere in the western part of Botswana. Ghanzi is an important stop-over on the Trans-Kalahari Highway for self-drive tourists as it is in reach of Moremi and Shakawe to the north, the Central Kalahari National Park to the east and the Kgalagadi Transfrontier Park to the south. It is also less than a day's drive from Windhoek in Namibia, all on excellent tarred highway. In Ghanzi you can replenish stocks, find affordable luxury accommodation as well as camping facilities and generally freshen-up before heading off into the wilderness again.

TRAVEL INFO:

If you need a doctor, you will have to see one at the hospital. There is only a Shell garage in town.

TOWN INFO:

Hospital:	+267 659 6334	Police:	+267 659 6222
Doctor:	+267 659 6333	Tow-in:	+267 659 6107
Tourist Info:	+267 659 6704		

Photo:Loureen Bester

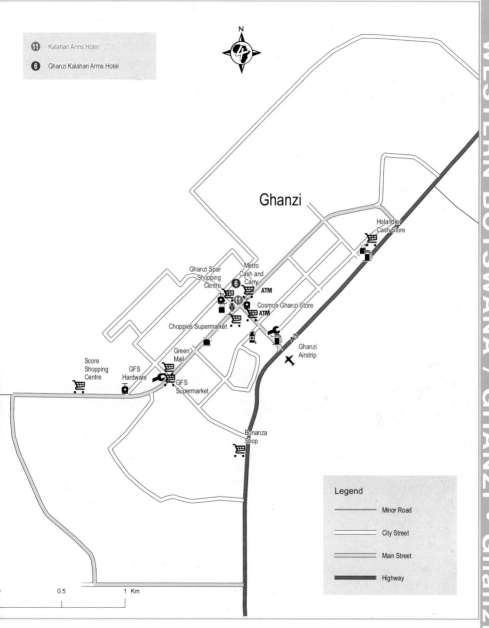

Ghanzi

11 Kalahari Arms Hotel

6 Ghanzi Kalahari Arms Hotel

Holandier Cash Store

Ghanzi Spar Shopping Centre

Metro Cash and Carry

ATM

Cosmos Ghanzi Store

ATM

Choppies Supermarket

Green Mall

Ghanzi Airstrip

Score Shopping Centre

GFS Hardware

GFS Supermarket

Bonanza Shop

A3

Legend

Minor Road

City Street

Main Street

Highway

0.5   1 Km

GHANZI

Chobokwane Community Camp — 1

Community Camp   w179209

85km or 52min SW of Ghanzi

We don't have any detailed information available on this listing because we were unable to contact them. However, it has been visited by our Tracks4Africa community of travellers.

Dqae Qare Game Reserve (camps) — 2

Park Camp   w179172
BWP 60.00 pp (2012)
42km or 55min E of Ghanzi

Fax: +267 72 527 321, Cell: +267 72 527 321
dqaeqare@gmail.com
www.dqae.org

Dqae Qare is a community based project of the Bushmen. There are two campsites, one near the lodge and a bush camp on the far end of the farm near a pan. The bush camp is rustic and hot water is supplied by donkey boiler.

Languages: English

Facilities:

Activities:

Dqae Qare San Lodge — 3

Lodge   w179173
BWP 273.00 to 499.00 pp (2013)
32km or 28min ENE of Ghanzi

Fax: +267 65 97 703, Cell: +267 72 527 321
dqaeqare@gmail.com, www.dqae.org

Dqae Qare is a Bushmen community project. This game farm has a main lodge, it includes en-suite double bedrooms in an old farmhouse and twin bed traditional Bushmen grass huts with outdoor ablutions. Cultural activities can be experienced.

Languages: English

Facilities:

Activities:

Edo's Camp — 4

Tented Camp   w195863
USD 390.00 pp (2013)
42km or 37min NE of Ghanzi

Cell: +267 72 120 399
edosbooking@gmail.com
www.edoscamp.com

Accommodation is offered in en-suite Meru-style tents overlooking a pan. Electricity is solar-powered. Children under 12 only allowed on request. Guests need to phone before arrival as the gates are locked.

Facilities:

Activities: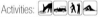

El-Fari Bush Camp — 5

Transit Camp   w204795
BWP 70.00 pp (2013)
67km or 44min NE of Ghanzi (4WD)

Fax: +267 71 59 1968, Cell: +267 72 12 0800
web@elfari.co.za
www.elfari.co.za

Campsites can accommodate up to three tents and have braai areas and water on tap. Firewood is supplied. Ablutions are clean and lighting is provided by solar panel and batteries.

Languages: English, Afrikaans

Facilities:

Activities:

Ghanzi Kalahari Arms Hotel — 6

Lodge Camp   w195855
BWP 50.00 pp (2012)
In Ghanzi

Tel: +267 659 6532, Fax: +267 659 6532
kalahariarmshotel@botsnet.bw
www.kalahariarmshotel.com

Ghanzi Kalahari Arms Hotel offers campsites with clean ablutions with electricity. Campers can use the facilities at the hotel.

Facilities:

Activities:

Ghanzi Trail Blazers — 7

Self-catering   w226707
BWP 80.00 to 460.00 pp (2013)
14km or 21min SSW of Ghanzi (4WD)

Tel: +267 659 7525, Fax: +267 659 7525,
Cell: +267 72 120 791
trailblazers@botsnet.bw, www.ghanzitrailblazers.co.bw

Accommodation is available in en-suite chalets or Bushmen grass huts that share communal ablutions. Each hut has stretchers with mattresses and mosquito nets. Self-catering, B&B or full inclusive stay options are available.

Languages: English, Afrikaans, Setswana

Facilities:
Activities:

Ghanzi Trail Blazers — 8

Tour Operator Camp   w226708
BWP 60.00 pp (2013)
14km or 20min SSW of Ghanzi (4WD)

Tel: +267 659 7525, Fax: +267 659 7525,
Cell: +267 72 120 791
trailblazers@botsnet.bw, www.ghanzitrailblazers.co.bw

At Ghanzi Trail Blazers guests can interact with the San/Bushmen and learn more about their culture. There are clean ablutions and braai areas at the campsite.

Languages: English, Afrikaans, Setswana

Facilities:
Activities:

Grassland Bushman Lodge — 9

Game/Safari Lodge   w187002
USD 336.00 to 400.00 pp (2013)
99km or 01h59min E of Ghanzi (4WD)

Fax: +267 72 104 270, Cell: +267 72 104 270
degraaff@it.bw
www.grasslandlodge.com

Grassland offers accommodation in en-suite chalets. The lodge has an indoor and outdoor dining area and a bar. Guests are treated to traditional dances and bushmen walks. E-mail bookings preferred. Rates are all inclusive.

Languages: English, German, Afrikaans

Facilities:
Activities:

Photo: Grassland Bushman Lodge

Grassland Bushman Lodge — 10

Lodge Camp   w195853
BWP 150.00 to 400.00 pp (2013)
101km or 02h06min E of Ghanzi (4WD)

Fax: +267 72 80 4270, Cell: +267 72 104 270
degraaff@it.bw
www.grasslandlodge.com

There are four campsites with clean ablutions. Hot water for the ablutions is supplied by 'donkey'. Guests are advised to bring their own drinking water.

Languages: English, German, Afrikaans

Facilities:
Activities:

Photo: Grassland Bushman Lodge

GHANZI

Kalahari Arms Hotel   11

Hotel   w179163
BWP 560.00 to 840.00 pu (2012)
In Ghanzi

Tel: +267 659 6532, Fax: +267 659 6311
kalahariarmshotel@botsnet.bw
www.kalahariarmshotel.com

Ghanzi Kalahari Arms Hotel offers comfortable en-suite rooms with satellite television and air conditioning. Rooms are fully serviced. The hotel has a beautiful garden and lapa.

Facilities:

Activities:

Motswiri Lodge   12

Lodge   w195858
BWP 1250.00 to 1715.00 pp (2013)
33km or 43min WNW of Ghanzi (4WD)

Cell: +267 72 118 811
reservations@kanana.info
www.kanana.info

Motswiri Lodge is situated in the Kanana Wilderness private game reserve. They offer luxury tented accommodation as well as campsites with hot water ablutions. They specialise in photographic safaris.

Languages: English

Facilities:

Activities:

Tautona Lodge   13

Lodge Camp   w150937
BWP 100.00 pu (2013)
7km or 16min ESE of Ghanzi (4WD)

Tel: +267 659 7499, Fax: +267 659 7500
tautonalodge@botsnet.bw
www.tautonalodge.com

Tautona Lodge has campsites for caravans with clean ablution facilities. Campers are welcome to use the facilities at the lodge. Activities offered at the lodge include bushmen dances. Pre-booking required.

Languages: English

Facilities:

Activities:

Tautona Lodge   14

Lodge   w179215
BWP 245.00 to 1870.00 pu (2013)
6km or 14min E of Ghanzi (4WD)

Tel: +267 659 7499, Fax: +267 65 97 500
tautonalodge@botsnet.bw
www.tautonalodge.com

Tautona Lodge offers comfortable accommodation with modern amenities. Guests can enjoy cultural dances. They do great breakfasts and buffets and have an a la carte menu available. Pre-booking is essential.

Languages: English

Facilities:

Activities:

Thakadu Camp and Safaris   15

Tented Camp   w150709
BWP 220.00 to 770.00 pu (2013)
8km or 12min SSE of Ghanzi

Fax: +27(0)86 219 4619, Cell: +267 72 120 695
info@thakadubushcamp.com
www.thakadubushcamp.com

The camp is situated on a private game reserve and the bar, restaurant and swimming pool overlook a pan. Accommodation is offered in en-suite Meru-style tents on rock plinths or in dome tents with shared ablution.

Languages: English

Facilities:

Activities:

Photo:Thakadu Camp and Safaris

Thakadu Camp and Safaris

Park Camp w151041
BWP 35.00 to 70.00 pp (2013)
8km or 14min SE of Ghanzi

Fax: +27(0)86 219 4619, Cell: +267 72 120 695
info@thakadubushcamp.com
www.thakadubushcamp.com

The camp is situated on a private game reserve and overlooks a natural pan. Campsites have electricity points and share clean ablutions. Campers are welcome to use the facilities at the tented camp.

Languages: English

Facilities:

Activities:

Photo:Thakadu Camp and Safari's

Photo: Sonja Joubert

Rental Companies

NAME	TEL	CELL	WEBSITE
Mckenzie Self Drive 4x4	+267(0)68 618 75	+264(0)71 303 788 +264(0)71 697 209	http://maunselfdrive4x4.webs.com
Travel Adventure Botswana	+267(0)68 612 11	+264(0)72 311 132 +264(0)71 327 070	http://www.traveladventurebotswana.com
Self Drive Adventures	+267(0)68 637 55		http://www.selfdriveadventures.com
Come-Along Safari	+31(0)507 200216	+31(0)683 209498	http://www.come-along-safari.com
Safari Drive	+44(0)14 88 71140		http://www.safaridrive.com

Tour Operators - Adventures

NAME	TEL	CELL
Liquid Giraffe Travel Services	+267 680 1054	+267 71 756 413
Drive Botswana	+267 492 3416	+267 71 781 665
Explore Africa Travels	+267 71 791 360	+267 71 791 360
The Booking Company	+267 686 0022	
African Animal Adventure Safaris		+267 76 550 191
Limpopo Valley Horse Safaris		+267 72 320 024
Makgadikgadi Pans Horse Trails	+267 76 550 191	+267 73 366 461
Adventure Safaris	+267 370 0166	+267 71 274 376
Kaie Tours	+267 397 3388	+267 72 261 585
Swampland Safari Trails	+267 686 5081	+267 72 765 735
Drifters Safaris Botswana		+267 72 304 472
Kalahari Skies Botswana	+267 686 2898	+267 72 299 523
Kgato Safaris	+267 686 4028	+267 72 524 566
Dumela Botswana (Pty) Ltd		+267 75 001 315
Letaka Safaris	+267 680 0369	+267 72 110 493
Okavango River Safaris	+267 684 1016	+267 74 442 313

Car	4X4	Camping equipped 4X4	GPS	Satellite phone
✓✓	✓✓		✓✓	✓✓
✓✓	✓✓	✓✓	✓✓	✓✓
	✓✓	✓✓	✓✓	✓✓
	✓✓		✓✓	✓✓
	✓✓	✓✓	✓✓	✓✓

WEBSITE	Quad Biking	Hot Air Ballooning	Sky Diving	Horse Riding	Hiking	Scenic Flights
http://www.liquidgiraffe.com	✓✓			✓✓		✓✓
http://www.drivebotswana.com	✓✓			✓✓		✓✓
http://www.exploreafricatravels.com		✓✓	✓✓	✓✓	✓✓	✓✓
http://www.thebookingcompany.net				✓✓	✓✓	
http://www.africananimaladventures.com				✓✓		
http://www.lvhsafaris.co.za				✓✓		
http://www.africananimaladventures.com				✓✓		
http://www.adventure-safaris.com				✓✓		
http://www.kaietours.com					✓✓	
http://www.swampsaf.com						✓✓
http://www.drifters.co.za						✓✓
http://www.kalahari-skies.com						✓✓
http://www.kgatosafaris.com						✓✓
http://www.dumelabotswana.com						✓✓
http://www.letakasafaris.com						✓✓
http://www.okavangoriver.com						✓✓

Tour Operators - Specialist

NAME	TEL	CELL
Liquid Giraffe Travel Services	+267 680 1054	+267 71 756 413
Swampland Safari Trails	+267 686 5081	+267 72 765 735
Kalahari Skies Botswana	+267 686 2898	+267 72 299 523
Dumela Botswana (Pty) Ltd		+267 75 001 315
Explore Africa Travels	+267 71 791 360	+267 71 791 360
The Booking Company	+267 686 0022	
Okavango River Safaris	+267 684 1016	+267 74 442 313
Ker & Downey Safaris	+267 686 1226	
Letaka Safaris	+267 680 0369	+267 72 110 493
Kaie Tours	+267 397 3388	+267 72 261 585
Makgadikgadi Pans horse trails	+267 76 550 191	+267 73 366 461
Kgori Safaris	+267 686 2049	+267 71 309 024
Rann Hunting Safaris	+267 686 1821	
African Animal Adventure Safaris		+267 76 550 191
Travel Adventure Botswana	+267 686 1211	+264 72 311 132
Dreams Safaris	+267 625 0332	+267 71 846 965
Drifters Safaris Botswana		+267 72 304 472
Kgato Safaris	+267 686 4028	+267 72 524 566
Drive Botswana	+267 492 3416	+267 71 781 665
Kalahari Holiday Tours	+267 625 0880	+267 71 448 780

WEBSITE	Photo-graphic Safaris	Fishing	Bird Watching	Star-gazing	Hunt-ing
http://www.liquidgiraffe.com	✓✓	✓✓	✓✓	✓✓	
http://www.swampsaf.com	✓✓	✓✓	✓✓	✓✓	
http://www.kalahari-skies.com	✓✓	✓✓	✓✓	✓✓	
http://www.dumelabotswana.com	✓✓	✓✓	✓✓	✓✓	
http://www.exploreafricatravels.com	✓✓	✓✓	✓✓	✓✓	
http://www.thebookingcompany.net	✓✓	✓✓	✓✓		
http://www.okavangoriver.com	✓✓	✓✓	✓✓		
http://www.kerdowneybotswana.com	✓✓	✓✓			
http://www.letakasafaris.com	✓✓		✓✓		
http://www.kaietours.com	✓✓		✓✓		
http://www.africananimaladventures.com	✓✓			✓✓	
http://www.kgorisafaris.com	✓✓				✓✓
http://www.rannsafaris.com	✓✓				✓✓
http://www.africananimaladventures.com	✓✓				
http://www.traveladventuresbotswana.com	✓✓				
http://www.dreamssafaris.com		✓✓	✓✓		
http://www.drifters.co.za		✓✓	✓✓		
http://www.kgatosafaris.com		✓✓	✓✓		
http://www.drivebotswana.com			✓✓		
http://www.kalaharichobe.com			✓✓		

Tour Operators - Tours and Services

NAME	TEL	CELL	WEBSITE
Kalahari Holiday Tours	+267 625 0880	+267 71 448 780	http://www.kalaharichobe.com
Kaie Tours	+267 397 3388	+267 72 261 585	http://www.kaietours.com/
Drive Botswana	+267 492 3416	+267 71 781 665	http://www.drivebotswana.com
Kalahari Skies Botswana	+267 686 2898	+267 72 299 523	http://www.kalahari-skies.com
Ker & Downey Safaris	+267 686 1226		http://www.kerdowneybotswana.com
Wilderness Safaris	+267 686 0086	+27 83 960 3391	http://www.wilderness-safaris.com
Explore Africa Travels	+267 71 791 360	+267 71 791 360	http://www.exploreafricatravels.com
Okavango River Safaris	+267 684 1016	+267 74 442 313	http://www.okavangoriver.com
African Animal Adventure Safaris		+267 76 550 191	http://www.africananimaladventures.com
Drifters Safaris Botswana		+267 72 304 472	http://www.drifters.co.za
Swampland Safari Trails	+267 686 5081	+267 72 765 735	http://www.swampsaf.com
Letaka Safaris	+267 680 0369	+267 72 110 493	http://www.letakasafaris.com
Dreams Safaris	+267 625 0332	+267 71 846 965	http://www.dreamssafaris.com
Adventure Safaris	+267 370 0166	+267 71 274 376	http://www.adventure-safaris.com
Liquid Giraffe Travel Services	+267 680 1054	+267 71 756 413	http://www.liquidgiraffe.com
The Booking Company	+267 686 0022		http://www.thebookingcompany.net
Kgato Safaris	+267 686 4028	+267 72 524 566	http://www.kgatosafaris.com
Makgadikgadi Pans horse trails	+267 76 550 191	+267 73 366 461	http://www.africananimaladventures.com
Magic Adventures	+49(0)26 077 130 100		http://www.magicadventures.net
Jenman Safaris	+27(0)21 683 7826		http://www.jenmansafaris.com
Dumela Botswana (Pty) Ltd		+267 75 001 315	http://www.dumelabotswana.com
Travel Adventure Botswana	+267 686 1211	+264 72 311 132	http://www.traveladventuresbotswana.com
Limpopo Valley Horse Safaris		+267 72 320 024	http://www.lvhsafaris.co.za

River Cruises	Guided Tours	4x4 Tours	City Tours	Camping Safari	Desert Excursions	Game Viewing	Donkey Cart Rides	Boat Trips	Mokoro Trips	Guided Walks
✓✓	✓✓	✓✓		✓✓		✓✓		✓✓		✓✓
	✓✓	✓✓	✓✓	✓✓		✓✓				✓✓
	✓✓	✓✓		✓✓		✓✓		✓✓	✓✓	✓✓
	✓✓			✓✓	✓✓	✓✓		✓✓	✓✓	✓✓
	✓✓			✓✓		✓✓		✓✓	✓✓	✓✓
	✓✓			✓✓		✓✓				
	✓✓				✓✓	✓✓		✓✓	✓✓	✓✓
	✓✓					✓✓		✓✓	✓✓	✓✓
	✓✓								✓✓	✓✓
	✓✓									✓✓
				✓✓		✓✓		✓✓	✓✓	✓✓
				✓✓		✓✓		✓✓	✓✓	✓✓
				✓✓		✓✓		✓✓		✓✓
				✓✓		✓✓			✓✓	✓✓
					✓✓	✓✓	✓✓		✓✓	✓✓
					✓✓	✓✓		✓✓	✓✓	✓✓
					✓✓	✓✓		✓✓	✓✓	✓✓
					✓✓		✓✓			
					✓✓					
					✓✓					
						✓✓		✓✓	✓✓	✓✓
						✓✓		✓✓	✓✓	
						✓✓				

Preparing for your trip A - Z

Camping & Lodging per Region

CENTRAL KALAHARI
Camping
Bape Camp (CKWIL-02) p104
Deception Camp 1 - 6 p104
Kang Ultra Stop Lodge p110
Khutse 1 - 10 p114
Khutse Khanke 1 - 4 p114
Khutse Maharushele 1 - 3 p114
Khutse Molose 1 - 4 p114
Khutse Moreswe 1 - 4 p114
Khutse South Gate Camp p115
Kori Camp 1 - 4 p104
Lekhubu Camp (CKWIL-06) p104
Leopard Pan p104
Letiahau Camp (CKWIL-07) p105
Matswere Gate Rest Camp p105
Motopi Camp 1 - 2 p105
New Kori Camp 1 - 4 p105
Passarge Valley Camp 1 - 3 p105
Phokoje Campsite (CKTAU-03) p105
Piper Pan Camp 1 - 2 p106
Qwee Pan CKWIL-01 p106
Sunday Camp 1 - 3 p106
Tsau Hills Camp p106
Xade Camp (CKWIL-05) p106
Xaxa Camp 1 - 2 p107
Lodging
Kalahari Rest Lodge p110
Kang Lodge p110
Kang Ultra Stop Lodge p110
Khutse Kalahari Lodge p114
Kukama Camp (CKWIL-08) p104
Nkisi Guest House p110
Tau Pan Camp (CKTAU-01) p106

CHOBE/KASANE
Camping
Chobe Safari Lodge p134
Ihaha Rest Camp p122
Kubu Lodge p135
Linyanti Rest Camp p122
Liya Lodge p135
Savuti Rest Camp p123

Senyati Safari Camp p136
Thebe River Safaris Camp p136
Toro Lodge p137
Lodging
Camp Linyanti p122
Chobe Game Lodge p134
Chobe Marina Lodge p134
Chobe Safari Lodge p134
Chobe Savanna Lodge p134
Duma Tau Luxury Camp (Linyanti) p126
Elephant Valley Lodge p134
Ichingo Chobe River Lodge p130
Ichobezi Safari Boats p135
Impalila Island Lodge p130
Kings Pool Luxury Camp (Linyanti) p126
Kubu Lodge p135
Kwalape Lodge p135
Kwando Lagoon Camp (Kwando Res) p126
Kwando Lebala Camp (Kwando Res) p126
Liya Guest Lodge p135
Liya Lodge p136
Mogotlho Safari Lodge p126
Motswiri Ketumetse Camp (Selinda GR) p126
Mowana Safari Lodge p136
Muchenje Safari Lodge p122
Ngina Safari's Rest Camp p136
Savute Safari Lodge p122
Savuti Elephant Camp p122
Savuti Luxury Camp (Linyanti) p127
Savuti Tented Camp p123
Selinda Camp (Selinda GR) p127
Senyati Safari Camp p136
The Garden Lodge p137
Toro Lodge p137
Water Lilly Lodge p137
Zarafa Luxury Camp (Selinda GR) p127
Zovu Elephant Lodge p137

Camping & Lodging per Region

SOUTHERN BOTSWANA/ GABORONE
Camping
Lodging

WESTERN BOTSWANA/GHANZI
Camping

INDEX

Camping & Lodging per Region

Lodging A -Z

INDEX

Lodging A - Z

INDEX

Camping A - Z

INDEX

INDEX

Notes

Notes

Notes

TRAVEL TIME AN...

Travel time in hrs:min	Francistown	Gaborone	Ghanzi	Gweta	Hukuntsi	Jwaneng	Kang	Kanye	Kasane	Letlhakeng	Lobatse	Mahalapye	Mamuno
Francistown		436	773	288	938	588	830	521	491	509	504	236	9
Gaborone	04:45		667	724	509	158	401	90	927	118	70	201	7
Ghanzi	07:55	07:10		489	374	508	267	586	888	537	637	861	2
Gweta	03:05	07:45	05:05		863	876	756	809	403	796	792	523	6
Hukuntsi	10:55	06:25	04:20	09:20		350	108	428	1185	379	479	702	4
Jwaneng	06:30	02:00	05:15	09:30	04:25		242	78	1079	214	130	353	6
Kang	09:10	04:40	02:40	07:40	01:50	02:45		320	1155	271	371	594	3
Kanye	05:50	01:15	06:10	08:50	05:20	01:00	03:40		1012	147	51	286	7
Kasane	05:15	09:55	09:10	04:20	13:30	11:40	11:45	11:00		999	995	726	1C
Letlhakeng	06:05	01:40	06:15	09:00	05:25	02:40	03:45	02:00	11:15		181	273	6
Lobatse	05:35	00:55	06:50	08:30	06:00	01:40	04:20	00:45	10:45	02:25		269	7
Mahalapye	02:35	02:15	09:10	05:35	08:25	04:00	06:40	03:20	07:45	03:35	03:05		9
Mamuno	09:55	08:20	02:05	07:05	05:25	06:25	03:45	07:20	11:10	07:20	08:00	10:20	
Martins Drift	02:55	04:00	10:30	05:50	10:05	05:45	08:20	05:05	08:05	05:20	04:50	01:45	12
Mata-mata	17:50	13:20	10:00	15:00	11:55	11:25	11:50	12:15	19:05	14:00	13:00	15:20	08
Maun	05:05	09:25	03:00	02:15	07:20	08:10	05:35	09:05	06:20	10:05	09:45	07:15	05
Mohembo	09:10	12:10	05:00	06:20	09:20	10:10	07:35	11:05	06:50	11:10	11:45	11:20	07
Molepolole	05:20	00:55	07:00	08:20	06:10	01:55	04:25	01:15	10:30	00:50	01:40	02:50	08
Nata	02:00	06:40	06:00	01:05	10:15	08:30	08:30	07:45	03:15	08:00	07:30	04:30	08
Ngoma Gate	06:15	10:55	10:15	05:20	14:35	12:40	12:45	12:00	01:15	12:15	11:45	08:45	12
Orapa	02:25	05:40	06:30	03:45	10:45	07:25	09:05	06:45	07:15	06:20	06:30	03:30	08
Palapaye	01:50	03:00	09:20	04:45	09:10	04:45	07:25	04:05	07:00	04:20	03:50	00:50	11
Parr's Halt Gate	03:35	03:20	10:15	06:35	09:25	05:05	07:45	04:25	08:45	04:40	04:10	01:10	11
Rakops	03:50	07:05	05:25	02:40	09:40	08:50	08:00	08:10	06:45	07:40	07:50	04:55	07
Ramatlabama	06:10	01:35	07:10	09:10	06:20	02:00	04:40	01:05	11:20	02:50	00:40	03:40	08
Ramokgwebana	01:05	05:45	08:55	04:00	11:55	07:30	10:10	06:50	06:10	07:05	06:35	03:35	10
Selebi-Phikwe	01:45	04:30	09:40	04:45	10:40	06:15	08:55	05:35	06:55	05:50	05:20	02:20	11
Serowe	02:20	03:35	08:55	05:20	09:25	05:15	07:45	04:35	07:30	04:05	04:20	01:25	10
Serule	01:00	03:45	08:55	04:00	09:55	05:35	08:15	04:50	06:10	05:05	04:35	01:35	10
Shakawe	09:00	11:55	04:50	06:05	09:10	10:00	07:20	10:55	07:00	11:00	11:35	11:10	06
Tlokweng Gate	05:00	00:25	07:25	08:00	06:35	02:15	04:55	01:30	10:10	02:00	01:10	02:30	08
Tshabong	10:15	05:45	06:45	11:45	05:55	03:50	04:15	04:45	15:55	06:25	05:25	07:45	07

The above values are based on a **shortest travel time** route calculation as opposed to a **shortest distance** route calculatic...

Numbers marked in blue indicate measurement along a route that exits the borders of the map and involves at least one bo...

Numbers in the above travel time table should be used as indicative values only. Road conditions may vary from time to tim...